PRAISE

ALL ROADS LEAD TO AUSTEN

"An Austenesque journey of a lifetime! The power of Jane Austen recounted through humor, poignancy, adventure, and, naturally, romance. You won't put it down, trust me!"

—Sharon Lathan, bestselling author of
Mr. & Mrs. Fitzwilliam Darcy and other
Darcy Saga sequels to *Pride and Prejudice*

"An illuminating insight into other cultures and a testament to Jane Austen's relevance in the modern world. Fascinating."

—Amanda Grange, bestselling
author of *Mr. Darcy's Diary*

"A journey through both a physical landscape and the geography of the human heart and mind, *All Roads Lead to Austen* deftly explores the universal themes of Austen's work while telling the story of Smith's own search for understanding, friendship, and, yes, love. Delightfully entertaining and often deeply moving, this book reminds us that Austen's world—and her characters—are very much alive."

—Michael Thomas Ford,
author of *Jane Bites Back*

ALL ROADS LEAD TO AUSTEN

A YEARLONG JOURNEY WITH JANE

AMY ELIZABETH SMITH

ILLUSTRATIONS BY LUCIA MANCILLA PRIETO

*For my fabulous, understanding mother and
the memory of my father—the beloved Old Welshman.*

Published by Sourcebooks, Inc.
P.O. Box 4410, Naperville, Illinois 60567-4410
(630) 961-3900
Fax: (630) 961-2168
www.sourcebooks.com

Library of Congress Cataloging-in-Publication Data
Smith, Amy Elizabeth.
  All roads lead to Austen : a yearlong journey with Jane / Amy Elizabeth Smith.
    p. cm.
  (pbk. : alk. paper) 1. Austen, Jane, 1775-1817—Appreciation. 2. Austen, Jane, 1775-
1817—Influence. 3. Books and reading—Latin America. I. Title.
PR4037.S54 2012
823'.7—dc23

                    2011047106

    Printed and bound in the United States of America.
        BG 10 9 8 7 6 5 4 3 2 1

Contents

AUTHOR'S NOTE

This all happened—*All Roads Lead to Austen* is nonfiction. I've changed some names (and in one case, the identity of a stuffed animal) for privacy. I may have gotten a few details wrong, but I did the best I could from memory and extensive travel notes. I recorded all of the reading groups, and because they were done in Spanish, I had to translate. I haven't caught all of the subtleties of the original conversations—which ranged from two to six hours each—but I've tried my best. For narrative flow, at times I've changed the sequence in which certain things were said (long conversations tend to meander, with lots of interruptions and backtracking). For the same reason, I've occasionally changed the sequence in which conversations took place.

My discussions of literature from each of the six countries are *very* selective. I could have used standard literary histories to be more comprehensive, but that's not what this trip was about—I wanted to learn about local literature by letting bookstore clerks recommend titles or having new friends hand me things they felt I'd enjoy. Latin American literature is endlessly beautiful, rich, and rewarding. What I discuss here is just the tip of the iceberg! (For more detail on some of the authors I mention, see www.allroadsleadtoausten.com).

A few technical points. There's a custom in Spanish to capital-
ize only the first word of book titles—so in English it's *Pride and
Prejudice,* but in Spanish, it's *Orgullo y prejuicio.* For consistency's
sake, I'm using the English style for titles both in English and
Spanish. Also, it's standard in scholarly publications to use ellipses
to indicate if you've shortened a quote. I've done so silently in a
few spots for flow (but never to change the meaning).

GETTING STARTED

Jane Austen just won't stay on the page.

I enjoy everything I teach at a small university in California, but I especially love my Jane Austen course. The students and I read her novels together, discuss Austen's historical context, and explore the amazing ways Austen keeps coming to life through sequels, updates, and spin-offs—Bridget Jones, Bollywood, zombies, and all. Instead of writing final papers, students do Austen projects that we showcase in December at a public Jane Austen Night bash. We've had *Northanger Abbey* in rhymed heroic couplets, a short play with the Dashwood sisters transformed into gay brothers, a sign language lesson using Austen plots, and my favorite, a marriage of Kafka and Austen: *Emmamorphasis*, wherein Emma wakes up one fine day as a giant cockroach (just *imagine* what her exoskeleton does to her best muslins!).

Austen moves her readers. Semester after semester, when my students talk about Austen's novels, they transition seamlessly between their own lives and Austen's fictional world. "My sister is such an uptight Elinor, she makes me crazy!" somebody will always say after we start *Sense and Sensibility*. Or, "Yeah, I've met a Willoughby or two." Or with endless variations, "Marianne needs a *serious* dope slap." By the end of each semester I can compile a list of the most smackable characters from student feedback: topping the charts are always Marianne, both Eltons from *Emma*, John Thorpe from *Northanger Abbey*, and of course, Mrs. Bennet.

Students just don't react this way to novels I teach in other classes, such as *Wuthering Heights* or *Jane Eyre*. Austen's post-mortem rivals wrote great novels, but not a single student has read Emily or Charlotte Brontë and reported back to the class, "That Heathcliff is *just* like my ex-boyfriend," or "Rochester's wife reminds me of my aunt," or "Somebody ought to pop Jane Eyre a good one!" Not once. Brontë World is to be viewed and enjoyed at a distance, but Austenland is a place where people feel inclined to get cozy with the locals, even give a few verbal wedgies. Or a dope slap.

It's not only my students who react this way to Austen. After a rough divorce, my friend Larry, a fellow native Pennsylvanian, went into an emotional tailspin. He ditched his job and, out of the blue, retrained as a railroad engineer. This led to long hours in hotel rooms between runs, either brooding alone or phoning me for where-did-it-go-wrong debriefs.

"You're an English teacher—what should I read?" he asked one evening, realizing we needed *something* to talk about other than his still-broken heart. "Would I like Jane Austen?"

Pride and Prejudice, her best-paced work, seemed a good recommendation for a man spending too much time staring out of train windows wondering how his marriage had gone off the rails. After a longer than usual silence, I got his first post-Austen call. "I liked it. Took a little getting used to the style, though," he said in his endearing Pittsburgh twang, *à la* "let's go daahntaahn 'n watch a Stillers game."

"You know," he went on, "I thought I married a Lizzy Bennet, but maybe I really picked a Lydia?" Well, so much for diverting him from divorce talk. As Larry made his way through all of Austen's novels—even *Mansfield Park*, whose heroine he dubbed the most "smackable" of all—our long conversations became populated by Emma, Captain Wentworth, Fanny Price, and others.

What is it about Jane Austen that makes us talk about the characters as if they're real people? People we recognize in our own lives, two centuries after Austen created them? When my first development leave from the university rolled around, I decided it was time for me to try my own Austen project, just like my students do. Something creative, something fun. So I got to wondering: the special connection that people feel with Austen's world, this Austen magic—would it happen with people in another country, reading Austen in translation?

Azar Nafisi's *Reading Lolita in Tehran* is one of the most moving books I've ever read on how literature matters in people's lives. She covered six different authors with the same group of students in post-revolution Iran. Inspired, I decided to try a new twist. Why not read the same author but shift through six different countries, instead? Jane Austen reading groups, on the road.

Growing up, I envied Nancy Drew's jet-setting ways, which set me on a course to travel at every opportunity as an adult. I spent a year in Prague in the early 1990s, and since my brother Shawn has an even worse travel bug than my own, I've tagged along like a good little sister to visit him when he lived in Italy, then South Africa, then Egypt. With that year's leave from the university ahead of me, I wanted to explore new territory: Central and South America.

In *Clueless*, the nineties update of Austen's *Emma*, the heroine

Cher offends her family's Salvadoran maid by assuming that any-body who speaks "Mexican" must *be* a Mexican. But Cher's no worse than the average clueless North American. Central and South Americans are our neighbors, but all too many of us can't tell one country from another south of the border. At work I'd met *latinos* and *latinas* from a host of countries I couldn't locate without studying a map.

So, on the road I could pick up some firsthand knowledge while seeing what Latin Americans would make of Jane Austen. Would they identify with her characters? Or maybe want to smack a few? Plus, I could find out who *their* Jane Austens were—which authors are beloved in Central and South America, which novels come to life off the pages. It would be a whole new world of books (and bookstores!).

Unfortunately, the only lesson I remembered from high school Spanish was that *pero* means "but" and *perro*, "dog." Thanks to my university's ties with a language school in the city of Antigua, I settled on Guatemala for both a warm-up and a starting point. The plan was to take five weeks of Spanish lessons during my winter break, then return in July to begin my "year with Jane" in earnest; I'd do my first reading group there.

The second country would let me mix business with plea-sure. I'd made two short trips to Puerto Vallarta prior to cook-ing up my Austen project. In fact, maybe that influenced my planning—because in Mexico I'd met Diego, a cheerful, hand-some taxi driver who also happened to be a booklover. We were both eager for a much longer visit. I wasn't a fan of long-distance relationships, but there was something special about Diego. I was willing to jump in and see how things might turn out.

For country number three, I decided on Ecuador, where I

could visit a friend-of-a-friend in Guayaquil. The next and longest stop would be Chile. I signed on to teach with a study abroad program for a semester in Santiago, where I was sure I could find some interested Austen readers. After that I'd head for Paraguay to stay with another friend-of-a-friend. Even without a connection, who could resist a mysterious, allegedly dangerous place almost nobody can find on a map? For the big finale, I'd spend a month in Buenos Aires, Argentina. I didn't know a soul there, but it seemed fitting that Jane Austen should wrap up her Latin American tour in the city many consider the literary capital of South America.

With five weeks in Antigua under my belt (and plenty of practice), I had a foundation for speaking Spanish. As I read and planned, I could see that each country would be unique, but the five-week language trip offered me a taste of what to expect. I walked the cobbled streets of a colonial Spanish city; I saw looming, active volcanoes; I heard marimba music at midnight; I learned to make my way through Conan the Barbarian stories in Spanish.

Come that May, there wasn't a student on campus more eager than I was to bolt. Was I nervous about spending a year away from family and friends, trying to function in a foreign language I had a tenuous grip on while convincing several dozen people in six different countries to join me for book groups? You bet. Was I excited about the trip anyway? *You bet!* When classes were done, I packed up my worldly goods and found new homes for my chickens—three Cochins, a white Silkie hen, and Nikolaus-Nikolaus, a strutting Frizzle rooster named after a stern German ancestor. Stopping through in Pennsylvania, I bought my mom a computer so we could use email along with phone calls; she's a worrier. And I visited my father's grave.

One evening a few years back, he'd set down the book he'd been reading and a heart attack took him fast, right there at home with the woman he'd loved for fifty years. The book was a novelization of *Casablanca*, a film he'd seen repeatedly, so as my dad slipped away, he wasn't even troubled with any nagging questions about how it would all turn out. To me, that's kind of a big deal. Unless I go in my sleep, I fully expect to be dragged off to eternity with at least three half-read books around somewhere, wryly wondering the genre-appropriate version of "Damnation, *whodunit?!*"

Raised by booklovers, I'll be a booklover 'til the end. In fact, now that I'm back from Latin America, I regret only one thing connected with my year's travels—that my father, the man who built me my first bookshelves, won't get to meet the devoted reader I'm about to marry, someone who played a role in my Austen adventure. Diego from Mexico? Maybe. Maybe not. But I will say this: as Austen fans know, when Austen's in the picture, somebody's going to end up hitched.

My dad would have loved my fiancé's sense of humor and his insight. After I'd returned to the States and was talking to some people about the book groups I'd done, one of them frowned and said, "That was superimposing European literature on those people, you know." The man didn't outright call me a Yankee Imperialist Pig-dog, but that seemed to be the subtext. When I passed this comment on to my fiancé, he was both annoyed and amused.

"Sounds like he's confusing you with the CIA in the 1970s," he said. "So *latina* cultures are so feeble that we can't enjoy a Jane Austen novel without our literary world collapsing? Somebody needs to learn a bit about Latin America."

Austen was a fan of not making assumptions—of avoiding

prejudices—of making sure you're reading a situation (or a person or a place) very carefully. She never set foot outside of England, but what she has to teach about astute reading applies across time, across borders, and even, as I came to learn, across languages.

I wish I could say that I never made any gaffes of my own while traveling, that I never brought too much old baggage to new places or into relationships with people I met. But thanks to bad judgment (and at times, bad Spanish), I wound up in quite a few bonehead situations. Like fleeing from a ghost in a Mexican bookshop—putting a scare, myself, into some unfortunate Ecuadorians in a grocery store—fending off an amorous senior citizen in a Chilean laundry room—and on one stellar occasion, barely escaping a good hard soaking from a police water cannon.

Fate stepped in at times too, independent of my own blunders, to deal some painful surprises. I struggled for months with the most serious illness of my life, much to my poor mother's distress. I made it through—but not all of the smart, warm, incredible new friends I met along the road were still around by the time I reached the end of it.

Yet, as Austen well knew, life's challenges and sorrows help us appreciate what goes *right*. No amount of stumbling on my part could spoil the pleasures of drinking rooster beer in Guatemala; of floating in the gentle sea at Puerto Vallarta; of feeding a hoard of tame iguanas in an Ecuadorian park; of seeing the snowcapped Andes in Chile; of riding a rocking horse in a Paraguayan nightclub; of watching seductive Argentineans tango on a narrow street in Buenos Aires on a chilly afternoon.

In every country I visited, I had the pleasure of not just learning but living a new language, along with the nerdy fun of browsing bookstore after Spanish-language bookstore. And the

Austen reading groups—each so different from the others, each letting me see Austen in surprising, enlightening, amazing new ways. On top of it all, I wound up with a nice old-fashioned happy ending, one that still leaves me and my fiancé marveling at our own dumb luck for having crossed paths in the first place.

It was a wonderful year, mistakes and all. The funny thing is, I made my very biggest mistake before I even hit the road: I set off on my travels thinking of myself as a teacher, just because that's how I earn a living.

So clueless. What a lot I had to learn.

GUATEMALA:

GIRLS' NIGHT OUT

In which the author returns to Guatemala and the language school, buys books, tries not to get impatient in restaurants, reads some great Guatemalan literature, drinks rooster beer, offers a few reflections on travel, and, at long last, discusses Pride and Prejudice *with five bright, lovely Guatemalan women and (separately) one astute male misanthrope.*

CHAPTER ONE

I can be a little…impatient. And as much as I love traveling, I'm prone to get panicky about the logistics. Watching all but a handful of passengers from my flight claim their bags and disappear while mine were nowhere in sight would usually have made me pretty twitchy. But I'd been in the Guatemala City airport before; since they'd lost my bags the first time, too, it felt kind of like a little "Welcome back!" I was too excited about the visit ahead to fuss over how long my luggage might take to catch up (first trip: four days).

Ahead of me was the beauty of Antigua, the challenge of more lessons at the language school, the hours I would spend with friends I'd met in December. For some people, travel is about adventure, something different at every turn, constantly seeing new places. But anyone who's read an Austen novel more than once—or any good novel—knows the pleasure of treading familiar ground. With a book as good as *Emma* (or *Great Expectations* or *To Kill a Mockingbird* or *Fear and Loathing in Las Vegas*), you can pick it up knowing how it ends but still discover something fresh and engaging each time around.

Mindful reading takes time and attention; so does mindful travel. A typical four-day stay just isn't enough to begin to understand a city and the people who live there. Extended travel—time to really *read* a place—is a luxury of the best, most rewarding kind. A whole year of it now lay ahead of me.

Antigua is about fifty minutes southwest of Guatemala City, so during the ride I caught up with Gustavo, the van driver I'd hired on my earlier stay as well. About my age, thoughtful, pleasant, and handsome, Gustavo is the proud father of three daughters. He updated me on his oldest, who was studying medicine. Getting into a university in Guatemala is tough; there aren't affordable state schools and community colleges around every corner. For female students in a culture with traditional, sharply defined gender roles, the road is tougher still. Gustavo had plenty of reason to be proud.

On this Austen-inspired trip, I couldn't help but wonder how the history of literature would be different if Austen's father hadn't been equally thrilled with his talented daughter. What if, instead of doing his best to help her publish, the Reverend George Austen had pushed harder for more grandkids and told Jane to leave the writing to her brothers? Scary thought.

"Are you back for more lessons?" Gustavo asked. He spoke slowly on purpose, his Spanish clear and easy to follow—he'd spent lots of hours ferrying students to and from the language school. I'd vowed to use only Spanish on my travels, and it was a pleasure to return to the fluid, beautiful language I wanted so badly to master.

"I'm back for more lessons and for something special," I answered (and since my own Spanish wasn't exactly so fluid or beautiful yet, I'm touching things up here in English). "I'll be holding a reading group with five teachers from the school, to talk about an English novel called *Pride and Prejudice*."

"Are you reading the book in English?" he said in surprise. Most of the teachers at the language school didn't speak English, since language immersion is its specialty.

"No, in Spanish. I want to see how well Austen translates." There was much more encompassed in that word "translates" than I could explain to Gustavo in my gritty Spanish—I meant not only Austen's language but her social vision, her fabulous casts of characters, her peerless ironic voice. How well would these flourish, transplanted to beautiful but troubled Guatemala, with a decades-long civil war in its recent past? Would readers here see themselves in Austen the way so many English-speaking readers do? Would they *recognize* these mothers, fathers, sisters, friends, and neighbors? Maybe even itch to manhandle a few of them, the way Larry and my California students often did?

These were the questions driving my travel, not just to Guatemala but to every country I would visit over the upcoming year. And I was willing to follow—wherever the answers might lead.

Settled into my hotel, the first order of business was a call to the States. There were several dozen ways grim fate could have snatched me up between my mother's Pennsylvania living room and my Guatemalan hotel, so I had to demonstrate that I had survived them all. I'd recently celebrated my forty-second birthday. By that age, my mother already had a grandchild—but I was the youngest of four and as they say, once the baby, always the baby.

"You have a good sun hat, don't you?" she asked.

The stores were full of them…how evil would it be to say yes, in the spirit of, "one is available if I need it?" Hopefully not too. "Yes, Mom."

"Please be careful! Don't forget what happened to Albert's sister," she reminded me (again) as we hung up. Albert was one of my high school boyfriends, and his sister died of a tropical fever during a Christian mission somewhere in Latin America. Which country, we never heard for sure. I can't imagine how his poor parents dealt with it; as for Albert, losing his younger sister was heartbreaking.

Since we never did get the full story on the tropical fever, this local tragedy transformed the entire map of Latin America, in my mom's concerned parental brain, into The Place Where Albert's Sister Died. To her credit, she never *once* tried to talk me out of my plans. And anyway, my love of books was inextricably tied to spending hours in the small local library where she'd worked for more than twenty years. Mom had her hand in my desire to travel two continents with Austen, intentionally or not. But I knew she would worry about me nonstop, so lots of calls and emails were in order. If that seems juvenile for a forty-something, so be it.

The next morning I had a warm reunion with Nora, my point-person for the Austen group. With some people you can pick up a conversation seamlessly even after months of separation; that's how it was with Nora. At the language school, teachers are assigned by the week, and during my initial visit, Nora was my second teacher. Cheerful, curvy, and feminine, she had a mile-wide smile and a serious appreciation of harmless gossip.

Before working with Nora I'd studied under Élida, a delicate, petite woman in her sixties with enormous, solemn eyes. With Élida, who would also be in our Austen group, I'd felt inspired to behave well. She reminded me of the "old-school" teachers I'd had back in Pennsylvania, ones who knew how to earn students' respect without coddling or pandering. But with Nora I felt free to share details about our love lives, the love lives of other teachers and students, the love lives we wish we had, etc. All in the name of education—you've got to use a lot of Spanish vocabulary to describe people's love lives.

Nora had rounded up the other three readers for the Austen group, fellow teachers from the language school, which from here on out I'll call *La Escuela*. Two months earlier, I'd mailed her five copies of *Orgullo y Prejuicio*, otherwise known as *Pride and Prejudice*, and she'd distributed them. Not Austen's best, in my opinion, but as her most popular novel it seemed the natural point of departure for Austen's Latin American travels.

"Everybody's excited about getting together for the group," Nora assured me with a grin. "How do you want to organize it?"

"Let's save it for the end of my visit. Every lesson counts for me! I'll be able to do a better job with our group if we hold off a bit. I know you're all really busy, so let's make it one session only," I suggested. The relief on her face was obvious. American women have our complaints, but the average American guy who cooks and cleans would be worth his weight in gold-wrapped chocolate in Antigua. Pretty much every woman I met there told me that she automatically has two full-time jobs if she works outside the home.

Classes would start up bright and early the next day, so Nora and I made the most of our time that beautiful Sunday catching up on gossip. After I found out how things were with her family and her daughter's upcoming wedding, she quickly steered things around to my own love life.

"So, are you dating anybody?" Her open, inviting gaze encouraged me to dish about Diego, even though I hadn't meant to quite yet.

"Yes and no. I've spent some time with somebody I really like, but it's long distance, so I'm not sure where it's going."

"How long is long?"

I hesitated a beat. "Mexico."

"Aha!" she laughed. "So that's why you're staying less time this visit! You want to run off to see your honey in Mexico!"

She had me there. I'd emailed Diego earlier that morning, knowing he wouldn't worry if a day or two passed before I could find an Internet café. He was the soul of contented cheerfulness. One day he'd pointed out, as we floated on our backs in the sea and I had been fretting about something, that the Spanish verb for "worry" is *preocupar*. In other words, to be "occupied" with something before you need to. I am my mother's daughter; I fret. But maybe with more time around Diego when I got to Mexico, I could learn to lighten up.

As Nora and I strolled toward the Parque Central, I was struck by how magically similar a July day felt to a January day—sunny, pleasant, no serious humidity in sight. Apparently it never gets too hot or too cold in Antigua, although there's more rain in the summer. And green—always so achingly, beautifully green. If I had dreamed up the place, I couldn't have done it better.

There was a downside, however. Once upon a time, Antigua was the country's capital. Then a devastating earthquake in 1773 killed a large percentage of the population and left many of the beautiful churches, government structures, and houses in ruins; the capital was moved to Guatemala City. While many structures in Antigua were rebuilt, to this day numerous buildings remain as they'd been left in the wake of nature's wrath, silent reminders of the city's past and the ever-present threat of more destruction. A 1976 earthquake killed more than 20,000 Guatemalans, wiping out entire villages in the mountainous areas, although the impact in Antigua was minimal.

There's nothing attractive about a deadly earthquake—but there's something undeniably picturesque, at this remove in time, about Antigua's eighteenth-century ruins. Catherine Morland, the heroine of Austen's *Northanger Abbey*, would have adored exploring them. In Austen's day wealthy Brits had a real taste for crumbling monasteries and shattered battlements, a fad Austen pokes fun at in her Gothic parody. Antigua is full of intriguing ruins of churches, convents, and other structures that time and abundant greenery have woven into the fabric of the city's present life, among the stuccoed and brightly painted houses.

The busy Parque Central is one of the prettiest, most inviting town squares I've seen. The climate allows for lush trees and flowers year-round, and attractive buildings frame the park on four sides, one of which is occupied entirely by police administrative offices. Upon inspection, the impressive colonial façade of the police station proves to be just that—a façade. View the building from the side and you'll discover that it gives way, two rooms deep, to colossal piles of rubble, the remains of its pre-earthquake stature. From this base, roving police maintain order to the point of telling people to keep their weary feet off the numerous benches.

As we settled by the central fountain for some people watching, a girl of seventeen or eighteen approached Nora with a bright smile of recognition on her pretty face. She was dressed in the universal teen costume of T-shirt and jeans. While she had the warm, dark complexion of many Guatemalans, the shape of her eyes and the lines of her cheekbones were somehow distinctive. Middle Eastern? After a noisy exchange of kisses and greetings, she and Nora began speaking at a pace I couldn't follow. Then, with a parting kiss and a wave, the girl tripped off.

Nora, who's got four children, sighed like only a mother can. I had to ask: "Where is she from?"

"Turkey," answered Nora. "She was at *La Escuela* for a while. She moved here on her own because she didn't like her home, but she's had some troubles."

"Are her parents here? Other relatives or friends?" No and no.

Wow. There I was thinking myself quite the adventurer for cutting loose in Latin America for a whole year, although with a university post awaiting at home—and here was a girl less than half my age cutting loose indefinitely, picking up and saying, "The heck with Turkey, how about Guatemala?" I looked around the park at the local girls in braids and beautifully embroidered clothing, people once referred to as "Indians" but now, more respectfully (and accurately) as indigenous. Their roots were in place well before the Spaniards showed up.

How inconceivable this idea would be to most of them, to disengage from a tightly knit family and try one's fortune in an alien country. According to what I'd learned at *La Escuela*, they would no more consider this than Austen herself would have. I'd spoken with some young indigenous women on my first visit who couldn't grasp why I'd chosen to travel alone. "But your *family*? How can you leave your *family*?" they'd repeated, clearly distressed on my behalf, as if I'd somehow stepped out of my hotel without my head on my shoulders.

Austen traveled very little in her lifetime—a move from her

birthplace of Steventon to Bath, some beach vacations to Lyme Regis, a few trips to London—and always accompanied by family. Americans are so enamored of "finding ourselves" that it's hard to imagine life in a culture where your place, *who* you are, is defined first and foremost by family. What would it be like never to feel driven to ask the questions that keep American therapists busy? To have a true and profound sense of belonging? You can find close communities in the States, but these days you have to look hard.

Maybe Austen would translate just fine for Antiguans. Maybe they'd be able to understand her better than a restless traveler like me or that high-spirited young girl disappearing through the crowd in the Parque Central.

Monday morning dawned—back to school! I was always one of those nerds who looked forward to school starting, to breaking in crisp new notebooks, color-coded by subject, to using shiny new pens. I remember with vivid intensity the childhood pleasure of stepping back into the classroom after a summer of sunburns and roughhousing. Returning to *La Escuela* that July morning felt the same, seeing the motivated morning bustle, checking to find which cubicle I'd been assigned, which teacher.

If you seriously want to learn another language and can pull together the cash, attend an immersion school with one-on-one instruction. Finding a pretty one, while you're at it, is easy to do in Antigua since most have outdoor classrooms. The grounds at *La Escuela* were idyllic. Neat cement paths wove between the beds of well-tended flowers and bushes that separated the three long rows of outdoor study cubicles. At capacity, the school accommodated dozens of students, but the layout and the semienclosed cubicles allowed for the sense of privacy you find in a well-designed restaurant. The school was enchanting—nothing like fresh air and flowers to make a classroom more pleasant.

As for teachers, I'd requested Luis, a man known for both his profound love of literature and his bile, especially toward women. I'd seen him during my initial five-week visit back in the winter but had never spoken to him. Unlike most of the teachers at *La Escuela*, Luis, who was fiftyish, simply didn't look friendly. His expressions were sharp, his features and the tone of his voice were sharp, the lines of his slender body, sharp, and his mind, as I came to see over the course of the week, sharpest of all. When students and teachers would gather for coffee breaks, he tended to hang back and watch the others—and I was intrigued.

Thinking about Luis's reputation led me to remember how one of Austen's neighbors compared Jane to a fireplace poker: an ever-present part of the furnishings, silent, stiff and upright, sharp and dangerous. This doesn't exactly square, however, with the many descriptions by Austen's nieces and by friends who found her pleasant and fun. In all likelihood the comparison to a poker had less to do with Austen being a cold bit of hardware than with the neighbor in question feeling roundly and soundly jabbed by Austen's now-famous wit.

A colleague from my university who'd already studied with Luis had asked me to bring him half a dozen novels in English as a gift. Luis eyed the stack I placed on the desk between us with thinly concealed desire as I introduced myself. Clearly he was a book person to the core, no doubt thinking, "Mary, mother of God, why can't I run home with these books right now? Why must I work for a living?" Every time I hear about somebody who wins a never-work-again sum in the lottery but keeps his or her day job I think, *not* a book person.

I don't fear death—I fear dying before I've read Dickens end to end.

Luis posed some standard questions and I worked through the answers: born in Pennsylvania, job in California, two brothers, one sister, mother living, father passed away. It was both a polite routine and a way for him to gauge my level in Spanish.

"You have children?" he asked.

"I've got nieces and nephews. That's enough for me."

This earned me my first real smile from Luis, a confirmed bachelor in a child-loving land. "We don't all need kids," he nodded. When I explained about the Austen reading group, he looked more interested still.

"Who's in your group?"

"Teachers from this school," I explained. "Nora, Élida, Mercedes, and two other women." At that point, I'd not yet met the other friends Nora had invited (or corralled?) to join. "Ani and Flor, I think."

"Which Mercedes?" Luis pursued, his eyes narrowing. "The fat one?"

Now, I knew one Mercedes at the school *was* bigger than the other but neither was fat. He maintained eye contact, unapologetic for his question, watchful for my response.

I decided on a frontal assault. "What a question! She's not fat. Don't you like her?"

A little smile wrinkled one side of his lips and he shifted tack. "I'd be very curious to know how your group goes with those women."

I got the distinct impression from his tone that he wasn't so sure they'd say much of interest. Sure myself that they *would*, I considered inviting him to join us. I had extra copies of *Orgullo y Prejuicio*. No doubt he could wolf it down fast, and I would love to know what such a widely read man would think of Austen.

Then my better judgment kicked in.

Just like the physical ruins in back of the administrative building on the Parque Central, that school had an ugly pile of rubble behind the façade in the form of the male/female relations. Various female teachers had let me know on my first visit that they feel disrespected by their male colleagues, and salary inequities were a big issue.

While I empathized, I wouldn't allow gender politics to prevent me from working with a teacher who interested me, and Luis interested me. But I also couldn't allow the Austen group to implode by inviting him and his incendiary jibes to join us. The ladies, I felt sure, would be outraged.

"I've got an extra copy of the book," I offered. I could discuss Austen with him, if he'd like, independent of the main group. "I brought a film version, too. Do you think they'd let us watch it here?"

For a teacher who spends seven hours a day, five days a week across a desk from foreigners butchering his beautiful mother tongue, watching a film could be a welcome change. We were due for a coffee break anyway, so we made arrangements. Wednesday, any and all interested parties could join us in the main office of *La Escuela* to see Jane Austen's *Pride and Prejudice*, dubbed into Spanish, with Keira Knightley as Lizzy Bennet and Matthew Macfadyen as Mr. Darcy.

As we resumed our conversation, refreshed with caffeine, Luis asked me about Austen and her novels. Lapsing in English was a serious no-no, but given the lack of subtlety in my Spanish, I quickly snarled up trying to show why Austen was worth discussing in Guatemala and elsewhere in Latin America. Not wanting to spoil *Pride and Prejudice* for him, I launched into a description of *Emma*.

"Emma's a rich girl, you see? And she's a, a"—drat, "matchmaker" was not in my Spanish vocabulary—"a person who finds husbands and wives for other people to marry." A simple statement can drag out endlessly as you pile up ten or twelve words you do know to substitute for the one you *don't*. "She's got a young friend, well, who's not really a friend because she's poor, but Emma wants to find a husband for her anyway, because that's the way she is, and when she finds a man who can be her husband, a husband for the friend, that man falls in love with her instead. With Emma."

Wow—stripped down to the plot, this sounds pretty sappy! "It's not just about what she says in the novel, it's the *way* she says it," I added, struggling to ignite some interest in Luis's critical eyes. "It's the way she sees things, the way she says them, it's her, her...*voice*."

It's not about the plots, I wanted to cry out. It's about the subtle commentary of the narrative perspective, the cutting inflections, the linguistic smirks! It's about those twists of the satiric knife that you can read right past unless you're really attentive—it's about the ostensibly innocent reporting of dialogue that nonetheless directs how we interpret that dialogue through the seamlessly clever framing. All of this I wanted to say, and so much more.

"*Su voz*." In Spanish, this was all that came out. "Her voice."

What a long way I had to go. There was *so* much I wanted to tell Luis about Austen, all of it trapped in my head in English and unable to make its way out along the extremely thin, badly rutted pathway my Spanish provided at the moment between my thoughts and my speech. Maddening!

I needed a nap. Spanish made my brain hurt.

I've already mentioned how beautiful Antigua is architecturally, but what makes it the loveliest place I'd ever been is that the city is completely ringed by green mountains, among which are two enormous volcanoes. Real live volcanoes! Well, one of them is live, anyway—the other, dormant.

Volcán Agua, the dormant one, is visible from any point in Antigua, a city without skyscrapers. Even my mother—the most directionally challenged person I know, bless her heart—could steer by this landmark. Volcán Fuego is about the same height as Agua, but since its base is situated lower, it appears shorter. It wins back the edge, however, by periodically growling and belching threads of smoke. During my first stay, early one morning shortly after lessons had begun, Fuego let out a series of low rumbles. I had never heard a volcano before, but I didn't have to ask what that immense, biblical sound was. Impressive. Very impressive. Involuntarily I shot to my feet as had every other student in sight. The teachers, volcano veterans, smiled and kept their seats.

When I returned for my second visit, I'd requested a room with a view of Volcán Agua. After checking in, I'd mentioned my Austen project to Roberto, the hotel manager. He was interested, since he'd been a high school teacher before going into the hospitality business. But when I mentioned that I also wanted to learn about his country's literature, to see if Guatemala had its own Austen, he lit up like a pinball machine.

"We've got so many great writers! Come, come here!" Warm and open, Guatemalans pretty much lack most Americans' shyness about touching strangers. Roberto seized my arm and hauled me to a table, patting his pockets with his free hand in search of a pen. "These are authors you'll like. You'll learn about Guatemala from their books." His eyes were full of the pleasure one booklover takes in sharing recommendations with another.

On the back of my flight itinerary, he wrote down several names, among them José Milla and Ana María Rodas (and if you know Guatemalan literature and are wondering about Miguel Asturias, rest assured; we'll get to him). "You won't have any trouble finding these authors here," he added.

Antigua has several bookstores on the main square and others near The Arch, a beautiful Spanish colonial structure that spans one of the streets bordering the cathedral La Merced. A signature landmark, The Arch was left standing—some say, miraculously—after the 1773 and 1976 earthquakes. There are a few coffee shops that allow people to swap books in English, a common practice in cities frequented by *gringos y gringas*, but finding Spanish books in such places is hit or miss. There's also an enticing used book fair on Fridays and weekends outside of the buildings that front the Parque Central.

Of the three authors on the list, José Milla, whom Nora and Élida had also recommended, was the most famous. Milla, born in 1822, came up most often when I asked Guatemalans about classic writers. I decided to read *Historia de un Pepe* when Roberto told me how he and his boyhood classmates had to recite it aloud in school, round robin. In the United States, school kids who'd rather be anywhere but in class are tormented with *Pride and Prejudice* or *Oliver Twist*—in Guatemala, with *Historia de un Pepe.*

Milla is a grand painter of tableaus, dramatic and unforgettable; reading him made me aware that I can rarely picture specific static images from Austen. Her work for me represents constant, typically gentle, motion—the passage of a polite visit, a fluid exchange of dialogue, the unfolding of ideas in the mind of a protagonist. Stylistically, Milla is more of a Sir Walter Scott. Scott himself acknowledged the contrast between his style and Austen's after her death:

> *That young lady had a talent for describing the involvements and feelings and characters of ordinary life, which is to me the most wonderful I ever met with. The Big Bow-wow strain I can do myself like any now going; but the exquisite touch, which renders ordinary commonplace things and characters interesting, from the truth of the description and sentiment, is denied to me. What a pity such a gifted creature died so early!*

A pity, indeed—although as history would have it, another famous writer came along a bit later to say, "It seems a great pity that they allowed her to die a natural death."

But that's a story for later.

CHAPTER TWO

The day for our school viewing of *Orgullo y Prejuicio* rolled around quickly. One of the administrators surrendered his office, and we set up our impromptu cinema. *Pride and Prejudice* is such familiar ground for Austen lovers that it brings back a certain thrill to view the movie with people who don't know if Lizzy and Darcy will manage to get together. When I saw the Knightley/Macfadyen version in the theater in California, I was seated behind two men and a woman in their fifties who could have been any of my more colorful Pennsylvania relatives or the grown-up equivalent of the fist-fightin' rednecks from my high school. The three treated the outing like a trip to a Steelers game, shouting encouragement and insults at the appropriate spots. I'm usually the first person to shush noisy viewers, but it was worth the ticket price to hear them respond to the story with such unreserved gusto.

"Who the hell does he think he is?!" barked the woman when Darcy snubs Lizzy at the dance.

"Ha! Guess she told you, buddy!" hooted one of the men when Lizzy takes him down a peg or two a few scenes later.

Every major plot twist prompted noisy feedback. "Oh yeah, Missy," cried the woman after Bingley has proposed to Jane and Lizzy sits outside, contemplating the proposal she rejected. "Yeah, that's right. Now you know you *blew it*!"

Imagine the surprise of all three when Darcy reappears to give it one more try—they were so happy they clapped and hollered. I felt like hugging them.

The teachers and students who clustered around the TV in *La Escuela* weren't quite so vocal, but they were clearly caught up in the Lizzy/Darcy battle. One of the teachers blurted out, "*Ay, no, no!*" in distress when Lizzy rejects Darcy and another actually flung her hands up and cried, "*Al fin, al fin!*"—"Finally!"—when Darcy makes his dramatic reappearance at the conclusion. Male and female alike had writhed in agony at Mrs. Bennet's machinations, the teachers elbowing each other to make comments in rapid Spanish that I couldn't entirely follow, beyond the sense that they'd seen her kind around Antigua. Mrs. Bennet translates particularly well across cultures, as anybody knows who's seen the mother dance down the steps in Gurinder Chadha's fabulous Bollywood adaptation *Bride and Prejudice*.

After the viewing, Luis and I made our way back along the garden path and sat down to debrief. "*Bien hecha*," he began. "Well made. Really a beautiful film." But the utter shamelessness of Lydia's behavior came under his fire, as well as her lack of repentance for the landslide of trouble her elopement caused. My hackles went up over the notion that Lydia was shameless when Wickham is the bigger wanker, for my money. But then Luis reached for a loose page of the meticulous notes he kept during each of our conversations and wrote down two words: *una mulada* and *una cabronada*.

"Austen's clearly interested in depicting shades of bad behavior," he explained, "not in drawing black-and-white portraits. As for this pair, they both ran off, but Lydia went off expecting to get married, and Wickham went off expecting to get laid. Her behavior was *una mulada* but his was *una cabronada*."

There's no way to translate these words exactly, but for starters, *una mula* is a mule and *una cabra*, a goat. The basic idea is that Lydia behaved like a stubborn mule, acting without a sense for the consequences, but Wickham behaved like a horny goat, with deliberate malice. One of the fun features of Spanish that English lacks is the capacity to create nouns that express behaviors out of other nouns or verbs. So, a dog is *un perro*, and behaving like a dog to somebody (see how many words that takes?) is *una perrada*. Behaving like *un burro* (donkey) translates into *una burrada* and *un cochino* (a pig), *una cochinada*.

"Very interesting, how the casting was handled," Luis continued. "There's nothing in the novel about Collins being short, but his height immediately conveys how small he is in character. A film can never provide the subtlety of characterization you find in a great book—and now that I'm reading it, I can see how subtle Austen is—but good casting helps."

As I agreed, he added, "Seeing a depiction of women's lives from that period was interesting. What do you think about the situation of women in Guatemala?" He leaned back against his chair and crossed his arms, watchful.

I could hardly think of a more loaded question from a man who hadn't exactly displayed the best attitude toward his female colleagues. I could also feel that late afternoon headache settling in, the one I got most days from struggling through hours of Spanish conversation.

Hell, I'm paying for this, I thought, so I went the easy route. "What do *you* think of their lives?"

The wry tilt of an eyebrow showed that he knew a dodge when he heard it, but he obliged me. "We got our independence from Spain in 1821." He leaned forward and wrote the date on our page of notes for that day, full on both sides with words, phrases, a few random sketches. "Where are Guatemalan women now?" He wrote another date: 1822. "Maids—that's what their parents raise them to be, maids. They're raised to do chores, not to use their minds."

Fascinating. A man so harsh on individual women nonetheless had a bead on what academic types call "social construction." The problem is not women *per se*; it's how women are raised. But Nora and Élida and their friends were obviously capable of using their minds, whatever social pressure may have tried to stop them from doing so, however much of their time was eaten up by "women's work."

Austen wasn't raised the same way as her brothers. She and her sister Cassandra only received about two years of formal education, while older brothers James and Henry were sent to Oxford. If Jane begrudged them a privilege her gender prohibited, no real trace of this sentiment survives. Disappointingly for scandal-seeking biographers, Austen's family seems to have been a happy one, inequities notwithstanding. Austen's determination to see her works in print bore fruit not only because her family supported her efforts but also because of her own determination not to let her talent go to waste, despite the constraints of her era.

Luis remained poised for my response. Judging from his expression, he was interested in knowing more than whether I could pull the words together in Spanish. Somehow I hadn't seen myself getting into a conversation like this outside of my Austen group, and I hadn't expected to encounter such harsh criticism of *latino* gender roles from a Guatemalan man. But what prompted me to think that way? What sort of assumptions was I making about Guatemalan men? Still I wondered: would Luis have spoken so openly on the subject with a Guatemalan woman?

Any Austen reader knows the dangers that lie in making assumptions and judging too quickly. Before setting foot off U.S. soil I'd given my feminist self an earnest talking-to: "Seriously *try* not to jump to conclusions about women's rights in Latin America! At least for a week or two." Now here was somebody who wanted to dish on the way women are shortchanged—and somehow, I balked.

Fact is, I'd already become defensive on behalf of the women I'd come to know in Guatemala, and I stared down at the date Luis had so provocatively written. 1822? Were Nora, Élida, and their friends nearly two centuries behind me, somehow? No way. On the other hand, they were the first to point out the exhausting struggles they faced to be taken seriously.

Arrgh! I so wanted to have this conversation, but I was torn on the subject and incredibly frustrated, yet again, with lacking the capacity to explain my thoughts properly.

"Complicated," I said at last. "The roles we play, taught to play." My head felt the size of a watermelon, and my Spanish decomposed into phrases and single words.

I fell silent, and we studied each other across the desk. Was I letting down women everywhere? Was I disappointing Luis? Could he *see* how hard this was for me, running the dull edges of my Spanish up against his sharp insights and questions? The bells of the nearby church began to toll.

"Enough for today?" I asked.

"Enough for today," he nodded, with a slow smile.

Okay. He saw.

After a lengthy nap I woke up, headache gone, then dressed and set off from the hotel feeling reinvigorated, ready for some nightlife. Antigua is full of wonderful restaurants, but for some reason that night, I didn't want any of the local fare, despite the quality of every meal I'd had in a Guatemalan restaurant across the price spectrum. I wanted something different. Something…

German. I stared at the sign, tickled to find a German restaurant in that decidedly laid-back, non-Teutonic setting. Johnny Cash was playing on the sound system as I took a window table across from the bar. A nearby wall was plastered with an eclectic mix of decorations: a scarf with the colors of a German soccer team, various cartoons cut from newspapers, magazine ads with busty young women, a photo of Che Guevara with Fidel Castro. A waitress eventually came by with a menu, and I ordered the tempting "*buffalo chili.*"

"Oh, the *buffalo chili*—very good!" The distance between my table and the bar wasn't large, and a smiling man seated there, tall and burly for a Guatemalan, bridged it with talk.

"I'm Osvaldo. Emmy? You're Emmy?" Spanish pronunciation, charmingly, turned me into an Austen character. "So, where are you from? The U.S.? That's nice! California? I like California!"

As he talked on, my buffalo eventually arrived and with it, a foamy stein of *Gallo*, a tasty Guatemalan beer I'd chosen because "*gallo*" means rooster. "Look at this!" Osvaldo said, slickly helping himself to the empty seat across from me. "Look at this stein!" The Gothic German script on one side read: "*Comedia Alemana.*"

I pondered the words while Osvaldo waited, an expectant look on his face. "Get it? Eh? Not *comida—comedia*! Not German food, it's German comedy!"

D'oh! And somebody had spent good money on those hefty steins.

I could follow most of what Osvaldo said as he chatted about his farm outside of Antigua, how good the local food is, how lovely the mountains are, his friendly flow of words interrupted only when other customers passed by and exchanged handshakes and greetings with him. Given the local norms, he had a wife and numerous children; if so, they got edited out of that evening's version of his life.

I wasn't the youngest or the prettiest woman in that restaurant, but I did have something special: a reputation. Many *latino* men, I'd been warned, assume that American women are "easy" in general and that when we're traveling, watch out—we're insatiable! At the risk of offending the delicate sensibilities of certain types of Austen fans, I'll admit I have had a foreign affair or two when the circumstances were just right. This was not one of those moments. But as I suspected, Osvaldo made his way around to his pitch. Really, pretty lady, the little towns outside of Antigua are so lovely, yes, and do you know how pretty your eyes are? How can you visit, pretty lady, and not see these lovely towns?—maybe this evening?

Time to finish my buffalo and go.

I set off without any particular plan in mind, passing numerous Guatemalans out enjoying the evening air. Eventually I found myself in front of Antigua's popular Irish pub, a favorite with foreigners of all stripes. On my first trip fellow students and I had come here to spend many hours and many *quetzales*, the local currency, named for Guatemala's exotically beautiful national bird. On my current trip I hadn't taken time to make friends among the students, so there were no familiar faces in the pub that night. Teachers, short on free time to begin with, tended not to hang out in tourist spots.

I took a seat at a table occupied by a woman named Ida who turned out to be, of all things, genuinely Irish. "My daughter's here studying Spanish," she lilted. "I'm just checking up on her, don't you know." A round of *Gallo* beer arrived and so did another foreigner, a young Welshman named Nevin. Germany, Ireland, and now, Wales—I'd managed to pull together all three elements of my ancestry in a single evening of dining and drinking.

"Are you here to visit or to study?" I asked.

He displayed his be-ringed left hand with a grin and said, "I live here. I came backpacking in 2004 and fell in love with a Guatemalan. Two weeks later, we were married." Impressive— quicker than even Charlotte Lucas and Mr. Collins!

After we'd exchanged some travel tales, I couldn't resist seeing if Nevin had a favorite Guatemalan author. "My favorite," he answered, "and my wife's, too, is Gaitán."

Dignified little Élida, my teacher before Nora during my first trip, had also recommended Hector Gaitán Alfaro, the author of collections of legends and ghost stories. Antiguans have a particular fascination with such tales. One famous apparition is the *Sombrerón*, a short fat man with a giant hat and a hair fetish; he sneaks into stables at night to tangle the horses' manes. When he's really feeling naughty he climbs into young women's windows while they sleep and braids their hair so tightly they can never get it loose. A teacher I'd spoken to at *La Escuela* insisted that this happened to one of his friends, who was forced to cut her waist-length hair off above the ears.

Élida had been a responsible, dutiful teacher. She had me recite verb conjugations; she corrected my pronunciation gently but firmly; she kept me on task when I tried to get lazy and let her do most of the talking. Her weak spot, I finally discovered, was stories about ghosts and spirits. A well-placed question and I could sit back and hear all about how an owl would visit outside the house of a person about to die or how a woman with a beautiful body but a horse's face—the infamous *Siguanaba*—lures unwary men to their doom if they catch her bathing in a public fountain at night. Élida assured me that these were legends and that only rural Guatemalans still believed them. Then again, a huge owl *had* hooted outside her family's house just before her grandfather died…

As the volume in the tourist-packed pub moved into the boisterous range, I checked my watch. I'd entered a gray area, given that the school's director had warned students not to walk the streets alone after 10:00 or 11:00 p.m. But Antigua, although it has its problems, is not Guatemala City. While fascinating culturally, the country's capital is noisy, dirty, and overcrowded; you can easily be robbed there in broad daylight. Nora had once seen a woman have her gold earrings—and half of her ears—yanked off in Guatemala City's central square.

Bidding farewell to Ida and Nevin, I started back to my hotel, alert to the city's somewhat eerie energy after dark; Antigua means "old" or "ancient" in Spanish, and the name is never more apt than at night. Rich with centuries of history, full of crumbling architecture just perfect for housing phantoms, Antigua has an ambiance that makes legends and ghost stories feel more plausible, somehow. Footsteps seem to ring differently on cobblestone streets, so quaint and narrow, and the fact that there are almost no buildings over three stories allows the night sky to retain a power it loses in most cities.

I passed the largest cathedral, as impressive in the shadows as it was in the sunlight, and started down the alley toward my hotel. Given a choice that night between encountering an earring snatcher or a roaming spirit, I'd go for the latter.

"I've got an idea," I said to Luis on Friday morning, the day before the Austen group and the last day of our lessons together. "Let me take you out to lunch, then we can skip the afternoon lesson. Does that sound good?" Normally the school has a two-hour lunch break so teachers can escape students, rest their weary ears, and see their families. I had a suspicion Luis would be willing to trade off his lunch to make it home earlier to his beloved books.

"If you'd like," he said, trying not to look too pleased.

We chose a Peruvian restaurant. Luis had seldom offered personal anecdotes during the week except when I'd asked him specific questions, but the lunch (or maybe the rooster beer) got him talking about California. He'd lived there for more than ten years in the late seventies and eighties with an American girlfriend. As new *Gallos* arrived to the sound of Peruvian flute music, we ranged over a huge variety of subjects but inevitably ended up back in literature territory.

"Austen's novels are excellent character studies," Luis said, sipping his beer. Somehow, I could hear the "but" before he said it. "But what about a writer's social responsibility? She was publishing while England was at war with Napoleon. Shouldn't a writer address current problems and politics?"

I was full of opinions on Austen's politics—in English.

"The question is," I plunged in, "what is literature for? It can address problems, but sometimes the last thing people want to think about is their problems. Sometimes they want to focus on something else. Maybe they don't want to think about fighting. Maybe they want to think what they're fighting *for*—their families and a peaceful England."

When my response earned a smile, I decided on a challenge of my own. "What about Guatemalan authors? Do you think they're more political? Which ones are important?"

"Asturias, of course. Miguel Ángel Asturias." He pronounced the full name ringingly.

If you've heard of any Guatemalan novelist, chances are it's Asturias, born in 1899. He won the Nobel Prize in Literature in 1967 shortly before his death. When I asked Guatemalans about literature, his was the first name, every time. Roberto the hotel manager didn't write Asturias down as a recommendation only because I mentioned I was already familiar with him.

"You know about our problems politically and with the U.S.?" Ever direct, Luis was unafraid to enter touchy conversational territory. I nodded. Some Americans dismiss our shadier foreign policy dealings in Latin America as "conspiracy theory," even covert actions the CIA has owned up to, as they have with Guatemala. The country's lengthy civil war extended roughly from the late fifties until 1996, with about 250,000 deaths and "disappearances." The United States didn't cause the war, but our meddling was part of the picture. I might still be struggling with Spanish, but I'd learned fairly quickly on the road that assuming all U.S. interventions have the moral soundness of the D-Day landings is a good way *never* to understand how people in Latin America feel about their northern neighbors (and I don't mean Canadians).

"You know about racism here," Luis expanded, "and about our military dictators, the U.S. companies who controlled our land, how your government interfered with our elections? This is what Asturias wrote about." He pulled paper from his brief-case beneath the table and began writing titles. *Hombres de Maíz* (Men of Corn) is perhaps Asturias's most famous, along with what's known as "The Banana Trilogy," on foreign agricultural exploitation. "Very powerful writer, very important. To realize how complicated this country is, you need to read Asturias."

Unfortunately, it's not just the country that's complicated—Asturias's texts are so rich precisely because his style and analyses are complex. For accessibility, the exception is *Leyendas de Guatemala* (Guatemalan Legends), produced early in his career.

Challenging topics and all, what a pleasure it was to linger over food and conversation with Luis. I was getting to like this leisurely two-hour lunch business. If you've ever traveled outside of the United States, the speed-eating capital of the world, you may have felt frustrated at the service in foreign restaurants. I've been as guilty as any American of wanting to scarf, pay, and dash, so I've done my share of glaring at staff oblivious to my desire to have the check right after my last bite of food. But to avoid a big howling heart attack while on the road (and thus confirm my mother's darkest fears that Latin America would kill me one way or another), I'd decided to stop pushing and to surrender as best I could to the local pace of life.

The previous evening, for instance, I'd been lounging around in a little park called the Plazuela Santa Rosa, enjoying the play of fading light over Volcán Agua, when a taxi van drew up. Driving was none other than Gustavo. He stepped out and we chatted for a good ten minutes before I asked him what he was up to that night.

"Oh, I'm taking these volunteers to their hotel. They're here to work with children." I'd seen one person emerge from the van when he stopped but failed to register until that moment that five more were still inside, each giving Gustavo and me an indignant look, that quintessentially American "why is this taking so long?!" look that I was working to eliminate from my facial vocabulary.

On that last lunch with Luis, our check arrived when it damn well pleased, without me fussing and twisting in my seat to hurry the service. After all, how often do I advise my California students to slow things down with Austen, to open up to the elegant pace of her novels? On first encountering Austen, some grouse that characters are simply talking and, therefore, "nothing is happening!" I urge them to see that a good conversation *is* something happening. Spanish even has a word we lack in English to describe those lingering conversations over a good meal—*sobremesa*. "Over table," literally, but the connotations in Spanish are much richer.

When Luis and I finally left the restaurant, we went to check out the book fair running in the main square. He made several recommendations, which I duly purchased. But along with local literature, I was hunting for something else: Nancy Drew in Spanish. Reading her in translation would be a nice way to revisit the dear old friend I'd first met long ago on a cold, rainy day in the library where my mother worked. But no such luck under the warm Guatemalan sun, as Luis and I browsed the tables in companionable silence. Luis selected several titles for himself and then announced, "I've got one more errand. Come along."

The errand was buying a fifth of rum. A good bottle and some good books—good plan.

"Will you come back?" he asked pointedly as we shook hands good-bye.

The intense look in his dark eyes felt like a challenge, as if the real question were much more profound. Will you be satisfied with your modest accomplishments or will you *really* learn to speak Spanish? After a jaunt through Latin America, will you return to an easy life in the United States and forget about the people here, about their struggles and their strengths, or will something get through? Will you be, in some way, changed? I felt transfixed by his gaze, by everything his question and demeanor implied at that moment. Luis was the best kind of teacher—the kind you don't want to disappoint.

"I can't promise how soon," I answered. "But yes, I will come back." I would show him I was a real traveler, not a tourist. "After all, you still haven't finished reading *Pride and Prejudice*. Just you wait until I can *really* argue with you in Spanish!"

A quick smile and a nod, then he and his books (and his bottle) were gone.

CHAPTER THREE

I paced the lobby of the hotel. Nora, Élida, and the others from the school were about to arrive, at long last, for the group. I wanted so badly for it all to turn out well! We'd had some visits during the week, including a dinner and a few coffee break chats, but with the weekend finally here, we could devote our time to Austen.

One by one the ladies arrived, and amid noisy greetings we commandeered the second-floor lounge. "Tell us," Mercedes prompted as she settled in on the sofa. "What do you think of Luis?"

Okay, so Austen could wait a bit. Clearly this was my invitation to spill. But recalling Luis's less-than-polite reference to Mercedes earlier, I felt wary of entering a minefield of co-worker gender politics.

"He's a very good teacher," I offered, already knowing that this simply wouldn't do.

"No doubt," Mercedes admitted, showing a bit of impatience at my disingenuous answer. "But as a man, what do you think of him as a man?"

"Definitely different. But he's never been married, like me. You know how odd we single people are." I recalled some of the revealing things he'd shared over *Gallo* beer but couldn't bring myself to tattle.

She shook her head and laughed at this newest sidestep. An "alpha" emerges from any group, and Mercedes was the early frontrunner. A traditional Brit would call her a handsome woman. With carefully coiffed black hair, a direct gaze, and an air of confidence, she somehow gave the impression of being taller than she really was. In fact, her demeanor reminded me of—Luis. A face-off between those two would be something to see; I got the feeling it was something the school grounds *had* seen on more than one occasion.

The arrival of the last of our crew saved me from any more probing questions. Happy, exuberant Flor, apologizing breathlessly for being late, was the youngest of us, strikingly pretty and a very sharp dresser, albeit a little on the daring side for a Guatemalan. Back in January *La Escuela*, coming under conservative leadership, adopted new policies and required all teachers to wear more formal dress. The original plan had been to permit only dresses or skirts for women, but a threatened Female Uprising nixed that idea. Nonetheless, Flor had to trade off her attractive-but-snug casual wear for dowdy professorial garb, a real disappointment, I suspected, for her admirers at the school.

Élida had given me a hug and kiss when she'd arrived, but she was somewhat distant that evening. I'd noticed the same thing earlier in the week when we got together with Nora for dinner. While Élida was always more reserved than Nora, she'd seemed especially withdrawn. At first I was concerned I'd offended her by studying with Luis rather than requesting her or Nora again. The situation turned out to be worse than wounded feelings about the school: her granddaughter, she'd told us over dinner, was carrying twins and having a difficult, dangerous pregnancy. I was glad our Austen group this evening gave her something else to think about, but her granddaughter's health couldn't be far from her mind.

The member of our group with whom I'd had the least contact was Ani, a shy, sincere woman in her late forties with short salt-and-pepper hair. According to Nora, years ago Ani had contemplated taking religious orders, and she definitely had the serene, centered bearing I've observed in many nuns. I was looking forward to hearing what this contemplative soul thought of Lizzy, her sisters, and their troubles.

Because the women had missed the film viewing at the school, they asked me to show the movie again before our talk, so we crowded around my laptop. Like most buildings in Antigua, the hotel had an open courtyard in the center, with the roof extending from the outer walls only far enough to overhang the passageways in front of the rooms. Because the lounge couch faced south, Volcán Agua provided a stunning backdrop to our viewing. The sounds of Antigua played counterpoint to the film's placid English countryside, as local children launched firecrackers with regularity, the noisiest ones setting off a return volley of car alarms. Roberto passed through periodically to show rooms to new guests ("Hot water's on the left, available from 4:00 a.m. to 9:00 p.m.!"). Random shrieks from the neighbor's colossal parrot made us all jump, and the chorus of local roosters periodically sounded off as well, for good measure.

What surprised me most about the viewing was how much the women adored seeing this particular Mr. Collins humiliated. My California students tend to find Tom Hollander's Collins either comic or a little sad, but there was a bit of a mean edge to the ladies' hoots of laughter over his blunders. "Ha! *Poco hombre*," snorted Flor when Lizzy arrives to visit Charlotte, who sweeps out of the room with her guest and leaves her husband pontificating, mid-sentence. In other words, "not much of a man." However rough life is for women in Guatemala, men have their own challenges if they've got to live up to a standard set by the likes of Mr. Darcy.

When the film swept to an end, we enjoyed a big girly group sigh as Darcy made his appearance in the mist—more Brontë than Austen, that cinematic touch, but it plays well. Before I could finish packing away the laptop, Mercedes took the initiative, patting the copy of *Orgullo y Prejuicio* resting on her lap. "So, tell us, what's the idea behind your Austen project? Why did you want us to read this book with you?"

"Well, I've been teaching Austen in the States for years, and I wondered how people in a different setting, a different country, would react."

"What reactions have you observed?"

"This is my first group, so you're my guinea pigs." The others laughed, but Mercedes pursued her line of thought.

"Okay, so what have you observed in us?"

"You all laughed a lot during the movie," I offered, somewhat flummoxed. Given my novice Spanish and my desire not to influence the group's responses more than I could help, I'd hoped to do less talking and more listening.

She shifted tack. "Why did you pick this particular book for us?"

"It's her most popular novel—people really love this story."

"But it's also important because it's about her life, right?"

"Not really," I began, wanting to clarify this complex issue, when she cut back in.

"No? It isn't about her life?"

Finally, another member of the group joined in and opened up the conversation; Ani suggested mildly, "It's about the time she lived in, about her epoch. Maybe some parts of it might be about her life, but it doesn't all have to be."

"Okay, what I want to know is if this is similar to her life, to how things were with her family," Mercedes explained.

"The biggest difference we know for sure," I said, "is that Austen stayed single."

"Ah," cried Flor, "an old maid!"

The word I'd used was "*soltera*," which means single. The word Flor used was "*solterona*," which also means single but with a negative connotation. There's no way to translate it exactly, although "old maid" or "spinster" are close.

"Please, for Austen's sake," I smiled at Flor, "*soltera* sounds better!"

We all shared a wry laugh over this bugbear of labeling for unmarried women. "People do use *solterona* here," Élida acknowledged, "but it's not very nice."

Mercedes persisted in connecting the novel to Austen's life. "So she was single. But surely, she wanted this kind of love, right? With an intelligent man, one who could respect her? This story is about love, about what love really is."

"About a love strong enough to overcome the prejudices on both sides—they both had prejudices," added Élida.

"They're such a good couple, Elizabeth and Darcy," Mercedes responded. "They're good for each other. And they're both intelligent. Austen was intelligent; you can see it. Whether she had a formal education or not, she was as intelligent as any man."

Nora, who'd been offering noises of agreement at various points, officially joined in. "She must have read a lot—it always makes a difference, reading."

As I nodded, Élida frowned and said, "The father, he was intelligent, but he read *too* much. He was careless with educating his daughters. Look at Lydia and Kitty. And that mother, that Mrs. Bennet. All she's got on her mind is finding husbands, improving their position."

Agreement and dissent erupted all at once.

"Definitely empty headed!"

"What's she supposed to do? She's a mother!"

"Something I noticed," Nora attempted to calm the storm, "is that the film focuses more on just the two oldest sisters. The book lets you see more about the whole family, how they all interact."

With an eye to Mercedes's interest in the life/works connection, I took up this line, "Yes, and Austen had one sister, with whom she was very close her whole life."

A rash of cross-talking broke out again, the others still interested in either defending or attacking Mrs. Bennet, until Mercedes cut back through it to say, "*Hasta la fecha*, mothers have this concern about the reputation and status of the family."

This was the first use somebody made of the expression "to this day" (or literally, "to the date"), but it wouldn't be the last. I had deliberately avoided any questions about how the book might connect to their own lives, wanting to see if, when, and how the question might come up naturally. And here it was.

"Unfortunately," Élida added, "lots of them are more concerned about status than they are about the happiness of their children."

On this point, there was no dissension. "And when a *ladino* marries a Maya, watch out!" *Ladino* is the word often used to describe Guatemalans of Spanish, nonindigenous descent. While not all indigenous people are Mayan, many Guatemalans use the term "Mayan" broadly to mean indigenous.

"It's the big prejudice we have here! I've actually heard people use the expression 'Hay que mejorar la raza,'" Mercedes said indignantly. "'We've got to improve the race.' We shouldn't mix with the Maya. But we're already mixed, we're all a *mezcla*!"

Élida echoed, "*Hay que mejorar la raza*," shaking her head sadly while the others nodded yes, they're a mix, *una mezcla*.

"Ask anybody here and, of course, they're pure Spanish. Nobody wants to admit to being Mayan," Mercedes added. "Why are people ashamed of this? Look at how sophisticated their civilization was. Students are always interested in the Maya, and they ask us so innocently, 'Are you Mayan?' They don't understand what that *means* to people here, how angry some people get if you ask them that!"

"It's so common, this prejudice," Nora and the others agreed. Given the role of race in Guatemala's civil wars—indigenous people were systematically oppressed by the various military leaders—the discussion took on a somber feel until Mercedes moved us into more neutral territory.

"Too many marriages are just like contracts," she said. "They're for appearances, for status. *Hasta la fecha*, it's what happens here. That marriage between Charlotte and Mr. Collins—terrible! I don't like that a bit."

A chorus of "me neither's" filled the hotel lobby, along with variations on "Money's not going to make you happy," uttered simultaneously. Their disapproval of the match was so strong, I couldn't resist playing devil's advocate.

"But look how it helps Charlotte's family," I pointed out. "And now she's got her own household." Heads were shaken and brows were furrowed; they weren't buying it.

I was surprised by their attitude. Parsing through my reaction,

I confronted an ugly assumption—not the first one I'd made in Latin America (and, unfortunately, not the last). As the conversation swirled on around me, I realized I'd assumed that their frustration with men would lead them to, well, get a little *cynical* about relationships. If men see women as lesser beings and objectify them, then why not objectify men right back? Why not marry the man who's going to inherit Longbourn? What's the difference between one provider and another, as long as he's providing enough?

But these women hadn't fallen into the trap of objectifying the objectifier, however much they resented being taken less seriously than they deserved. I knew that two wrongs don't make a right, so why would I think that these women would behave as if they did? Badly done, Amy.

Sheepish but still curious about the relationship question, I waded back in with arguments I'd heard from former students, since the Charlotte/Mr. Collins match always finds defenders in California. "Can't there be more than one kind of marriage? Why do we have to assume that everybody's looking for the same kind of thing in their married life?"

Still not buying it. "Without love, it's not a marriage," Flor pronounced bluntly.

The other four defenders of love concurred. Then two began to waffle.

"Her husband is a preacher, after all, and that's a good thing," said Nora.

"I hope for her sake Charlotte will grow to love him," Ani added, a look of compassion on her kind face. There it was, again, just like I'd seen over and over again in the States—Austen's characters bursting the seams of her novels as if they were real people.

I couldn't help but smile, thinking about my students (and a slew of Austen sequel writers, eager to chronicle Charlotte's fate).

"Love doesn't work that way," Flor insisted firmly, moving forward in her seat for emphasis. "In a couple, if from the outset one doesn't love the other, they're never going to."

That love is necessary, all agreed. But the question of whether love can grow provoked yet another flurry of debate.

"We've all had our different experiences here," Mercedes declared. "Me, I'm a widow. And you've been divorced, you've been divorced, you've been divorced," she pointed in turn at Nora, Élida, and Flor. "And Ani, single. We all know now that when it comes down to it, you've got to ask yourself, how will I feel by this person's side?"

"Can you really *live* with them?" seconded Élida.

"The biggest problem here is that we all worry too much what other people think about our decisions," Mercedes said. "We say we shouldn't, but we do."

As for Austen, she was fading further into the background, but I had no intention of steering us back. I didn't want to turn this into a lecture; I wanted to see where Austen would lead us.

"But it can be hard to make good decisions about men, because we grew up with so little information," Mercedes continued. "I didn't spend *any* time with men until after I finished school. That's how we were raised here, right?" Nods all around. "My very first school was a convent!"

Flor giggled and the rest joined in, sharing memories of conservative Catholic schools and encounters with nuns.

"My school was *so* strict," Nora said. "But actually, I wanted to be a nun!"

As Flor laughed even harder, Mercedes added, "I did too! I really did! But my grandmother talked me out of it. She told me to make sure that I understood the commitment."

"Yes, since it's like a marriage," I offered.

Suddenly five sets of eyes were fixed on me. "It's not *like* a marriage," Ani said gently but firmly. "It *is* a marriage."

As much as we had in common, I was reminded with a jolt, we came from different worlds. I'd been raised Catholic but not in a Catholic country. I wondered how many combinations of five women you'd have to pull together in the United States to produce a group in which not one but three had seriously considered becoming nuns. Quite a lot, I suspect.

We transitioned from how little interaction they'd had with men while growing up to how one adjusts to living with the troublesome creatures (male readers, please reverse the genders here). Our conversation then began fracturing off into chat between pairs. Somebody began a juicy story about somebody's sister getting pregnant by some real so-and-so, and would you believe that—

Suddenly Mercedes put on the brakes.

"That thing, that recorder—is that still on?"

Knowing I could never keep up with the whole conversation, I'd been taping us. We all laughed in mutual acknowledgment that we'd come quite a way from Austen.

"Time for dinner," I said, shutting off the recorder.

As somebody completed the story about somebody's sister and the so-and-so—off the record—we made our way to the restaurant, *La Fonda de la Calle Real*. It was noisy and festive, crowded with happy weekend diners. We had trouble finding a table for six but at last located a spot in the open central patio area.

"Ah, those musicians, I know them!" cried Mercedes, indicating two guitar players and a singer circulating among the tables in a side room. "They played a serenade for me on my birthday!"

We ordered drinks, enjoying the music and gossiping. After we hit one of those moments of companionable silence, again Mercedes took the initiative. "Did you have any more questions for us? What else should we talk about?"

Glad to return to a thread I'd wanted to pursue, I asked if they had any thoughts on the differences between the novel and the film.

"I liked the film," Nora said, "but the message, the idea that appearances can be deceiving, is clearer in the book. It also made me think more about how all of these problems the characters faced are exactly the things we all face in our lives and our relationships. The novel is set in England, but it's just the same as if it were here. It could all be happening here."

This is *exactly* what I had been wondering, and I was glad to get this response without any prompting. Before I could pursue it, however, Mercedes added, "I liked the emphasis on families and romance. I don't want anything to do with stories with blood and crime; we've got too much of that here."

I exchanged a look with Nora and recalled her story about the gruesome earring (and ear) snatching, as well as another she'd told me a day or two before our Austen group. Six armed gunman had stormed her daughter's school on the day parents paid tuition, in cash (public schools are so terrible that many people work two jobs to pay for private education). They'd ordered the kids to the ground, roughed up the terrified secretary, and bolted with the money. Armed robberies are a common enough occurrence that store delivery trucks carry guards armed with machine guns; even the brightly painted rural "chicken buses" full of low-wage commuters get ransacked periodically.

If indeed many of Austen's contemporaries enjoyed her books as a respite from all the talk about Napoleon and the war, ugly realities beyond their immediate control—likewise, in Guatemala.

"In this novel, love conquered pride and prejudice both." Ani's contented look as she spoke suggested that she'd had this point in mind for some time. "Despite all the things that could have prevented a happy ending, love triumphs."

"The book's also a demonstration of good behavior," Mercedes said. "Young people today have such bad manners."

The others nodded agreement, relishing the perennial middle-aged complaint, apparently not unique to the United States, about "young people today." She added somewhat archly, "I've seen plenty of people who are supposedly well educated but are *very* rude and others, people with no formal education, who are very courteous."

I had the feeling Mercedes was hedging a bit on who some of those "*very* rude" people might be, so I baited her: "I'm sure none of the U.S. students at *La Escuela* have bad manners."

All eyes were on me. Humor is hard to pull off in another language and sarcasm in particular, because it relies so much on tone. Tone is not something you can learn from a book.

Since Nora knew me best, after a beat she nudged me, laughing, and the others joined in. I may not teach in the same school, but I was a teacher, after all.

"Yes, it's true, there are *norteamericanos* at the school who aren't very polite," Mercedes said. "Let's face it—our students are living at a different economic level from us, a better level."

"And some are arrogant, very arrogant," Élida murmured as Mercedes talked, unable to resist seconding the point.

Nora overlapped her as well. "Rich people sometimes actually have the worst behavior, like Darcy and Bingley's sister at that first dance. Other people were just trying to be nice to them!"

While I let the conversation unfold naturally, there was one specific thing I wanted to ask. "Are there any elements of this story that are specific to England, things that wouldn't happen here?"

Élida shook her head. "There are some differences with our lives today but that's more because of the times, not culture, I think. People back then were much more formal and ceremonious."

"We're courteous but not so formal," agreed Mercedes. "Even husbands and wives referred to each other then as *Señor, Señora.*" I was glad I'd asked, because before our food could arrive to shut down conversation, the roving musicians did.

"'You're like a thorn in my heart,'" Nora leaned over to translate the lyrics of the ballad. "I think this song is Mexican. A lot of the best songs are."

"Well, anyway," Mercedes again took the initiative as the talented musicians moved off to serenade other diners, "I wanted to say that I like how Austen shows you that some pride is good, like pride in your accomplishments or your family. But you can't let pride make you think you're better than others."

"That's our problem here," Nora offered. "That's exactly where discrimination comes from. Whether it's because of money or because of race, it's no good."

Élida, Flor, and Ani nodded agreement, and we fell into a satisfied silence. The flow of our discussion had led us there, it seemed, as a kind of conclusion about the novel's themes and Austen's contemporary relevance. I thought back to Larry and to my California students and the many connections they'd drawn between their lives and Austen's romantic entanglements and family dramas. While no one in Antigua had offered to smack any of the characters, they'd certainly enjoyed seeing Mr. Collins knocked down to size by Lizzy and Charlotte.

And it was clear that for these women, Austen's world—however far from Guatemala—was still familiar territory.

After the meal, as we savored our coffee and desserts, I noticed Flor surreptitiously check her watch. Better get to the presents. The whole evening I'd been toting along a large paper bag with string handles, which each of the ladies would eye at random moments. One by one, I removed smaller festive bags from inside and placed them on the table.

"Flor, this is for you!" I started with her, and soon each member of the group was carefully removing tissue paper and probing into a package.

If you're really an Austen fan, a true Janeite in the nerdiest sense, you know that there's quite a lot of Jane stash out there. Before the Internet, to get it you had to visit hot spots like Bath, where she lived for a stretch, or Chawton Cottage, her last residence, or Winchester, where she died. Now from the comfort of home you can order Austen coffee cups, tea cozies, aprons, kitchen towels, key rings, pens, necklaces, notepads, mouse pads, pillows, bobbleheads, and for the adventurous fan, the Jane Austen action figure (complete with quill pen and paper). I'm proud to say, however, that every goodie I'd brought to Guatemala came directly from hallowed ground, either from the Winchester Cathedral gift store or the shop at Chawton Cottage.

"Wow, thank you, how adorable!" cried Flor, holding up her Austen key chain, a small portrait of Jane carved onto a delicate oval of wood. Soon an Austen tea towel was revealed and passed around to be admired, then some Austen stationery, a set of Austen coasters, a fancy Austen pen.

They all seemed taken aback—not that I'd given them presents, as Guatemalans are great gift givers, but that these Austen items *existed*. I tried to explain about Janeites, those devotees who write sequels, set up websites, hold dances and tea parties. The ladies could understand the novels themselves being popular, but since the notion that anything people like is ripe for marketing hasn't taken hold in Guatemala, they remained puzzled but pleased about the fan toys. Needless to say, I never ran across any "I'd rather be reading Milla" bumper stickers or Miguel Asturias coffee mugs.

But now came the beginning of the end, because Flor did have to go. I was so happy she had been in the group, keeping things light with her musical laughter.

"*Que te vayas bien*," she smiled, departing with a kiss and a hug. This friendly send-off translates literally as "go well," but the idea is more a general wish that things work out smoothly for you, that your trip (whether one block to your home or 3,000 miles to Chile) is all you hope it will be.

"You're going to learn so much when you travel in South America," Mercedes said, giving me a hug. "When you come back, my home is your home. You just tell us when you're ready to return!" She hailed a *tuk-tuk*, one of Antigua's noisy little golf cart taxis, with space for two passengers (or three, if you *really* like each other). On the rutted cobblestone streets a trip in a *tuk-tuk* is like riding on a donkey running at top speed, but they're cheap and popular. "*Hasta pronto!*" she called out, disappearing into the night.

Since Élida had back problems and couldn't ride a speeding donkey, Nora and Ani were going to walk her home then catch a *tuk-tuk* themselves, heading south while I went north. Nora and I had lunch plans for the next day, but I knew it would be quite some time before I'd see Élida and Ani again. "I'm so glad you liked the novel," I told them, "and I'm *so* happy I could talk with you about it!" If only I had more eloquence in Spanish to show them how much I appreciated their insights, their ideas, their personal stories, their laughter, sharing a chummy girls' night out.

But I think they could tell—we don't only communicate with language.

"I'm not sure exactly when, but I will be back," I promised earnestly. "And with better Spanish!"

That final Sunday morning, as I waited at the café for Nora to join me, I enjoyed the memory of how well the group had gone. But I also thought about the price. For weeks, Nora confessed, she'd had to steal moments for Austen, because she shared her house with twenty people. *Twenty.* Guatemalans take care of each other—so if your sister needs to move in with you, you let her, without staring at the calendar and waiting for her to move along. Austen would have approved. This means that cousins get to know each other better and are often more like sisters and brothers.

It also means that both privacy and time for books are a luxury. How can you read with a houseful of people who want to be fed, to have their clothes washed, to visit and talk? To finish the book, Nora had to wake up before anybody else, hide in her cubicle during the coffee breaks at *La Escuela*, and come home an hour later than usual, lingering in the school gardens to see if Darcy would lighten up, if Lizzy would learn about Wickham's lies, if Bingley would come back to Jane.

And me, swooping down on my big year's adventure. I'd been, quite frankly, clueless. I had no idea what I was asking when I invited Nora and the others for the book group. I assumed everybody had plenty of time to lounge around with Austen. In my defense, this was a mix of cross-cultural cluelessness with ain't-got-no-kids cluelessness. A fellow *soltero* like Luis could make his way through stack after bedside stack of books. But people with families—especially extended families—were hard-pressed to justify time for Jane Austen when dinner's not ready and a daughter, son, nephew, or niece scrapes a knee and needs a hug. Even the time to see me off was one more small theft from Nora's loved ones.

"So, we didn't get to talk about your daughter's wedding last night," I said when she arrived, her usual bright, bustling self.

"Oh, it was lovely. But," she added, looking pained, "the groom's family is a bit…well, they've got more money than us. We worked *so* hard to make everything nice, but for some of them, it wasn't enough. People here can be really critical about things, about the dresses, the dishes, what food we had."

I nodded sympathetically, recalling the previous night's discussion on marriage as a way to "better" your family and on placing too much emphasis on material things. Money, the ladies had pointed out, doesn't automatically bestow good manners. Nora had vigorously condemned the class prejudices that threatened Lizzy and Darcy's happiness and just as vigorously supported unions based on love, not the desire for a successful merger. Clearly, none of this was theoretical for her.

"*Chica*, what about you?" she asked, sipping her coffee. "Tell me more about that Mexican."

I gave her the nutshell version of how I'd met Diego more than a year ago on an impromptu beach trip to Puerto Vallarta, before I'd had any Spanish lessons at *La Escuela*. A year later I went back for a week's stay with him right after I'd finished my classes that May, so my upcoming visit would actually be trip number three (I do love repeat journeys). "He's really a great guy—very handsome, very easygoing. I'll be doing my next Jane Austen group with him and his friends."

She clasped her hands together gleefully, just as Ani had done the night before when Darcy proposed a second time to Lizzy. "That's so romantic! We don't find love when we're looking for it, you know. That's not how it works. Love finds *us*."

"*Vamos a ver*," I smiled, using a favorite phrase I'd heard there: "We'll see."

"Now I have something for you," Nora smiled. From her enormous purse, the kind mothers always seem to carry, she pulled a neatly wrapped package. Inside was a glass plaque inscribed with a saying, on a carved wooden base.

"You didn't have to do this, Nora!" I protested. "You've done so much for me already, giving your time and organizing everything here!"

But you can't stop a Guatemalan from being generous. "It wasn't work, it was *fun*. We all enjoyed it! And reading Jane Austen gave us something special to talk about even before you arrived."

We gossiped on, but the time finally came, even by leisurely local standards, to pay the check. I lingered just a bit more; it's easier to say good-bye to someone when you've got a clear idea of when you'll be saying hello again.

"I will be back," I promised. "I'm just not sure when. Maybe next Christmas?"

"*Que te vayas muy, muy bien, chica*," Nora said with a hug and a kiss—travel very, very well. "I'll be here!"

Seeing Gustavo the driver's familiar face raised mixed feelings since this time he signaled my departure, not my arrival. I wondered if he'd notice how much heavier my suitcases were, stuffed to the gills with books I'd bought.

"Things are going well with your daughter's studies?" I asked.

"Very well, thank you! And your reading group?"

I summed up my lively exchanges with Luis ("Ah, that Luis!" he laughed), my conversations with the ladies, and the reading I'd been doing.

"Did you call your mother?" he asked with a smile. We'd talked about her nervousness on the ride in.

"Absolutely. She knows that as of this morning, I'm still alive." And Diego knew that I'd be there with him in Mexico soon.

As we eventually reached the sprawling outskirts of Guatemala City and Gustavo needed to concentrate on navigating the heavy traffic, I reflected back on the "girls' night out." I wasn't planning to do any of the other sessions as single gender, but it had turned out to be a fun and comfortable arrangement for the first venture.

When I'd asked them whether *Pride and Prejudice* could have taken place in Guatemala, just as it was, with appropriate name changes, the ladies' unanimous answer was yes. Now I asked myself if our reading group conversation could have taken place in the United States just as it was, substituting Ann for Ani, Mercy for Mercedes, and so on. Or were there elements specific to this setting, this culture, specific to Antigua, Guatemala?

I've never heard U.S. students shift from Austen into racial prejudice—but within the recent memory of all five women, the Guatemalan army was wiping out entire indigenous villages while indigenous guerillas were picking off soldiers and perceived collaborators in response. I'd spoken with one Guatemalan who said they should disband their army altogether, like Costa Rica had done. "We can't possibly defend ourselves from foreigners with it. The government just uses the army to push its own *citizens* around." This is an alien reality for most people in the United States, who, whatever their thoughts on foreign policy, see the military as there to support us, not oppress us.

As for gender, traditional roles for men and women are more sharply marked in Guatemala than in the United States. Where I teach, someone trying to impose a skirts-or-dresses-only code for women would be laughed off campus; the women at *La Escuela* fought off just such a measure, proposed with a straight face.

I couldn't help but think that these realities, these struggles, made Austen's world even more accessible in Antigua. Sometimes my young California students just don't get how Lizzy has gone out on a seriously shaky limb by rejecting not one but two marriage proposals. They don't see why Lydia's premarital jaunt with Wickham is a Very Big Deal for her family. Granted, TV shows like *Sex in the City* and movies like *Bridget Jones's Diary* wouldn't exist if Anglos weren't jumpy about singledom too, and our sexual double-standard is still alive and well. (I'd love to see the day when a film like *Easy A*, an adaptation of *The Scarlet Letter*, wouldn't make sense any more: "A guy who has sex is a hero but a girl who does is a *slut*? On what planet?")

So maybe the difference is one of degree, not of kind. But in a country like Guatemala where marriage and motherhood remain the gold standard (unless one takes the nun option) and a woman's expiration date rolls around very early, in a country where a woman's reputation still seriously affects her entire family, *Pride and Prejudice* just might resonate on more levels.

So maybe because of the differences—not in spite of them—with no prompting from me the women all felt the connection between Austen's world and their own. They'd transitioned seamlessly from Mrs. Bennet to meddling mothers in Antigua, from the tribulations of Lizzy and Darcy to their own varied marital experiences, from class prejudice in England to racial prejudice in their own country. Austen was, to them, more familiar than foreign.

Would it be the same in Mexico and Ecuador, in Chile and Paraguay and Argentina? To a greater or a lesser extent? *Vamos a ver*. We'll see.

I was taking away so much, and not just in the bulging suitcases—wonderful memories, great experiences with Luis and with the women, a world of fabulous new authors to enjoy. And safely stowed in my carry-on was Nora's engraved plaque, a gift with a message suggesting I'd also be leaving something precious behind:

Gracias a ti, mi mundo seguirá siendo un lugar lleno de posibilidades y esperanzas.

"Thanks to you, my world will continue to be a place full of possibilities and hope."

I'll confess that Nora's gift brought tears to my eyes, given that

I'd learned a hell of a lot more from my new Austen buddies than they could have from me—and I don't just mean Spanish, either. Still, making time to read and discuss Austen drew Nora, Élida, Mercedes, Ani, and Flor out of their usual routine, and now the book club bug had bitten them. They all assured me they'd make more such opportunities, with or without me around.

But I couldn't really take credit for that "*Gracias a ti*." Thanks were due instead to a woman who wrote an incredible future for herself, one page at a time—although if anybody had told her a group of ladies would be laughing over Mr. Collins two centuries later and half a world away, Austen probably would have suggested they lay off the laudanum.

MEXICO:

SENSE IN THE LAND OF SENSIBILITY

In which the author rejoins a long-distance sweetheart in Mexico, buys more books, offers a few reflections on Mexican writers and fun fotonovelas, gives Austen's Catherine Morland a spin around the block, sees a ghost, is verbally assaulted by a poet, and, after three depressing weeks sick in bed, emerges to discuss Sense and Sensibility *with smart and interesting folks.*

CHAPTER FOUR

Guatemala was not my first venture into Latin America. More than a year before my Antigua Austen group, I flew to Puerto Vallarta for an end-of-semester beach break. That's when I met Diego, my driver for the half-hour ride to the hotel. He was tickled, he later told me, by my pre-*Escuela* Spanish, as I bounced from window to window in the backseat to take in the gorgeous sights, sputtering out gems like "Very good ocean! Very! Mountain pretty!"

Smiling into the rear view, midway through the ride Diego invited me to go dancing that night.

"No," I said flatly. I was *not* dashing off with the first man in Mexico who spoke to me. Yes, he had handsome dark eyes, thick, closely trimmed black hair, and an adorable droopy Pancho Villa mustache. Yes, his skin was incredibly close in color to milk chocolate. Chocolate! But *no*.

"You don't like to dance?" he pursued.

"I like. But with you, no dance."

He took one more shot after he'd set my bags in the hotel lobby, switching to his rudimentary English for my sake. "Here's my number. I honestly don't ask out every woman who gets in my taxi. But I'd really like to see you again."

"Maybe," I said, meaning "no," despite how sincere he looked.

Still, as the week slipped by I found myself remembering his cheerful, handsome face. How about if I hired him my last day to drive me to nearby Mismaloya, the lush film location of *Night of the Iguana* and a number of scenes in *Predator*? He could take me there then deposit me at the airport for my departing flight. That was innocent enough.

And so it went. Diego was pleased to show off the sweeping seascape of Mismaloya and the verdant hills, noisily alive with birds. And if I liked hills, how about a view of all of Puerto Vallarta?

"There's time before your flight. I want to show you where I jog every day."

Off we went up a dirt mountain road so rutted and narrow I feared for the vehicle. Part way up we pulled over to let a man descending with a burro pass by.

The view at the summit was worth the trip—there was all of Puerto Vallarta below and the sparkling ocean. And here I was with a complete stranger just a bit taller than me but from the muscular look of him, considerably stronger. Perhaps this was the part where he would jump me then toss my body into the thick vegetation, to be eaten slowly by the fist-sized spiders hanging from the surrounding trees.

What on earth was I doing up here with this man? This was precisely the sort of risky behavior that would lead my poor mother to have one fewer child. But I'd traveled a lot over the years, and I trusted my instincts. They told me that here was a person who wanted to show off the best view going of the idyllic place where he was born and raised.

"Beautiful, isn't it?" He smiled proudly. "I never get tired of seeing it from here."

Diego took me to the airport, wrote down my email address, and our lengthy correspondence began. It didn't take much prompting for me to return the next May for another week's vacation, prior to my trip to Guatemala. And that's how, a year after he'd first asked, we finally went dancing. Diego was amazed at how much better my Spanish was, and we agreed on a no-English rule so I could keep improving. At the end of a ridiculously happy week I asked him two very important questions:

"Would you like to read a novel by Jane Austen? And…have you got four or five friends who'd like to, also?"

Yes and yes. So now I was back yet again, this time for a three month stay. The passionate Marianne types of the world might be hoping for something juicy on our reunion at the airport. I've always been more of an Elinor, myself, when it comes to sharing detail—not big on kiss-and-tell. I will say that it felt *right* to be there. Seeing Diego poised to grab me for a hug as I cleared customs made me happier than I'd felt since I'd left the States. And I was certainly pleased, as we reached his taxi, to see the copy of *Sentido y Sensibilidad* I'd mailed him before setting off for Antigua.

One of Diego's friends had a house for rent, cheap, because it was under construction. When we arrived there Diego watched my reaction closely with a hopeful smile. The house was supposed to have been closer to done by the time I arrived, but…*así es la vida*. Such is life.

I couldn't help but see the house reflected through Diego's happy gaze. It radiated color and warmth. The covered entryway was draped with trailing branches of vivid purple bougainvillea, and in the straight line of sight from the front door to the rear patio, I could see newly planted greenery out back. The rich dark woodwork of the staircase was identical to the wood of the interior doors, carved with different aquatic scenes. Dolphins sported on the bathroom door, seahorses on one bedroom door, sea turtles on another. The floors were tiled, a mocha brown on the ground floor, sky blue on the second. The beautiful tile ceiling of the master bedroom made its way from one wall to the other not as a flat surface but rather as a series of three long, gentle arches that mirrored the form of the individual tiles themselves.

"So, what do you think?" he smiled.

As if on cue, a neighborhood rooster crowed somewhere nearby. How I missed the pet chickens I'd left behind in the States! I sighed happily at the familiar sound. "It's perfect."

"You haven't seen the best part yet!" He gave me a squeeze and led me up to the house's top level, an unfinished, covered roof patio, which he called the *azotea*. "It's got something for me and something for you. Guess which is which!" he laughed. A hammock strung between two cement pillars and a punching bag suspended from the ceiling—not much guesswork there. Diego had been an amateur boxer for years and still served as a trainer and sparring partner in a local gym. This *was* the best part of the house! I could lie there with a book, catching the sea breezes and watching him work up a nice, attractive sweat.

"So does this mean you'll stay here and keep me company?" We hadn't discussed a joint living arrangement, but I'd been secretly hoping he would just move in with me for the three months I'd be there.

As I settled into the swinging hammock, he gave me a hand-in-the-cookie-jar smile. "I brought a bag of clothing over before you got here."

Diego headed off to work the next morning and suddenly, the house felt huge and empty. As much as I love to explore new places, over the years I've been prone to panic whenever I relocate. It's a sort of traveler's stage fright, an intense anxiety that always goes away but not before I spend anywhere between a day and a week hiding in my bedroom, typically with a book, thinking, "What the hell am I *doing* in this place?!" It had hit me the hardest when I lived for a year in Prague, owing to the huge language barrier, but it happens whenever I find myself in new surroundings. On my first visit to Antigua I'd lived in closer quarters with other people, so it was less intense than usual.

Now I was rambling around a three-story structure—alone.

I abruptly stopped seeing the house through Diego's eyes and saw it through a different pair: my mother's. Not a window on the ground floor had glass. There were bars to keep out prowlers, *but all sorts of things could fit through bars, you know.* The second-floor passageway between the bathroom and the bedrooms was gated at either end but had no walls or glass either. *That just can't be safe! And how on earth will you keep things clean?* As for the outdoor cement staircase leading to the roof patio, it had no railing. My maternal grandmother, born in the United States after her parents emigrated from Germany, had died a decade earlier, but the sight of that spectacular two-story drop from the roof patio down to the back yard would have led my mother to channel an extra generation's worth of maternal concern: *Gott in Himmel—it's a death trap! Don't they have a law against people moving into houses that aren't done yet?!*

So I wouldn't be sending any photos of the house to my mom. Except maybe a nice close-up of the flowers over the entryway. But the least I could do was venture out and find a pay phone to call her—that would keep me from hunkering down in the house all day like a ninny. She had no doubt been staring at her phone since an hour before my plane took off for Mexico, perhaps wondering if there had been a crash so devastatingly horrible they were afraid to talk about it on the news.

As I dressed and set out for the bus stop to the center of town, I felt my panic receding. I'd been here twice already, for Pete's sake; I knew my way around. No call for alarm. After finding a pay phone and assuring my mother that I was indeed still alive, I went to hunt for *fotonovelas*.

Anyone who wants to learn Spanish should know about *fotonovelas*. Some Mexicans turn their noses up at these popular works, but they're hugely helpful for learning the language. Essentially they're novels told via sketches (not photos, despite the name), similar to comic books but the size of small paperbacks. There's an infamous subgenre people used to call "Tijuana Bibles," cheesy porn with lurid sketches. While the porn business is still booming, the other main genres are romances and westerns.

For romance, there are three biggies: *El Libro Seminal* (Weekly Book), *Amores y Amantes* (Love and Lovers), and *Libro Sentimental* (Sentimental Book). These are the series names; each individual volume has its own catchy title, like "My Father-in-Law, My Lover!" "He's Shameless but He's Mine!" and "Endless Suffering!" *Libro Seminal* is the most realistic, *Amores y Amantes*, the boldest and sauciest, and *Libro Sentimental*, tear-jerkingly maudlin.

To give you an idea how the three differ, let's take an underrated Austen heroine, the one who would have adored Antigua: Catherine from *Northanger Abbey*. In Austen's novel, sheltered country girl Catherine travels to Bath with family friends, where she meets a witty clergyman and learns to behave in proper society. Visiting the abbey home of the clergyman, she's led by an overdose of Gothic novels to suspect that his father, the widowed General Tilney, has done in his wife. Embarrassment, then marriage, ensues.

Fotonovela authors crank out a new title every week. If they got their hands on Catherine, the story would unfold something like this:

Caterina, from humble San Sebastián, travels to exciting Puerto Vallarta with the González family. While there:

Libro Seminal: Caterina gets invited to dinner by a mysterious yet somehow familiar man and finds herself attracted. She wakes up on the weekend still thinking about the mystery man. To distract herself, she goes with Señora Gonzalez to the commercial center and both buy attractive new dresses.

Amores y Amantes: Caterina gets seduced by a college boy on holiday and feels guilty yet somehow fulfilled. She wakes up on the weekend, only to discover she's been abandoned. To distract herself, she seeks comfort in the experienced arms of a retired army officer, recently widowed.

Libro Sentimental: Caterina gets a job as a maid for a *gringo*, who drugs and frames her for pushing his five-year-old daughter from a window (a crime actually committed by his drunken wife). She wakes up in jail surrounded by hardened female prisoners. To distract themselves, they beat and abuse her for killing a helpless child.

Never has life been so exciting for Caterina! And when she least expects it:

Libro Seminal: Caterina discovers that the mysterious man used to be her best friend's parish priest but renounced his vows when he saw Caterina at a wedding and doubted his calling. Returning to quiet San Sebastián, Caterina is unable to forget the fallen priest. Is it a sin to love a man who has renounced his calling?

Amores y Amantes: Caterina discovers from the retired officer's handsome son that her new lover is hiding a desperate secret in his palatial house—about his recently deceased wife. Returning to quiet San Sebastián, Caterina is unable to forget the retired officer's handsome son. Is she a bad woman for desiring the son of a woman who died so mysteriously?

Libro Sentimental: Caterina discovers that she's been assigned a top defense lawyer—then learns that the lawyer's only sister died in a fall from a window owing to negligence and is determined to see Caterina hang. Returning to her quiet cell after the trial, Caterina prays humbly, regretting only that she must die without having any children. Will her misery never end?

Clearly, all hope is gone! But finally:

Libro Seminal: The fallen priest pays Caterina a surprise visit and begs her to forgive him for not wanting to live a lie in the church; moved by his sincerity, she consents to be his wife, and they live happily ever after.

Amores y Amantes: The retired officer's handsome son pays Caterina a surprise visit and confesses that he hinted at dark secrets in order to separate her from his father. Moved by his ardor, she consents to be his wife, and they live passionately ever after.

Libro Sentimental: The prison chaplain pays Caterina a surprise visit to hear her confession; moved by her piety, he assures her that true repentance will earn her a place in heaven where she can be a godmother to the many children called home early by their maker. She dies happily after all.

The house felt more like home after I set up the cozy little library of *fotonovelas* on the built-in bedroom shelves, one of every current title, along with a huge number of back issues I'd found at a secondhand store.

Diego finally returned that evening, filling the house back up with sunshine and dispelling any doubt about my decision to come to Mexico. I felt as comfortable and content with him as if we'd already lived together for months. Some men might be irked to come home and find an empty refrigerator and no food on the table, but Diego laughed out loud to see that I'd spent my day buying bargain reading material instead of groceries.

"Let's go out to eat," he said, kissing the end of my nose.

My Spanish might be rough, but that man definitely understood me.

Puerto Vallarta was a quiet fishing village until the 1960s, when John Huston decided that Mismaloya, just north, would make a perfect setting for his film *Night of the Iguana*. Elizabeth Taylor and Richard Burton began their tempestuous relationship during the shooting. Dick bought Liz a house in Puerto Vallarta and then, more or less, tourists starting showing up. But while the population has expanded to about 250,000, the town center remains compact. There's a small central square, which often has free entertainment and dancing on the weekends, and close by is the town's loveliest church, Virgin of Guadalupe, with a huge lacey metal crown where you'd expect to find a steeple.

Directly across from the square, extending north and south along the shore is the Malecón, the attractive beach walkway where folks go to see and be seen. Soon after my arrival Diego and I went for a stroll and a swim so that I could reacquaint myself with the sea. After a leisurely day, we went to deliver *Sentido y Sensibilidad* to the first couple in the group. I was curious if *Sense and Sensibility*, less popular with U.S. students than *Pride and Prejudice*, would be more appealing to Mexicans.

On the bus ride there, Diego explained that he'd been friends since childhood with Salvador, whose wife Soledad was a perfect match for him. Both were sincere, hardworking, intelligent—and "*chiquititos*." Very, very small. Then he squeezed my hand and said, "Their house is simple." His emphasis gave me pause. Many of the houses I'd seen outside of the tourist center struck me as simple, so clearly he wanted to prepare me for a bit more. Was he afraid that I would be uncomfortable or that I'd make his friends uncomfortable? Or both?

Midway there we switched from bus to taxi, leaving behind the city's main traffic artery. The houses became smaller, the neighborhoods more ragged, and the terrain increasingly steeper. Diego pointed out a left turn to make but when the taxi driver saw the street, he balked and let us out. What used to be a road had disintegrated into dust, chunks of concrete, and stones from the local river. From there, we walked.

The small army of waiters and waitresses, taxi drivers, maids, clerks, and vendors who work in the tourist industry—that is where they live. Puerto Vallartans were around well before the crowds arrived in the wake of Taylor and Burton, but many local jobs now depend on tourism. *Septiembre* is jokingly dubbed "*sept-hambre*," *hambre* meaning hunger, for the lean times between the summer and the high season beginning in November.

Salvador and Soledad's neighborhood wouldn't be appearing on the cover of any tourist brochures, but all of the people with whom we exchanged a *buenas noches* as we passed looked at ease, lounging on plastic chairs in the dusty streets with friends and family, surrounded by miscellaneous dogs, enjoying the evening breeze and the music from competing stereos.

Salvador greeted us just outside the door, and as we entered, introduced Soledad. She was as warm and open as her husband and just as tiny. *Chiquititos*, the pair of them. Salvador was about five feet; Soledad, under. I often felt like a horse around Mexicans, and now I was a serious Clydesdale. I was happy to fold my bulk into the chair Salvador offered and stop towering impolitely over our hosts.

Their two even-tinier sons Juan and Salvador Jr. shimmied up to be admired then went off to play on a blanket spread over the concrete floor. On the kitchen wall I spotted several *cuizas*, bulgy-eyed pink lizards that look exactly like they're made of rubber. Salvador and Soledad's *cuizas* were even bigger than the ones living in my house. I almost pointed this out—then I realized they might not take it as the compliment I meant it to be.

After greetings, we worked our way around to Austen. "Tell

them about the book," Diego prompted, as he handed two copies to Soledad. Salvador was eyeing the size of them, and I thought of my friend Nora in Guatemala, snatching moments to read with such difficulty. Could these busy people find time for Austen?

"It's longer in Spanish" was the first thing I could think to say.

Laughing, Soledad exchanged glances with Salvador. "Almost four hundred pages," he mused, thumbing through the book. "Soledad will help me." He looked at her with pride. She had more formal education, having attended one of the many universities in Guadalajara for a year.

I didn't want to prejudice their reading, but I also didn't want them to feel at sea with an unfamiliar writer. So I told them a bit about Austen's life, cautioning them to have patience with *Sense and Sensibility*'s opening chapters.

"Sorting out who's married to whom, who's related to whom, which are the sisters and half-brothers is frustrating for my students in the United States."

"So it's like the Bible," Salvador said. I must have looked confused because he clarified, "Like the genealogies in the Bible where you find out about the family lines. Then it gets easier after that."

Not a comparison that had ever occurred to me before, but certainly apt.

Eventually the conversation turned from Austen. When Soledad asked about my education and I explained that I have a PhD, she and Salvador got a wary look in their eyes I'd seen before. At my university in California, at least once a week I bought a bacon and egg breakfast sandwich at the student union and gossiped with the person at the grill making it, usually a Mexican American named Luisa. One morning a student interrupted with a question, addressing me as "Dr. Smith."

Luisa stopped, spatula poised, and gave me the same look that had just flashed across Salvador's and Soledad's faces. "You're a professor," she blurted out, half accusingly.

"Yep," I answered.

Her brow furrowed. "You've always been a professor here?"

"Yep. The whole six years you've known me," I answered.

"I thought—" She examined me intently then gazed down at the grill. "I thought you *worked* here."

I'd wandered off with my sandwich, equal parts proud and bemused—proud of being mistaken for a staff employee (translation: normal human being) but bemused at her newfound discomfort with me and her assumptions about what it means to "work."

I didn't want any similar issues with this kind, earnest couple. I think Diego's warning about their house had been a warning not to judge, not to make assumptions about their capacities based on their living conditions. I didn't want any assumptions made about me either, that my education made me some kind of eyebrow-arching snob.

But as Austen delineates so clearly, you can't stop people from making assumptions if they're so inclined. You can only do your best to show your character through your actions and hope that other people will be capable of forming sound opinions. And if you're a realist like Austen, you'll also be wise enough to realize how many people aren't up to it.

As I fretted, suddenly wondering if *I* were making assumptions about *them* making assumptions, Soledad slipped into the back room then reappeared with a Ruth Rendell mystery and a historical romance by Jean Plaidy, both translated into Spanish.

With the wordless comprehension you see in a truly solid

couple, Salvador took the books and handed them to me. "You could read these," he said with a playful smile, "and we could also have a discussion about *them*."

I looked for a way to decline without rejecting the spirit in which they were given, responding truthfully, "What I'm really interested in is reading Mexican novels. Which authors do you like? If you give me suggestions, I'll definitely read them."

Soledad tilted her pretty head thoughtfully and said, "Rulfo, I think. Carlos Fuentes is more popular now, but I don't like his style so much. Juan Rulfo, *Pedro Páramo*." Salvador deferred to her, and they both smiled as I wrote down the names. Then we found our gazes shifting to the blanket on the floor where the boys were curled up against each other, sleeping soundly. Diego squeezed my hand and smiled. Time to go.

We each had our homework: Salvador and Soledad would read Austen, I would read Juan Rulfo. Equilibrium restored.

Puerto Vallarta has a number of nice bookstores, and working in them is the same mix of funky writer types and offbeat geeks you meet in bookstores across the world (I worked enough years in bookstores, pre-graduate school, to earn the right to say this). The largest one downtown, albeit tiny by U.S. megachain standards, was half a block inland from the Malecón, the city's lengthy boardwalk.

The tall, thin bookstore clerk nodded expressionlessly when I asked for Juan Rulfo and came up with three separate editions. He pulled them from completely different shelves, leaving me puzzled as to the organizing system.

"Have you read *Pedro Páramo*?" I asked.

"Of course. It's important." His Spanish was oddly flat in tone. "This edition has both of his only two books, *Pedro Páramo* and *El Llano en Llamas*" (*The Plain in Flames*).

Published in 1955, *Pedro Páramo* is one of the most famous novels written in Spanish and perhaps the best early example of Magical Realism. The plot is simple—Juan Preciado sets off to find his father, Pedro Páramo, but when he arrives in his father's hometown he's told Páramo is dead. A variety of odd characters share stories about his father, and the narrative slips seamlessly between past and present. But some of Rulfo's characters seemed to be not just memories but outright ghosts, hanging around people's windows at night, appearing and disappearing.

After pondering this for an evening, I decided to seek help. I headed back to the bookstore to see the thin, grim clerk rather than confess my difficulties to Soledad.

"Are some of the characters in this book ghosts?" I asked him.

He stared at me.

"I mean, are they dead already, some of them?"

"They're all dead," he said flatly.

"Pedro Páramo's dead, I got that, but the people in the town? Are some of them dead when Juan shows up?"

"Juan's dead. They're all dead." As I tried to think of a better way to ask for clarification, he repeated, "They're all dead."

My head full of questions I couldn't articulate, creeped out by his hollow stare, I edged my way slowly toward the door. Once outside, I resisted the temptation to look back. No doubt there'd be nothing but boarded up windows and a big "for sale" sign. *Sí, there used to be a bookstore there, a long while back. Sad story, what happened to that young clerk. Qué lastima.*

I headed straight home and started *Pedro Páramo* over from

page one. Sure enough, just short of halfway through the book were references to Juan being in his coffin—which before I'd assumed was some kind of metaphor. He was in his coffin, talking to other people in their coffins.

Dang. Maybe I'd better stick to books with pictures.

Diego and I had a second Austen drop to make. He'd known Salvador and Soledad for years, but Josefa was a more recently acquired friend from his church. She and her husband Juan and their sixteen-year-old daughter Candela, the other half of the Austen group, lived in an attractive neighborhood well clear of the tourist areas and close to the encircling mountains. Downtown, the ocean dominated; there, the river rushed through noisily, giving the neighborhood a more inland tropical feel.

Josefa, a soft-spoken woman about my age, ushered us into her living room. She had a quiet, unassuming type of beauty, her face glowing without a hint of makeup, her thick dark hair arranged appealingly, without fuss. Her house, while larger and more luxurious than Salvador and Soledad's, still felt just as homey and welcoming.

With thanks and a gracious smile, Josefa accepted her fat copy of *Sentido y Sensibilidad*. "I'm really looking forward to discussing this book!" she said, looking pleased.

Candela, as lovely as her mother, looked not-so-pleased at the size of the volume. She brightened, however, when she saw Austen's name. "This author wrote *Pride and Prejudice*, right?" She and her mother, it turned out, had seen the film version with Keira Knightley. "I loved that movie! Is this book as good?" she asked, eyes hopeful.

No, I was thinking. No, it's not. "Yes, it is," I said. "But it's… different. It's a little slower at the beginning." In other words, no, it's not. I plunged forward. "It's got a very good message. And it's funny, too, but more subtle than *Pride and Prejudice*. You'll enjoy reading about the sisters." Candela's older sister, married, no longer lived at home.

That workday had been particularly draining for Juan, who finally came in late, hungry, and visibly tired. Handsome and well built, about Josefa's age, he had thick, prematurely gray hair that made a striking contrast with his still youthful face. He'd worked for years as a bricklayer and construction worker and had recently managed to open his own business, where he sold building materials. He was too tired to disguise his alarm at the size of the book.

"Wow," he said, blowing out a big gust of air. "We've got a lot of time to read this, right?" He exchanged a look with his daughter, who seemed to share his concern. Josefa stroked his arm reassuringly. I got the feeling she had readily agreed when Diego approached her about the book group and had been working to convince Juan and Candela ever since.

"Definitely," I assured them. "I'll be here for three months. There's plenty of time!" Diego, knowing his busy friends better than I did, decided it was best not to leave things quite so open-ended and added, "How about the first week of November, two months from now? Would that be enough time?"

So, plans sketched out, we left Juan to a well-earned rest and headed off into the night, Austen mission accomplished.

CHAPTER FIVE

There was an upside to living in a house with almost no windows: free pets. For the whole of my stay in Puerto Vallarta an assortment of creatures came and went at will. Insects of all varieties and rodents were a given, and where there are rodents, there are cats. Various felines would drop by to startle me in the kitchen or interrupt as I sat at my desk in the upstairs hall making Spanish flashcards of words gleaned from *fotonovelas* (or when I was feeling sharpest, from Rulfo or Fuentes).

I adored the resident *cuizas*, the rubbery little lizards I'd also spotted at Soledad and Salvador's place. I'd randomly find them scurrying along the ceilings, dodging behind the bedroom curtains, staring at me from the showerhead. Before lights-out at night, bats would shoot through the hallway passage and sweep for insects. The least frequent but most exotic guests were *garrobos*, enormous lizards that would lounge on the rail-less stairs leading to the rooftop *azotea*.

But what entered the house uninvited even more than the many creatures was noise. The daily volume in a Mexican neighborhood took some getting used to.

Music topped the list. Shortly after arriving I spent a pleasant Sunday afternoon meeting Diego's family at his sister Manuela's house. Everyone was curious to see the strange traveling woman who'd entered their son's/brother's/uncle's world. Diego's mother had the same bright demeanor as his, and despite my paranoia that she and his sisters would give the stink eye to the hussy shacked up with him, all three women were kind and open. We enjoyed a wonderful dinner, complete with dessert coconuts that, when the meal started, were minding their own business up a tree in the yard. There was something darkly sexy about discovering that Diego could whack open a tough coconut with a single machete blow.

Ah, but the music! From the noise level, the average American passing outside Manuela's house would have assumed that nothing less than a wedding or a canonization was in progress. The only way to keep your neighbors in the United States from calling the cops if your stereo's up that loud is to invite them over and liquor them up. I wonder how many ugly feuds get started in the States from a basic cultural misunderstanding—with Mexican immigrants thinking their neighbors are hassling them, maybe out of racist motivations, and the neighbors thinking the Mexicans are giving them a very stiff middle finger by playing their music so loudly.

While my neighborhood was more tranquil than Manuela's, the family across the street had a colossal parrot-like *guacamaya* caged in their front yard. Many families had noisy birds, but this one was off the charts. It muttered to itself constantly then every hour or so would let out a bloody shriek that set off every dog and rooster around. At first this seemed to be its only trick. Then with the first really hard rain, the bird went into an ecstatic freefall of sound that lasted almost an hour. It whistled, hooted, and screamed, barking out unintelligible words and raucously imitating the sound of human laughter.

Each time thereafter, a hard rain drew me to the window. I would watch the *guacamaya* bob its gigantic blue head and sway on its thick wooden perch, transported, pouring out its song to the rain pounding the plastic cover of its cage.

~❧~

After the *Pedro Páramo* "They're all dead" incident, I felt too embarrassed to go back to the bookstore downtown, so I found another along the main stretch to the airport, one with a reassuringly animated young clerk named Marisol. After the requisite apology for my poor Spanish, we chatted, and I explained about my travels.

"It's your *job* to travel around learning Spanish?" she asked in surprise.

"Well, the other part is reading. I'm doing reading groups on Jane Austen."

"That's your job, too?" She sounded almost indignant. "You get paid to read and talk about books? In different countries?" She glanced around the shelves, her expression saying loud and clear how much she wished she had time to devour every volume in the store. While traveling, better yet. "How do you get a job like that?"

"Well, you study for years and years then fight it out with other people who want a job like that. There are very few university teaching spots and lots of people who want one."

She nodded, conceding that I hadn't simply won the lottery. "And you're reading Jane Austen? I've read *Pride and Prejudice*. *Sense and Sensibility*, too. I liked them both."

Ah ha! "What did you like about them?"

"The history—seeing another country, a place so different

from Mexico. I like reading about different customs, how people lived in the past. I like the style, too, something elegant, something that's not common and every day."

"Is there a Mexican writer who's like Austen, from that time period?"

"No." She shook her head sadly. "But for contemporary writers, there's Ángeles Mastretta. She creates wonderful characters, but the settings are realistic, so you learn a lot about our culture." Once again navigating a system that remained a mystery to me, she began pulling novels by Mastretta, born in 1949, from different locations on the shelves. "She's very popular." Marisol recommended *Mujeres de Ojos Grandes* (Women with Big Eyes), a book that shows how even the most ordinary women's lives have a touch of magic. Stories don't have to be about the siege of Troy to have value; quiet lives, surrounded by family, are worth sharing. If this sounds Austenesque, I agree—I think it is. As soon as I finished the book I put a copy in the mail to Guatemala for Nora and the others, each as special as any of Mastretta's magical Mexican women. For good measure, I sent off a Graham Greene novel to Luis that I thought he'd enjoy.

But despite what a nerd like me might lead you to believe, Puerto Vallarta's not all about books and bookstores. There's plenty of sociable fun to be had. Like boxing. Diego invited me to the fights, and after my time with Mastretta, some boy-oriented fun seemed appropriate.

While our tickets got us into the arena, there wasn't a seat to be had. Fortunately, half of the spectators seemed to know Diego, and after we stood a short while near the edge of the upper level deck, some friends spotted him and offered me a chair. The earliest matches were between young fighters in training. As the night advanced, the crowd got thicker, the arena hotter, and the collective voice of the fans drunker, louder, and more bloodthirsty.

Morbidly fascinated, I watched the boxers pound each other. Diego used to *do* this? On the ride there, upset by the Willoughby betrayal in *Sense and Sensibility*, he'd been urging me to tell him whether things improved for Marianne. Could this same warm-hearted man, so troubled on behalf of Austen's sensitive heroine, actually sock another human in the head with all of his strength, on a stage, in front of hundreds of screaming people?

As if reading my mind, Diego leaned down and shouted over the din, "I loved to box, but I was never as good as my brother Pancho. You should have seen him!" Their sister Manuela later told me she'd attended one—and only one—of Pancho's matches, bursting into tears and fleeing after two rounds at the sight of her brother's face being publicly bloodied (and since Pancho won, presumably the other guy's sisters felt even worse).

Yet among the roaring spectators were quite a few women, some with young children. And that very pregnant woman, standing...I yielded my seat to her, its wooden borders my one small protection from the growing press of the beyond-capacity crowd. After accepting the chair, the glowing mother-to-be accepted a bottle of beer from a disembodied arm. Then a shot of tequila.

"After these next two fights we'll see the *real* boxers!" Diego said into my ear, pressed solidly against me from behind, both of us soaked with sweat. I could barely see the ring, and strangers were plastered against me on three sides as intimately as Diego was against the fourth. I toughed out most of the next fight then succumbed to the heat and frenzy. "Stay and watch, Diego," I urged him. "I'll wait on the benches in front of the bathroom.

Stay!" I began unsticking myself from the crowd. But bless his kind nature, he followed me, too much of a gentleman to leave me waiting alone.

I was upset with myself for disappointing him, but as we snaked our way to the exit he squeezed my hand and smiled. "Now we'll beat the rush and get a taxi!"

Okay. Was there such a thing as being too cheerful?

If I'd taken Diego to something I enjoyed and he bailed just when things were getting good, could I have been as upbeat? Like, if we'd gone to the world's biggest outdoor flea market on a beautiful day and he begged off just before we hit the tables with all of the books? As content as I felt with him, over the last month I'd begun to worry about just how long I stay cheerful myself. Yes, I wanted to be open to new ways of doing things, but was it natural for me *never* to grouse and fuss? Seeing him happy made me happy, that much I knew, so I'd taken to biting back any snarky comments on life's little irritations just to avoid seeing hurt or disappointment in Diego's eyes.

"I've got an idea," he said, ushering me into the taxi. "It's a beautiful night. Let's sleep up on the *azotea!*"

Too cheerful? I must be mad.

While the tourist industry cashes in on foreigners' fascination with the Day of the Dead, for Mexicans it's a serious celebration—not of death, but of life. I went with Diego to visit his grandmother's grave on November 2, and I've never seen a happier bunch of people at a cemetery. The streets outside were lined with vendors selling colorful wreaths and enormous bouquets of flowers, and food vendors kept people fortified for their long vigils. Even before we entered I could hear the sound of *mariachis*, hired to play the favorite songs of departed loved ones. Young boys were giving the above-ground tombs fresh coats of whitewash, while older family members did the delicate work of repainting statues, repairing tiles, or tending live plants.

Diego's family had visited before we arrived, so his grandmother's grave was laden with colorful wreaths, fresh flowers, and a large image of the Virgin of Guadalupe. On the high, flat surface of the tomb I didn't see any food—until Diego lifted a large pink cross made out of flowers. Protected from the sun were bags of peanuts, potato chips, and candies.

"She loved potato chips," he smiled, laying the cross gently back in place.

The evening after the cemetery visit, Diego arrived home looking distressed. "I've got bad news about the Austen group," he said, sitting down at the kitchen table. We'd planned to get together that week, so I was all ears. "Salvador and Soledad are finished with the book, but not Josefa and her family."

I decided to be Diego-like and look for the positive. "We'll just have to set another date. I could use some rest, actually, since I'm not feeling so great right now."

That was an understatement. Some kind of illness was creeping up on me, turning me into an Ugly American; the day before, prior to visiting the cemetery, I'd had a genuine public snit. Numerous musicians and entertainers board the Puerto Vallarta city buses, perform, then pass the hat. That day as I sat wilting in a bus seat, hot, fussy, and in denial about getting sick, a lean young man entered.

"BAM, BOOOOM, BAAAAAM! Ratatatatattattattt!" he snarled in imitation of the police firing on unarmed demonstrators, belting out his poetry of protest directly next to my seat. Normally I was supportive of people trying to earn a few pesos, but on that day, the poet's assault on government abuse of power was an assault on my frayed nerves. Giving him my nastiest look, I made a big show of moving as far from him as I could get. Not my finest intercultural moment.

The day after we rescheduled Austen, I was unable to get out of bed. And the next day, and the one after that. I was burning with fever and wracked by the worst body aches I'd ever experienced. I was scared and miserable, and Diego grew increasingly concerned. By the morning of the fourth day he sat on the edge of the bed and stroked my hair, his habitual look of cheer long gone. "Maybe I should call your mother?"

Good lord—my mother! At least a week had passed since my last call. I'd been too fevered to think of her; she must be ill herself with worry. She'd been right all along—I *was* going to die in a strange foreign land. I wrote down her number and fell back into bed. Diego had only a local-use cell phone and needed to go to the neighborhood phone booth with a calling card. As I drifted back to sleep, I wondered how comforting my mom would actually find it to hear the broken English of a man she'd never met who, for all she knew, might have already sold me into white slavery and was fending off an investigation with placating phone calls.

There was a doctor in the neighborhood, and when I was strong enough to walk the two blocks, Diego led me there. The man prodded me and concluded that I needed more rest—and antibiotics, which he pulled out of a drawer. "No need to bring a pharmacy in for a cut on this." The doctor winked as he took Diego's cash.

The drugs didn't help. My mind stayed mush, and I could only sleep and watch addictive Mexican soap operas and *SpongeBob SquarePants* dubbed into Spanish. A break in the monotony came two weeks later when I woke from a nap one day with a huge crimson 3-D rash covering my entire right leg. Two of Diego's uncles lived in the neighborhood, and I'd met that wing of his family a month earlier when they'd invited us over for a party. I couldn't reach Diego when he was working, so I thought of his cousin Lucia, a smart, capable woman I'd met at the party. She was a mother; she'd know what to do about an alarming, itchy rash.

Every kid playing outside the family's house (and that was quite a few kids) stopped dead at the sight of the panicky *gringa* with one flaming leg staggering into the yard. Fear and discomfort had reduced my Spanish to Tarzan level. "Leg hurts!" I whined. "Very red!" Someone ran to fetch Lucia who, patting my shoulder and tsk-tsking, led me gently to a pharmacy. More antibiotics, once again ineffective. The strange rash disappeared after a few hours only to reappear randomly on various parts of my body for a week or so—one day on my back, another on my belly, then again on my leg. Very weird, *very* distressing.

My mother's not an effusive person when it comes to expressing affection; she's too old-school German for that (and while I'm stereotyping, I'll add that she's a quarter Irish, which gives her a warm heart and a great singing voice). When I could finally make the four blocks to the pay phone, she said simply, "I'm glad you're stronger, Amy." Someone who didn't know her well might think she seemed oddly casual, given the circumstances; I could hear the profundity of relief in her voice.

"It must have been scary to get calls about me from a stranger," I said.

"Well, a little bit, but you trust him, so he must be a good man." My mother's faith was better than medicine. I should have known not to underestimate her and assume she'd be mistrusting. I was reminded again of Austen. One of the reasons I love *Northanger Abbey* is the faith Catherine's parents place in her when General Tilney boots her out of the abbey. The Morlands know bad behavior when they see it, trust their daughter, and never assume Catherine had done something inappropriate (which she hadn't). For my money, they're the best parents in any Austen novel.

As we caught up on family news, a dogfight erupted outside of the phone booth. If there were leash laws in that part of Mexico, nobody obeyed them, so pet dogs (and cats and goats and chickens) had free range of the neighborhood. Typically the dogs formed themselves into friendly packs, rolling and playing on the brick and dirt streets, but occasionally the pecking order needed to be refined.

"What's that? Is everything okay? What's happening there?" my mom cried as the fight grew noisier and two of the dogs bowled into the phone booth. Yes, there it was, the old familiar sound of "Something terrible is going to happen to my daughter!"

My mother trusted me; she still wasn't so sure about Latin America.

But she was right about Diego. He was a good man. During the three long weeks of illness he was kind and loving, nonstop. He was patient and attentive in the evenings and when he had to work, he popped in between fares with marlin burritos, bowls of soup from his mother, and small stuffed animals (including an adorable stuffed Chihuahua). A good man, indeed.

Too much time alone with my own thoughts was forcing me to realize just how much I'd been denying the growing depth of my feelings for Diego. When we'd been constantly on the move—swimming, hiking, visiting with his family, romping on the *azotea*—it was easy to enjoy the moment and not worry about the future. But like it or not, thoughts of the future, of me preparing to leave and Diego needing to stay behind, were beginning to intrude.

But what could I *do* about it? At the moment, nothing. So, back to my uncomplicated relationship with Bob Esponja—otherwise known as SpongeBob.

When I was finally strong enough to get out of the house, we set another date for our *Sense and Sensibility* discussion. As a warm-up before our private evening of culture, Diego invited me out to hear a friend perform at a small café in what the flyers called "A Night of Poetry, Music, and Art!" Mexican hipsters strolled among the tables, trailing pot smoke. Diego and I were uncool enough to order fruit juice, which we were sipping when a young man detached himself from a cluster of artsy types and approached, greeting Diego laconically. Then he fixed me with a haven't-I-seen-you-somewhere? stare, just as I thought, "Jesus H., no way!"

"This is Tito the poet," Diego announced. Ah yes, I'd heard Tito and his poetry.

Now there he was, smiling wickedly, pulling up a chair. I was cornered. "Glad you came, Diego! We've got to keep the arts alive. But it's hard in a town with so many tourists," he said pointedly, his gaze locked with mine. So you remember where you've seen me before, Señor Guerilla Bus-Poet!

Fortunately the show started, and Tito slipped off. Two singers took the stage in succession, then Tito made a grand reentrance. He performed poems about the death of culture, ducking off periodically to change costumes. He was a wrestler, an old indigenous man, a sashaying prostitute. "*Hay que violarla, hay que violarla,*" he crooned, picking up volume with each repetition, "*HAY QUE VIOLARLA, LA CULTURA EN VALLARTA!*" You've just got to rape her, the culture in Vallarta!

I certainly agreed on the need to stage live events, to haul people away from their TVs, to keep the quirky owner-operated coffee shop alive. I couldn't help but wonder, however, about Diego's take on criticisms of the tourist industry in the town where he'd spent his whole life.

"Sometimes the politicians here cater to tourists at the expense of the citizens," he responded while we waited for the bus afterward. "But there's more culture now, not less. Before we were just a village. Now there are museums, bookstores, language schools. And *jobs*. There are lots of places in Mexico where there aren't. That's why so many Mexicans go to the United States. They don't want to leave their families, but people need jobs. Poets don't always think about these things."

Well put. Maybe that's why Plato didn't want poets in his Republic. But would you really want to live in a world without poetry?

"There's another problem with the Austen group."

By this point, I'd been in Mexico long enough to roll with the punches, so to speak. I waited for Diego to go on.

"Salvador and Soledad can't come on Thursday, because now her mother isn't free to watch the children that night. They'd like to meet on Monday instead, but Josefa and her family can't make it Monday, because of her husband's work."

After getting a veto on several alternative dates, I concluded, "Sounds like we'll have to do two meetings." Doing separate groups meant there'd be no opportunity for the families to interact and play off each other's ideas, but what can you do? *Así es la vida*.

"I was hoping you'd say that," he smiled in relief. "Josefa would like to have the group in her house, and I think it's best we do the other one here."

And so, at long last, the date for the first group rolled around.

Josefa led Diego and me into her comfortable living room, where we chatted until Candela joined us. Rather than have dinner afterward as I'd done in Guatemala, we decided to order pizza and eat first. Delivery pizza was still a novelty for many Mexicans, and I didn't want to put Josefa to the trouble of cooking. When Juan came home we shifted into the dining room. As we ate, I took note again of how gentle Josefa's manners were and how timidly she spoke. How on earth was my recorder going to pick up her soft voice?

But when the food was put aside and *Sentido y Sensibilidad* hit the table, she became a whole new Josefa. Clearly, she'd enjoyed the novel, had thought about it a lot, and was ready to go. Her husband and daughter let her take the lead in the conversation.

"Elinor is a wonderful character," Josefa opened. "So reasonable but also so caring. She's a good sister to Marianne, who needs the extra attention. Elinor is a good woman."

"That's what the book seems to be doing," Diego added. "It shows us something about the times and the customs, but it also shows us about the values that the sisters have, values that are good for people to have. Like loyalty."

"Definitely loyalty," Josefa seconded. "Elinor is a very loyal sister."

"But when it comes to the men, to Edward and, what's that other one?" Diego asked. Willoughby is a puzzling name for Spanish speakers. Too many unpronounced letters. "Willoughby, that one. At first I thought, hey, those two guys are just the same. They do the same thing—they're flirting, then suddenly they're gone. But Edward comes back, and you see that they're not at all the same. It makes you think about judging somebody's behavior before you've got the whole story."

"Do you think Willoughby ever really loved Marianne like Edward loves Elinor?" I asked.

"Definitely," Diego answered. "Why else would he come back and apologize to her sister, when there's no hope he could get Marianne back? It was his conscience, because he *did* love her and it bothered him that he'd hurt her so much." In Ang Lee's beautiful adaptation, this scene is compressed into a single mournful shot of Willoughby watching Marianne's wedding from a distance.

Josefa nodded. "Repentance is a very important theme. He's sorry for what he did to Marianne. And Marianne, even more so—her behavior caused a lot of problems for everyone. But you can see that she's truly sorry."

"The focus on values is important, and repentance is one of them," Diego said. "But I think Austen shows that women are better overall about this kind of thing. There's that scene where Marianne wants to talk about what kind of person Willoughby is, and all Sir Middleton can do is go on about his dogs. I think this makes her a feminist."

Not following the argument, I asked him to clarify. "How is Austen a feminist?"

"For focusing on people, forget about the hunting and all that guy stuff, for showing that women are more attentive to other people."

I was intrigued by this conception of feminism, but Josefa chose just this moment to switch tracks. "Sir Middleton and those others, all of these men with no jobs! Sheesh!"

Her husband sighed and rolled his eyes at the thought of a man with no job. The new family business consumed so much time and energy it was never far from their minds. Josefa's comment led us into work and class issues in the novel, which then led us into the question of how hard it can be to make ends meet or improve your financial situation. Diego, Josefa, and her family, just like the ladies in Guatemala, had no trouble steering back and forth between their own lives and Austen's fictional landscapes.

For good measure, I took the time to ask the question directly: "Do you think this story could happen here, in Mexico?"

"Every single thing that happens in this novel could happen here," Josefa answered without hesitation. She looked to Candela for confirmation on this, but her daughter smiled a little nervously and remained silent. "Marianne likes to study, to read," Josefa continued, "but it seems that most women then didn't. It was like that here, too, in the past. Even now, there are men right here in this neighborhood who don't think their daughters need an education. Why do girls need to read if they're going to be in the house cooking and cleaning and sewing?" At this Candela shuddered in distaste and nodded.

Diego agreed. "If there are differences from how we'd behave, it's more about class than about culture. Austen's characters are rich people, really, and rich people here act just the same, worrying about money all the time, about keeping it in the family."

"But any parent, rich or poor, worries about their kids having the best, being happy," Josefa said.

"And not having their daughters get stuck with a bad guy," Diego added.

"Someone hardworking," Juan spoke up for the first time. "You want your daughter to find a hardworking man."

"Without vices," Josefa concurred.

Juan immediately repeated his wife's words for emphasis. "Without vices."

"That's what's important for your children because you want them to be happy," Josefa continued, and she and Juan both smiled at Candela. "I liked that the book had a happy ending."

"With Edward getting the position in Brandon's church, the sisters get to stay close to each other," Diego agreed. I was struck that the sisters remaining close was top on his list for why the book had a happy ending and immediately recalled the Tito-the-Poet conversation we'd had about Mexicans forced to search for work, forced to leave their homes. "It was really good of Brandon to help them that way, and he's not even a relative," he added. "You expect your family to help, and so many people in this book don't even treat their family right."

While everyone around the table nodded, I decided to check in on a point that usually gets my students in the United States going. "What do you think about the match with Brandon?"

After a second of hesitation, Josefa said, as firmly as she'd said anything all evening, "I *didn't* like it. He's really better for Elinor. I kept thinking those two would get together." Diego looked over at me, nodding. He'd brought that up while reading the book, trying to wheedle details out of me in advance.

"So," I probed, "you don't think Marianne loves Brandon?"

"I've got my doubts," she replied. "It's hard to believe she could change so completely after all the complaining she did to her mother about how old he is."

"But think about what's happened to her," Diego cut in. "That big disappointment she's had with getting jilted. He's a faithful man, and now she knows the value of a faithful man."

Josefa continued to look dubious.

"A student in the United States once told me that this match seems like Austen's punishment for Marianne," I said. "She's got to marry the old guy for causing so much trouble."

"She's repented of her follies," Josefa argued. "She's already *been* punished. She nearly died! But the good part, like you said, Diego, is that she gets to be close to her sister. Too often, you see sisters fighting, not getting along."

"Well, you could definitely do a good film if you set the story in Mexico," Diego offered. "I think Antonio Banderas would make a good Willoughby. And I'd love to see Salma Hayek, too, but I'm not so sure she's right for any of these characters."

"Look," Josefa said abruptly, seeing that we were about to shift gears and not wanting to let the Brandon subject pass just yet. "Let me tell you why I don't like this match. My other daughter's married to a much older man, and I just don't like it." She let out a huge breath and sat back in her chair. There—it was on the table.

"Fifteen years," Juan added with disgust, not at all surprised by his wife's outburst, presumably because the same thing was on his mind.

Josefa glanced at Candela, who'd been sitting quietly with a "please, please, don't call on me" look all evening. I'd seen that look before; it almost always meant, "Sorry, Professor Smith, I haven't done the reading!" I didn't want to jump to any conclusions, but I was picking up a similar vibe from Juan.

"Who wants a drink?" Josefa asked abruptly, perhaps thinking twice about criticizing one daughter in front of the other. She disappeared into the kitchen.

"Fifteen years," Juan repeated, then shrugged. "*¿Quién sabe?* Who knows? Maybe when a couple's older, it's not such a big deal. But when the girl's twenty and he's thirty-five, that's just not good." No one had told me how old Candela's sister was, but I had the feeling Juan wasn't offering hypothetical numbers.

"Well, anyway, it's a love story, and love stories never go out of style," Diego said, taking the drink Josefa offered when she returned with a tray.

Josefa's flight from the table had shifted the mood, somehow, and the discussion became more casual and diffuse. Diego joked about casting boldly dressed *mariachis* in a film adaptation then we shifted topics to soap operas, to the number of *gringos y gringas* moving into their neighborhood, to the price of real estate in California. When it seemed we'd moved completely away from Austen for the evening, I turned off my digital recorder.

That's when Juan 'fessed up.

He hadn't finished the book. His admission emboldened Candela, who also confessed to giving up after six chapters, which was three more than Juan had read. Was it just their busy schedules or something about the book itself? Disappointed, I wanted to ask, but without sounding like a teacher about to hand out bad grades. As I pondered how to do this gracefully in my not-so-graceful Spanish, Diego stepped in.

"Well, Josefa, I can see you really liked it! And I loved it." He then steered us back away from Austen. It would be rude, I got the feeling, to press for answers. They'd done their best; I couldn't take it personally. And I shouldn't have been too surprised. My California students almost never like *Sense and Sensibility* as well as the other Austen novels; many find it slow and "preachy." But Diego and Josefa had liked how the novel promotes good values. Given how active both were in their church, I wondered how their frequent Bible reading, an issue Diego had discussed with me, might color their leisure reading.

Or—radical thought—was "leisure reading" too academic or restrictive a concept? Maybe for some people reading is reading, and they always look for the same things: lessons to be learned, examples to follow, cautionary tales to avoid. I tend to read two ways, either with or without a pencil in hand. Certain books I study and analyze, and others I read for pure pleasure. Tolstoy gets a pencil; I set the pencil aside and power down portions of my brain while savoring *Tomb of Dracula* comics or lewd pre-feminism "bodice rippers." Perhaps Diego and Josefa were reading with a different filter, with different goals. For people who took their Bible seriously, perhaps applying moral analysis and reading for pleasure were one and the same thing?

Even with two readers who hadn't made it to the end of the novel, the group had been very interesting, although it had gone more quickly than the discussion in Antigua. As we left talk of Austen behind, I found myself checking the clock, still feeling extra tired and knowing that Juan had been up well before the sun. I pulled out my camera to get a group picture, only to discover the batteries were dead. Diego frowned and scanned the room. Josefa's kitchen clock had two AA batteries, which we pressed into service for parting photos amid hugs and promises of future visits.

I loved Diego's quick Plan B thinking. Brandon was Plan B for Marianne, as was splitting our group into two. But as Diego often would say, *así es la vida*. Such is life—as Austen well knew.

"Happy with the group?" Diego asked as we crossed the wooden footbridge spanning the river that separated Josefa and Juan's neighborhood from the center of Puerto Vallarta. He pulled me to one side of the bridge, out of the path of foot traffic, for an embrace.

"Happy," I responded, folding into his arms.

And yes, with the group, too.

Chapter Six

When I held my fortieth birthday party in Las Vegas, one of my closest friends arrived from Virginia looking dazed, even before the drinking started. In order to party with the girls, Susan had left her two small children for the first time since they'd been born. Periodically, in the midst of Vegas hijinks, I'd catch her with that faraway look. *What are they doing right now? Will they get to bed on time? Did I leave enough juice? Do they miss me?*

When Salvador and Soledad arrived at 9:45 p.m. for Group Number Two a few days after the first group, they were very sharply dressed—and had that same distracted air about them. This was the first evening Salvador Jr. and Juan were spending away from their attentive parents. We were starting up so late in the evening specifically because the couple wanted to put the boys to sleep then slip out, so as not to cause a panic.

"Everything's okay with the kids?" Diego asked as we settled in around the table and I passed around plates for delivery pizza; I'd felt too tired to cook, and Diego had been working all day.

The couple exchanged nervous smiles. "They're asleep. Everything will be fine," Salvador said, as much to comfort Soledad as to answer Diego. Because there was very little beer in the house, I'd been about to make a run before they arrived, but Diego had assured me they didn't drink.

But thank god there were two bottles left because tonight, Mom and Dad both needed a beer.

"So did you like the book?" I usually don't start a discussion with such a subjective question since it puts people on the spot. For some reason, it just popped out that way, but what the heck, I was sure they'd liked it.

Dead silence from both.

Salvador cast a sideways glance at Soledad, who made a face, shook her head ruefully, and said, "Well, more or less."

Salvador jumped in. "Yes," he said firmly. "I really did like it. It was very interesting to learn something about the period when it was written, about a place that's different. I liked the character development, too. And especially," he added energetically, "I *loved* the way the plot unfolded, all the surprises. I was so glad when it worked out that Marianne will have the same happiness as Elinor, after all she went through."

"Diego mentioned while you were reading it that you were upset about Marianne," I nodded.

"I was so upset about what that guy, that—" Again, the pronunciation problem, and it finally came out sounding like an insult. "That *Willoughby* was very cruel. I almost wanted to stop reading, it was so depressing. She was so sad when he left her! And that letter, that terrible, cold letter he wrote. That was very bad."

Salvador cast a glance at Soledad, to see if she wanted to comment. She took a sip of her beer, so he went on. "This whole problem of people not keeping their word was important throughout the book. Starting with John Dashwood. What an awful brother, not caring for his sisters. And the way he lets himself get talked out of his good intentions by his wife, that was just terrible."

Diego had actually read this passage out loud to me in bed one evening, laughing uproariously at Fanny's greedy machinations and John's slow crumble. The brilliant handling in Ang Lee's film brings out the vicious humor of the scene. But Salvador was not amused.

"Women do that here, too, talking their husbands out of their good intentions," Diego chimed in, and I had to bite my lip. Only women do this? "It's a problem, I think, because people only have so much money, and it's basically a competition for resources. Sometimes the wife wants more money or attention for her own family, when he wants to share it with his. But that Fanny, she's just shameless. She's so greedy, she didn't even want the mother and sisters to have some nice china!"

As Diego, Salvador, and I laughed over Austen's eye for selecting the perfect detail to make a character ridiculous, Soledad finally spoke up.

"Well, I just kept reading and reading and reading," she said somewhat impatiently. "I read and read, waiting for *something* to catch my interest. Finally, in the middle, it got more exciting when things started to go badly for Marianne." I thought back to the question of the Bible and the lenses through which we read. Salvador was caught up immediately by the moral questions of the novel, such as John Dashwood's treatment of his mother and sisters. Had Soledad's time at the university influenced her reading habits? Could developing a taste for Juan Rulfo and similar writers make Austen's ethical dilemmas seem flatfooted—especially in translation? I waited for her to continue, but that was it.

I hope the kids are still sleeping, I could practically hear her thinking.

While the first chapter can be a drag, most people are engaged quickly with the contrast between the sisters. "Have you got any sisters?" I asked, wondering if maybe this was the issue.

"Yes." *What if they wake up and we're not there?*

"Well, lots of my students in the United States have a preference right away for one sister or the other. Did you?" I asked, working to draw her mind back to Austen.

"Elinor." *Did I show Mom where I left their favorite toys in case they get up?*

"Why?" I prompted.

"Because she didn't let herself get carried away with her emotions, because she always tried to make life easier for her family," she said, finally starting to warm to the subject and let go of concern for her sleeping sons, safe, after all, under the watchful eye of their *abuela*.

"I feel the same way," Salvador seconded. "Actually, at first, I liked Marianne better for her sincerity, her openness. But after the first half I could see how giving in to her feelings was making things hard for her family, and I didn't like that. And there's something else, something I *really* didn't like—how that Lady Middleton wasn't taking care of her own children, how people liked to have someone else watching their kids all the time. Children need their own parents, not somebody paid to care for them. It's no wonder some of those kids in the book behave badly."

I did a quick mental scan, trying to remember if any of my U.S. students had *ever* commented on parenting in the book. But with the talk on parenting, suddenly Salvador and Soledad both had that *are the kids really okay* look, so I switched gears again.

"Are there things in this novel that wouldn't happen in Mexico?"

Just as confidently as Josefa had several nights before, Soledad responded, "No, the book's really relevant. I'd already thought about that. Things then, in her country, are just the same way here and now. Look at Willoughby, taking advantage of women. Men here do that all the time. And Marianne, marrying more for the sake of getting married than for being in love. Women here are afraid to be single. It's very hard."

"So you don't think that's a good match?" I asked.

"Well, maybe she'll come to love him, like the book says, but she certainly doesn't at first."

"I think lots of marriages back then were more like contracts," Diego said.

"Definitely," Salvador agreed. "Think about Edward's mother, Mrs. Ferrars. That marriage surely must have been some kind of arrangement between families. Imagine being married to her." Another score for Salvador. With the father out of the picture, I'd *never* thought about Mrs. Ferrars as a wife, only as a mother.

"What was it she wanted Edward to do for a living?" Diego turned to me. "She didn't want him to be a minister, right?"

"A soldier, a lawyer, something more grand, that's what she wanted."

"Well, if his father had been around, he would have gotten him to focus better. Not having a father is a problem. He would have given him better motivation, helped him be more successful."

"It's not just the fathers who want their children to be success-ful, you know," Soledad said firmly.

"But they've got more authority," Salvador began, and Diego cut in.

"Fathers are more convincing, like when your mother says, 'Just you wait until your father gets home!'"

So this familiar threat is alive and well in Mexico, too; we all shared a good laugh.

We talked on for a while about parents and parenting styles, about some of the other twists in the plot, like Lucy's surprising but welcome defection to Robert and how furious Mrs. Ferrars must have been, thinking she was thwarting Edward, only to lose her favorite to Lucy! We got on to the subject of movie adaptations, too, and once again played with some Mexican casting choices.

Soledad, now definitely settled comfortably into the conversation, suddenly turned to her husband. "Was there somebody in the book you identified with?"

"Colonel Brandon," he answered without hesitation. "He's reserved; he's serious; he's got good intentions. He never wants to cause problems, but he understands his duty. Like with that scene about the picnic. He really didn't want to leave, but he had to. He's never selfish, but sometimes you've got to choose between two responsibilities."

They exchanged a quiet smile, then she turned to me. "What about you? Who do you identify with?"

I was pleased to see her taking the initiative. "Elinor," I said. "She's always focused on other people, and she's not selfish either. I can't claim to be as good as Elinor, but of the two sisters, I've always liked her more. In all honestly, Marianne kind of irritates me."

Nodding in agreement, she turned to Diego. "Who do you identify with?"

"Willoughby's pointer," he responded, setting us all laughing again. "No, really, I like that dog! She's alert; she knows what's going on around her. And she doesn't cause any trouble, like all the humans are constantly doing. She enjoys nature, too—that's big for me."

We drifted into an entertaining sidetrack about all the places to go hiking in the area, and again it was Soledad who pulled us back to Austen. "Something I think is interesting is how many authors never were famous during their lifetime but become more famous later," she commented. "Was that true with Austen?"

The Austen background I routinely share with students in the United States was harder to explain in Spanish, but I muddled through. They were all surprised to hear that Austen never put her name on any book in her lifetime, instead inscribing them "By a Lady." But eventually word got out, and Austen drew the attention of the prince regent, poised to take the throne when his father George III finally got around to dying. The prince thought it would be lovely if Austen would write a historical romance about his family line, or so his personal secretary implied in a letter to Austen. Her wry response is priceless. She insisted she couldn't do it "under any other motive than to save my life, and if it were indispensable for me to keep it up and never relax into laughing at myself or other people, I am sure I should be hung before I had finished the first chapter." Pretty bold for a humble subject! She did bend enough to dedicate *Emma* to the prince, but the dirty dog never even acknowledged the honor.

"So basically," I wrapped up, "she had some success in her life-time, but nothing like the cult fame she has now with Americans and the British."

"And Canadians," Diego added. "I had the novel in the taxi, and one of my clients was surprised to see it. She told me Austen is very popular in Canada, too."

I brought out my laptop. "Here are some photos of a sea-side village she visited," I said, showing them Lyme Regis. I also pulled up shots of Chawton Cottage. "Here's the house where she lived after her father died. It was officially a 'cottage,' just like what the family in *Sense and Sensibility* moved in to, because it's the smaller property on a large estate. But you can see it's not so small." Salvador and Soledad nodded, impressed. Their own neat little house would fit into Chawton Cottage several times.

"Here's Chawton House, where her brother Edward lived." One of Austen's brothers had been adopted by wealthy, child-less relatives. When they died he hit the inheritance jackpot, landing, among other properties, the entire Chawton estate. I explained how the mansion is now open to the public for the first time ever, thanks to a generous philanthropist who is also a die-hard Austen fan. She took a lengthy lease on the property from Edward's descendents, and now her pet Clydesdales, named after various Austen characters, graze the grounds. Officially, it's a research library focusing on women's literature with visiting hours for the public.

My photos were from the initial limited-invite opening, an academic conference in 2003 that drew Austen scholars from around the world. We roamed the buildings freely before the public descended; some eager beavers were, in fact, being turned away at the gates while the conference was still going on. At one point I had timidly asked a guard if I could pretty-please sit for a moment in the second story window seat overlooking the front drive, apparently a favorite reading spot of Austen's. My nerdy wish was granted; it was a happy, quiet moment of communion.

"How many novels did Austen write?" Salvador asked. "She didn't live very long, did she?"

"She'd been writing since she was young, but she didn't actually publish until 1811. Since she died in 1817, her public career was short. She published four novels in her lifetime—*Sense and Sensibility, Pride and Prejudice, Emma,* and *Mansfield Park*—then *Northanger Abbey* and *Persuasion* were published by her family after her death."

"That's a lot in a short time," Salvador said with a look of respectful surprise.

"What about Mexican novels from the same period?" I asked. "Were there Mexican writers producing similar work?" I'd struck out on this question with Marisol at the bookstore and also got a unanimous *no* from Josefa and her family.

Salvador deferred to Soledad, who replied, "Austen's writing about people, about families. All the writers I know about from this time were concerned about politics and war. And they were all men."

"There's Sor Juana," Diego offered. "But she was writing much earlier." Sister Juana Inés de la Cruz is the great anomaly of Mexican literature, a seventeenth-century nun who wrote spellbinding poetry, theological essays, and feminist arguments. She later renounced her work in a document signed in her own blood, under pressure from the church. If you've seen the portrait on a Mexican two hundred peso note, that's her.

Despite starting this second group much later in the evening, we ended up talking longer. By midnight I was seriously fading, still not fully recovered from my illness, and I could see Soledad lapsing back into longer and longer silences. *I hope we tired the kids out well enough during the day,* her look was saying again. Salvador noticed as well.

"It took me a while to get into it, but I did like it, after all,"

Soledad conceded with a smile as she and Salvador headed for the door. "It was fun to do something different like this!"

"Well, I've got a copy of *Pride and Prejudice*, and it's yours to borrow whenever you want," Diego offered. With his characteristic directness and sincerity, Salvador quickly thanked him. "Yes, I'd like that."

As for Soledad—*vamos a ver*. We'll see. I thought she was coming around, but I couldn't be sure she was an Austen convert yet. At least she'd finished the book, so there was definitely hope!

To toast the success of the groups, Diego took me to the city's annual celebration in honor of Saint Cecilia, the patron saint of music. The main square was filled with dashing groups of *mariachis*, all performing at once, competing for attention. An especially clever group one-upped the others by bringing an adorable little girl dressed in a wee jet-black jacket identical to theirs and a skirt with the same gold froggings that ran down the legs of their *mariachi* trousers. Not more than two, the girl danced as if every single person were there just to see her.

Although a few tourists milled about, the crowd was mostly a mix of locals and Mexicans on vacation from other cities. "There's a song I want you to hear," Diego said as we worked our way through the press, pausing to enjoy the different style and handsome costuming of each group. "I'm sure some of them will do it." But the hours passed and gradually, one group after another packed up, until only one group remained. Seeing how much it meant to Diego, I tried not to show him how exhausted I still felt from the illness.

"There," Diego cried, just when I was afraid I'd finally have to confess or collapse. "That's it! *El Mariachi Loco!*" "The Crazy Mariachi" was apparently everybody else's favorite, too. The crowd swayed and sang along merrily. There were quite a few drinks circulating, but that communal pleasure wasn't alcohol induced. It was about sharing something familiar, about being out with family and friends in a classic Mexican mix of the sacred and the secular. God bless the martyred saint—let's dance!

Diego seized me around the waist and twirled me joyfully, laughing aloud, then pulled me up close against his side again to watch the musicians. I suddenly experienced an intense wave of travel schizophrenia: happy to be sharing the moment—above all, sharing it with *him*—but bluntly aware of being an outsider.

It wasn't just that I didn't know the song lyrics being belted out around me—I could learn those fast enough. It was about the layering of experiences that each person there had, all of the associations with the song, heard from childhood onward, sung at weddings, parties, other festivals, completely embedded in a rich network of shared memories. I could learn Spanish, but I'd never catch up. The second time I sang the song would be Diego's forty-second; my fifth, his forty-fifth.

Diego smiled over at me. I sighed and smiled back.

My relationship with my sister Laurie blossomed when she finished high school and we no longer had to share a room, but growing up I was closest with my older brother Shawn. We logged many hours together watching *Star Trek* episodes and *Planet of the Apes* films; when he was feeling ornery, he'd chase me around to fart on me. As Laurie and our oldest brother David each hit eighteen, they got married, got jobs, and started families. Shawn, a book nerd like myself, got a PhD, became a teacher, and stayed single (and eventually stopped farting on me, although he still enjoys farting *around* me and exclaiming in a pirate voice, "Arrrr! Music to me ears!").

Before time and circumstances sent the Smith kids in different directions, we four spent many happy afternoons like millions of other youngsters raised in the sixties and seventies: playing Monopoly. At the celebration for Saint Cecilia, Diego had shared something quintessentially Mexican with me, something meaningful from his childhood. I wanted to share something other than Austen with him. Something 100 percent American, something from my Pennsylvania past. So I taught him how to play Monopoly.

Even in the Mexican version I'd bought, no game says "USA!" like Monopoly. The board's center was an attractive Aztec calendar, all the properties grouped by state. The good folks from the state of Guanajuato might not be too happy to know they housed the cheapie purple properties while Mexico City landed pride of place with the costly blue ones. Boardwalk was *el Palacio de Bellas Artes*, and Park Place, *el Castillo de Chapultepec*. The railroads transformed into the *Centro de Autobuses*. I hadn't played in a good twenty years and needed to consult the rules, but it all came back pretty quickly. I explained to Diego the central challenge of the game: the need to buy property while retaining enough capital to develop it so that you can then bleed your opponents dry.

Diego's good nature did not serve him well in Monopoly. It looked promising when he bought the third yellow property after I had the first two, but that was as cutthroat as he got. Since Puerto Vallarta is in the state of Jalisco, it was only fitting that I completed this block first, those red properties that everybody lands on. Diego looked distressed when he saw my money disappearing into the bank, just like on shopping trips when he'd catch me buying yet another brightly colored blanket or irresistible owl statue. "*Mi amor*," he asked, "are you sure you need that many houses?"

His distress changed to stunned denial the first time he landed on the *Plaza de Liberación* with three houses. How on earth could the rent go from $20 to *$750*? Now the money that had drained from my stash into the bank began flowing from Diego's stash back to mine. I had tried to explain the principle of investments and returns, but only cold hard reality could teach that lesson. When he counted out the crushing rent a second time, I held a hand flat out, palm up, signaling "gimmee gimmee gimmee!" with my fingers—just like big brother Shawn would always do to his beleaguered siblings, so many years ago on the orange shag rug of our family den.

Diego was crushed. Who was this woman, this cruel capitalist *gringa*, and what had she done with his bookish, impractical girlfriend?

The handwriting was on the wall for his first Monopoly venture. It was getting late, and I was still more tired than usual, so we packed it up. He swore that he'd enjoyed it and would play with his family. But in the land of *mi casa es tu casa*—and when they say it in Mexico, they really mean it—a game where you charge your loved ones eye-popping rents until they collapse financially may not be quite the thing. For me, the game had been a wonderful trip down memory lane, bringing back rainy Pennsylvania afternoons, Velveeta sandwiches, Shawn's maniacal laughter over each property acquisition, and debates over why the mice that visited the box at night only chewed the hundred dollar bills.

None of these layers of memory were there for Diego as he'd watched me fuss over the precise arrangement of the houses multiplying in my tiny empire. And anyway, he could never catch up. It was *El Mariachi Loco*, in reverse. The second time he played Monopoly would be my forty-second; his fifth, my forty-fifth.

Stacking the bills back in the box, I smiled over at him. He sighed and smiled back.

Good-byes are a long process in Mexico, so I started mine shortly after the celebration for Saint Cecilia. One by one I visited Diego's family members, thanking them for all their help during my lingering illness. Warm as ever, full of good wishes for the rest of my travels, one by one they asked the same thing—when would I be back?

A very good question, but one I couldn't answer yet. The fact was that over the past month, Diego had begun urging me to return to Puerto Vallarta—for good. His existence was completely woven into the fabric of the city where he'd lived his whole life. During a family dinner when someone had asked me about life in the United States, Diego's mother, seated next to me, suddenly turned to clutch my arm. "Please don't take my son away," she'd said quietly but with a depth of feeling that left me speechless.

I'd already uprooted myself from western Pennsylvania, but now I had a secure, tenured university position in California that had taken me years to earn. Could I give that up on the chance that things might work out between us long term? And what about the rest of the year's travels? Ecuador, Chile, Paraguay, and Argentina still lay ahead. Could we maintain a relationship over such time and distance?

The thought of leaving Diego, of traveling on without him, of not waking up beside him, of not hearing his happy laughter each and every day, made my stomach churn with fear. But how much of that was fear of being alone, of the unknown, and how much was about *him*, specifically? I'd known when I arrived in Mexico that I would have to turn around and leave again—how had I managed to get in so far over my head?

Feeling helpless and overwrought, I went to an Internet café to check my email, hoping for a bit of cheer from friends and family in the States. Instead I was hit with the hardest type of good-bye—the kind you don't get to say in person. Nora, who'd organized the Guatemala Austen group, had stayed in touch by email. She tried to break the news gently, but there was no way to say it except just to say it.

Luis, that sharp-tongued lover of literature, was dead.

"We were all sad at the school to hear that he passed away suddenly," Nora wrote. "It was really shocking! And such a shame." It turns out that Luis was diabetic. I immediately remembered the trip to the store I'd taken with him on our last day—to buy a fifth of rum. *Damnation, Luis.*

And what about his books? Luis had told me what an odd fish he was to his relatives, a life-long bachelor surrounded not by children and grandchildren but by hundreds and hundreds of books. What would his family make of them; what would they do with them? Someone I'd never met would come and carry off the translation I'd given him of *Pride and Prejudice*. Had he enjoyed it? The copy of Graham Greene's *The Power and the Glory* that I'd sent from Mexico a month earlier—was it there, too, among the piles? Had he read it? Had he liked it?

In the small private courtyard of the café, I had a long, hard cry. I couldn't help but lament all of the wonderful, challenging conversations—about Austen, about Spanish, about life and literature—that I'd never get to have with Luis. Antigua, when I returned, would not be the same without him.

The night before leaving Mexico, I tried to work up the nerve for a Relationship Talk with Diego. I usually didn't have trouble with this kind of conversation; I wasn't sure why I was finding it so difficult just then. When Diego saw me looking earnest over dinner, he asked what was on my mind. "You're still not feeling well, are you? Or are you thinking about your friend who died?"

"I'm still run down, but I'm getting used to that by now."

"Then what's wrong?"

"Well, it's just that I wanted to talk about"—I fidgeted with my spoon—"about this visit, about where I'm going from here. About…Austen. You don't know how much I appreciate your help with all of the planning and rescheduling!"

Chicken.

"It was fun!" he responded. "You know how much I love to read, but I've never done anything like this. Knowing we'd talk about the book with other people made me think a lot more about it." He reached over and grasped my hand firmly across the table. "Didn't the groups turn out the way you planned?"

"It was a shame about splitting into two but aside from that, I'm very pleased," I reassured him.

But even as I responded, I was struck with the answer to my reticence, because there *was* something that hadn't turned out the way I'd planned—Diego and I. Before I'd arrived, I'd imagined that we'd stay in touch via email but that I'd move on, that he'd meet another woman in his taxi or out dancing, or maybe on the beach or at church. I had never imagined that I'd develop such feelings for him, that he'd want me to move back, that the thought of leaving this warm, patient, loving man would make me feel like I was about to head for Antarctica, not the equator. Was there any way we could work things out after all? Could we actually find a way to be together in the end?

To disguise the depth of my concerns, I avoided his eyes and dodged back into Austen. "Anyway, I didn't really have anything specific planned for the groups, although I was curious about one thing. Lots of Americans tend to relate to Austen very personally, and I wondered if you and your friends would do the same."

"Wasn't that funny about Josefa and Juan's older daughter?" He caught my meaning immediately. "There's plenty of reason to think that things with Marianne and Colonel Brandon will work out just fine, but those two were both thinking about their daughter's older husband."

"Salvador brought up some points about parenting I'd never considered before, as many times as I've read *Sense and Sensibility*. That really struck me. He also spent more time talking about being honorable, on the value of being a good person."

"Salvador is one of the best men I know—you can trust him *completely*. And you can see what good parents he and Soledad are. If your students don't have kids, it's no wonder they don't bring that up. They're not going to think so much about parenting."

I carried a handful of dishes to the sink. Time for me to 'fess up to my latest cultural cluelessness. "There *is* another thing that surprised me. I guess I was going on stereotypes about Mexicans, but somehow, I thought you'd all like Marianne better than Elinor," I admitted. "She's much more emotional, warm, and spontaneous. That's the image Americans have of Mexicans, you know. That you're all passionate and crazy, that Mexican men are always getting into knife fights over women, that Mexican women are hanging out on their balconies or running off to war to follow their lovers. Marianne thought dying for love was the best way to go!"

"Only until she almost *did*," he laughed. "Well, Mexico's a big country. Maybe if you read the book with more people, you'd find some fans for Marianne. It's true we're passionate, but the problem with Marianne was the selfishness. We care about love, but we care about family even more. When you're hurting your family, that's no good."

Diego took over at the sink, washing the dishes while I leaned against the counter. "I've thought a lot about what you said on feminism that night," I told him. "The women in Guatemala liked how intelligent and strong Lizzy is in *Pride and Prejudice*, but nobody brought up feminism specifically. At first, I couldn't see how Austen focusing on domestic life and personal interactions was feminist, because getting women out of the house is exactly what so much feminism in the United States has emphasized. But I think I see what you mean more clearly now. Austen gave value to something that was undervalued—the daily lives of women, the things that mattered to them. In fact, there's a famous feminist from the States who argued that the personal *is* political."

"Really?" he asked, looking pleased with himself.

"Really."

"Will you read *Sense and Sensibility* with any of the other groups?" He abruptly turned his attention to the sink, piling glasses precariously and struggling to fit the last plate into the strainer. Men are supposedly better at spatial relations, but I've found that doesn't apply to dishes. Then again, given the sudden tense set of his shoulders, maybe he too was agitated about all the things that weren't getting said that night.

As he turned, I saw the solemn look on his candid face—his mention of the other groups raised the unavoidable topic of my going. Shame on me. I'd been so caught up in my own feelings, it hadn't occurred to me that he might be just as unhappy as I was.

I resituated his big scary tower of glasses and secured the plate, then took him by the hand. "We'll read *Sense and Sensibility* in Chile this spring, after I leave Ecuador. I'm reading each book twice this year to see what kinds of similarities and differences come up. I'll let you know what Chileans think of Marianne. But right now, I'd rather think about the *azotea*."

There it was, back again, that smile of his I loved so much. Diego was the one, after all, who'd taught me that "to worry" in Spanish was *preocupar*—to be occupied with something before we need to be. Tomorrow I would be gone. There was no way to know how we would feel about maintaining a relationship down the road until I *was* down the road.

No sense worrying about tomorrow, tonight.

ECUADOR:

Pride, Prejudice, and Tame Iguanas

In which the author goes to Guayaquil to visit a stranger who becomes a friend, buys even more books, suffers a setback in her Spanish, solves a few mysteries left over from Mexico, including The Case of the Itchy Red Rash, celebrates Austen's birthday in Iguana Central, meets a bonus reading group, and, best of all, joins an ongoing reading circle of fascinating folks to discuss Pride and Prejudice.

CHAPTER SEVEN

Usually I need very strong coffee to wake up. My first morning in Guayaquil, the view from the twelfth-floor balcony was enough. If I hadn't known the Guayas was a river, I would have sworn it was the ocean. Dotted with islands and fishing boats, it stretched as far as the eye could see, flowing powerfully, serenely to the Pacific nearly fifty miles south. I'd arrived well after dark the night before, so this first stunning vista was my introduction to my new home for the next month.

"The pirate port of Guayaquil," the city is often called in books on Latin American history, and that tantalizing phrase was half the reason I'd wanted to visit. Apparently for centuries every time the good citizens got their houses built and their gardens planted and their curtains hung just so, French and English pirates would sweep through to burn and rape and pillage. At the far left of my balcony vantage point was Cerro Santa Ana, St. Anne's Hill, from which citizens would mount watch for the marauders so they could save their skins, if not their possessions. In today's Guayaquil rows of brightly painted houses wind their way up the steep hill, crowned by a picturesque lighthouse.

Directly below the balcony and stretching for blocks along the river was the Malecón, a boardwalk even more elaborate and attractive than the one in Puerto Vallarta. Back at the turn of the millennium, the city gave it a complete face lift and now, along with the broad river walkway itself, the Malecón hosts gardens, museums, restaurants, upscale shops, and an indigenous artisans' market.

Pirates aside, I'd picked Guayaquil for an Austen group thanks to that classic traveler's resource, the friend-of-a-friend. Betsy, an American who'd married an Ecuadorian, had agreed to arrange the Guayaquil Austen venture. She'd managed to locate an ongoing reading group willing to add *Pride and Prejudice* to its December schedule. I was eager to see what perspectives on Austen Guayaquileños might have in common (or not) with Guatemalans.

I'd arrived gruesomely late the night before, but Betsy was as energetic and upbeat as her emails had led me to expect. A blue-eyed blond in her late sixties dressed casually but stylishly, she'd been easy to spot in the crowd at arrivals. She'd whisked me off then set me up in the apartment next to hers, one she and her husband also owned. That next morning when she invited me over for breakfast, I was still on the balcony taking in the singular view.

"This is just the most fascinating thing you're doing, reading Austen in different countries!" she said as she poured coffee. "I'm sorry I can't join you, but I know you'll enjoy both groups!"

This was news to me on two counts—"can't join you" and "both groups." I started with the first. "Why can't you join us?"

"We spend December at our house on the coast. Our grandchildren love the beach. We want you to come, too, every weekend, if you can! You'll love it!"

Then she handed me a sheet of paper with names and phone numbers, clarifying the "both groups."

"The first group I call 'Mrs. Gardiner.'" Betsy smiled at her own whimsy, a reference to Lizzy Bennet's kind, accommodating aunt. "They're all very warm, very smart. The other one I call 'Lady Catherine.' I'm not saying they're snobs—they're just a ritzier group, but they're very well read and interesting. Ignacio José coordinates both. You should talk to him first."

Ignacio José was, I discovered, a genteelly starving artist, a very talented offbeat writer paid by the groups to serve as a facilitator and literary critic.

"I only mailed six copies of the book," I said, mentally tallying the readers now involved.

"Mrs. Gardiner has them. I think Lady Catherine bought their own. Actually, even the six you sent almost didn't get here. The customs people assumed we were going to sell them. Why else would anybody want six copies of the same book? They tried to charge extra taxes, and my husband was so mad, he said, 'Fine, if you think they're so valuable, sell them yourselves!' So they let them through."

Soledad from the reading group back in Mexico had been curious about the degree of fame Austen achieved in her lifetime—and while Austen lived to see public acclaim, in her wildest dreams she could never have imagined that nearly two hundred years after her death, in a country of steamy jungles and skyscraping mountains half a globe away, men would be arguing in a crowded post office about a Spanish translation of her dear *Pride and Prejudice*.

Betsy then handed me several books. I hadn't mentioned via email that I wanted reading recommendations in each country, but she's such a devoted booklover she couldn't resist sharing.

"These authors are Ecuadorians," she said. "You'll learn a lot about the culture from them!"

Edna Iturralde was one and the other, Alicia Yánez Cossío. I tucked the books into my backpack purse, thanking her for getting me started on my newest course of reading.

Since Betsy and her husband were renovating the adjoining apartment, my night there had been a stopgap measure; I'd be spending the month in a comfortable back room in their office suite two blocks away. After helping me lug my fat suitcases the short distance, Betsy handed over the keys.

One of the secrets of long-term travel is to make every temporary abode feel like home, so I set about nesting. In Mexico I'd acquired more things than I could possibly haul away; most I'd left with Diego and his family. The items I'd kept were favorites—a violet-purple blanket adorned with multicolored fish, an owl statuette with huge, mournful eyes, a bird tile I used as a coaster. Last but not least was Diego's gift, Señor Guapo the stuffed Chihuahua—a poor substitute for Diego himself, but seeing it always brought back happy memories of the day he'd brought it home to me.

I found spots in my new room for each familiar item, and things seemed cozier already. Too bad there weren't roosters outside to greet me as there had been in Mexico—although over the course of the month I heard men *pretending* to be roosters on three occasions as the local bar shooed customers out for closing time (then again, maybe it was one man, three times).

Homestead established, I stopped at an Internet café to email Diego. There was already a message from him wishing me a safe arrival. I wrote a quick reply, afraid that if I lingered too long over how much I wished he were there with me right then, I'd end up in tears.

I also let my mother know I'd made it safe and sound. The

easy part of the café transaction was paying for it, since Ecuador uses U.S. currency, including the Sacajawea dollars that mysteriously disappeared from U.S. circulation. Understanding the clerk was not so easy. Here was a whole new version of Spanish, rapid and contracted, the ends of words often disappearing entirely. A useful phrase like *más o menos*, for instance, which means "more or less," turns into a single blur of *máomeno*.

I was reduced to the old trick of smiling, faking comprehension, and handing over a bill undoubtedly large enough to cover the total. Oh, boy—demoted to rank amateur in Spanish once more, unable to carry out the simplest transaction after months of work and slow but steady improvement.

The call in English had gone better. My mother picked up on the second ring, no doubt waiting anxiously since I'd left Mexico. She was pleased I'd made it safely to a new continent, but concern about new dangers surfaced quickly: "I heard on TV about an American farmer getting bit by a vampire bat. They said it came up from South America."

I could tell from the slight echo that she was using the speakerphone in her bedroom. I could just see her, seated on the bed, which was part of the suite she and my dad had scrimped to buy as newlyweds. The burgundy wood headboard, dresser, and vanity set, meticulously well cared for, had gone from serviceable in the fifties to dated by the seventies to stylishly retro for the new millennium.

Aside from a short stint in Vermont when my father was in the Air Force, my mom had lived her whole life within a fifteen-mile radius of the house where she was born (and I do mean house; my German grandmother considered hospital births a luxury). What had my kind, loyal mother done to deserve a daughter who couldn't manage to stay put? Who flung herself in the path of tropical diseases, battling street dogs, and winged death in the form of bats?

"I've seen lots of pigeons here and some seagulls, too—but no bats. Don't worry, I'll be careful!"

~⚬~

Ecuador was where Charles Darwin put two and two together on a few important issues when he visited the Galapagos Islands, roughly five hundred miles off the Ecuadorian mainland. My own discoveries weren't quite so dramatic, but it was satisfying for a woman raised on Nancy Drew to finally solve The Bookstore Mystery.

Back in Puerto Vallarta I'd been befuddled every time I asked for a title and the clerk, whether cheerful Marisol or the grim ghost of Pedro Páramo, would pull copies from various shelves around the shop—never from the same location.

That December morning in Guayaquil, when I asked the clerk for Jane Austen novels in Spanish and he began the now-familiar dash from one area of shelving to another, I blurted out impatiently, "Why do you have to look in more than one place?!"

My out-of-left-field bitchy tone stopped him cold, probably more than the question. Arm poised in midair reaching for a book, he stared in injured surprise.

"I'm so sorry!" I apologized, appalled at my own behavior. "I don't feel well." I was still frustratingly weak and tired—but I also felt genuinely irritated that I'd arrived in yet another country with an unfathomable system for organizing books. My mother was a *librarian*, for cryin' out loud. I was supposed to be good at this stuff!

He shrugged and laughed, saying something that resembled "Don't worry!" Then he handed me a copy of *La Abadía de Northanger*. Grateful for his patience and his Austen discovery, I repeated more calmly, "Why aren't all the Austen titles in the same place?"

It took me one more try to understand his accent, but finally the light bulb went on. *Organized by publisher.* It should have dawned on me sooner, but I just couldn't get my head around it.

"Why do you do that?" I asked.

He shrugged again and said, predictably, "Why not?"

So you don't have to look in five places for one title? Because most people care about the author, not the publisher? I was incapable of responding without sounding like a harpy, so I didn't. A core value of multiculturalism holds that there's no such thing as good or bad when it comes to cultures—just "different." On child labor laws and women's rights, I simply don't buy that, as much as I want to be open to difference. Shelving books isn't exactly a high-stakes venture, but I also didn't see myself returning to the States at the end of the year and reorganizing my books by publisher.

Still, I was pleased to finally know the lay of land and move on to safer territory: my standard request for reading suggestions.

"Nineteenth century?" The clerk's response had more words in it than that, but those were the ones I got. He handed me a volume published by Libresa, plucked from its rightful spot, by local standards, next to all of the other Libresa titles—*Cumandá* by Juan León Mera. "Classic," "school," "Indians," and "jungle" were four key words I picked out of his recommendation.

Deciding it was time to retreat to my room before my crankiness resurfaced, I thanked him and turned to pay for my books, but he took them from me with a smile. *Patience*, I urged myself, as he carried the books to a counter where he handed them to a clerk. The clerk wrote down the titles on a piece of paper, which she stamped and handed to me. Then she carried the books to a different counter by the store entrance, directing me to yet another counter. *WTF?!* My stamped slip had a dollar figure on it, so this must be the place to pay. I handed over cash, and Clerk Number Two stamped the slip again. Reporting with my stamped paper to the counter by the store entrance, I was finally rewarded with my books by Clerk Number Three.

What is this, the Soviet frickin' Union?

My head throbbing, feeling dangerously close to tears, I sat down outside on a doorstep to collect myself. So Ecuadorian bookstores are slow as molasses, so what? What on earth was wrong with me? Was I afraid to look like a dummy navigating the Byzantine sales system? Was I embarrassed at the setback with my Spanish?

Maybe it really was physical. But could I still be ill after so many weeks? Or was I *losing it* without Diego? Was I turning into a whiny hypochondriac because I missed his calming influence, his perpetual cheer?

There are few Austen characters less attractive than her hypochondriacs. The best known is Mrs. Bennet, with her "nerves," and Mary Musgrove of *Persuasion* is a royal pain, too. Emma Woodhouse's father is more endearing since at least he's equally worried on others' behalf, but in Austen's world, dubious health complaints are often shorthand for "Loser!" Apparently Austen's mother was prone in this direction. There are lots of theories as to why Austen's sister Cassandra burned so many of Jane's letters after she died; making sure that none of Austen's (no doubt hilarious) commentary on their mother's complaints survived is one of the more probable ones.

I didn't want to be an Austen Loser, but whatever the problem, I needed a nap. I stopped in a grocery store for some staples, deciding that a bit of chocolate wouldn't hurt either.

"You is beautiful, beautiful," a man's voice crooned in English just behind me. Knowing I was the only *gringa* in the small store, I refused to turn around.

"You beautiful, beautiful!"

I bought only half of what I wanted just to get the hell home before I bit somebody's head off. I placed the checkout divider between my items and those of the man behind me. The clerk reached over and placed it back in the slot running along the counter. "That's to show the counter is closed," he said.

I picked it up and set it behind my groceries again, pointing to the side that now faced him, which said "*cerrado*." "*This* side means your counter is closed. The side with the cigarette ad separates your groceries from the next person's."

"People don't understand. They'll think I'm closed," he answered, reaching for it. I slapped my hand onto the divider, glaring until he looked away, then turned to the man in line behind me.

"You understand that this divides our groceries, correct?"

Clearly in the presence of a *loca*, a pasty white fiend from the north, the man simply nodded, also refusing to make eye contact. The clerk silently resumed ringing up my goods.

And I walked out of the store and straight into a nearby emergency clinic I'd noticed that morning, groceries and all.

"How long have you been sick?" the doctor asked me, shining a tiny light into my ears.

"More than five weeks. My head is pounding, and I have no energy." And no patience.

Looking into my throat, he grunted one of those "this doesn't look good" noises. He felt the glands in my throat and said, "You've got a *really* bad infection. Your entire throat is swollen and covered with pus. I'm going to give you an oral antibiotic and an injection, too, to get something into your system as fast as possible. I want you to come back tomorrow for blood work and a throat culture."

Armed with antibiotics, my tail end throbbing from the shot, I headed back to the office for my nap. On the bright side, they hadn't leeched or bled me. Watching Ang Lee's *Sense and Sensibility*, my students always groan when they see poor fevered Marianne at the mercy of early nineteenth-century medicine. I tried to be optimistic that the antibiotics would work this time, but it was hard not to be worried after so many exhausting weeks of illness. Could this possibly be the same fever that had floored me in Mexico, or had I picked up something new?

Or maybe…it was travel stress. Maybe I just didn't have what it takes, after all, to spend a whole year on the road.

That was a grim thought.

Whatever my problem was, I had to keep any complaints from my mother. She'd definitely make herself ill, too, if she knew I was still in such bad shape. Sleep—that's what I needed. I was out as soon as I hit the bed, still clothed.

Waking hours later, I felt a little stronger and less panicky. I was in an intriguing new country, and if I didn't exactly feel like strolling the streets, I had books.

Among Betsy's recommendations was a historical novel by Alicia Yánez Cossío: *Sé Que Vienen a Matarme* (*I Know They're Coming to Kill Me*). Born in 1928, Cossío is one of Ecuador's most respected novelists. *Sé Que Vienen a Matarme* traces the life of Gabriel García Moreno, president of Ecuador between 1861 and 1875. While the Catholic Church has wielded political power throughout Latin America for centuries, Moreno established the only full-fledged theocracy, stripping non-Catholics of citizenship. He tortured and killed political enemies with a fury he felt was backed by the wrath of an angry god, although he also made important improvements to Ecuador's educational system. Still, his cruelty was so severe that when several would-be assassins converge on him on the same day—working independently, no less—you're rooting for whoever gets there first. Turns out it's the man wielding the machete rather than the ones with pistols.

I called Betsy to let her know I was enjoying her recommendations so far but had to bow out on spending that weekend at the beach with her family.

"I'm so sorry you're feeling sick! Keep in touch by phone so we know how you're doing."

I was determined to see more of Guayaquil, illness notwithstanding. A few days later I made arrangements to meet Ignacio José, the literary guru who coordinated the two reading groups and who was, according to Betsy, "quite a character!"

Arriving ten minutes early at the agreed-upon spot in a square facing one of Guayaquil's historic churches, I circled the area, noticing the contrast between the beautiful façade of the church and the uninspired mid-twentieth-century architecture of the surrounding buildings, including some U.S. fast-food chains. The Malecón area is striking, but the farther you get from the water, the more things seem to be built for use, not style. Then again, I was probably being harsh by comparison—Antigua is famous for its beautiful colonial architecture, and Puerto Vallarta had been completely colored by the rosy glow of Diego's company.

As I paced the square I began to realize I was drawing stares, so I found a spot on a bench next to two older women sharing a newspaper. They returned my "*buenas tardes*" with curious looks. I was the only *gringa* in sight, as I had been in the grocery store. Antigua and Puerto Vallarta are tourist destinations; Guayaquil is not. It's the jumping off point for the Galapagos Islands, but few tourists spend time hanging around the city, which has a reputation for more crime than Quito and other parts of Ecuador. More than once I was followed for blocks by taxis honking and persistently offering their services, the drivers apparently unable to believe I *meant* to be on foot, alone.

I waited forty-five minutes past my meeting time with Ignacio José then, growing tired of the stares, some idle, some flirtatious, some less friendly, I gave up. I stopped by the clinic to see if the blood work I'd had taken on my second visit was done yet. No such luck. *Grrr.* An hour after I'd popped more ibuprofen for my pounding head, the phone rang. Ignacio José, apologetic, with a strange and rambling excuse for his lateness. Would I give him a second chance?

He came to fetch me at the apartment, and I had no trouble recognizing him from Betsy's description. He was Starving Artist incarnate—tall, thin, shoulders stooped from hovering over books and writing desks, with light, thinning hair, a lopsided smile and bright, burning eyes. If I hadn't known he was

Ecuadorian, I'd have sworn he was Dutch; while the indigenous population of the country is very large, there are Europeans in the mix, and not just Spaniards.

"What a pleasure to meet you! I know you'll forgive me when you hear what happened!" He was off to the races with a story, different from his original phone version, about having slept in after being awake all night writing—surrounded by silence, in the throes of literary passion, consumed by the drive to create, etc.

Aside from a few practical tidbits about plots and settings, we don't know much about Austen's thoughts on writing as a vocation, but it's pretty clear she wasn't a suffering *artiste* type. Compared to colorful contemporaries like Mary Wollstonecraft, Lord Byron, and Percy Shelley, whose extremely public private lives were as dramatic as any of their literary creations, Austen was very dull indeed. From what evidence we have, she treated writing as a craft to be mastered, not a painful primal drive. She was an artist, not an *artiste*. The romanticized modern image of a writer as tormented by creative urges has its origins in the era when Austen was publishing, but I could well imagine the sort of cutting witticism she'd drop on the subject: *If one finds it so draining to write, a search for a more invigorating profession might be in order. Clergymen seem to live comfortably enough.*

The erring Ignacio José promised me a sight that would erase any lingering pique over being stood up, and he delivered. He took me to the Parque Bolívar. Flanked by Guayaquil's cathedral and national museum, this park is better known by its nickname— Parque Iguana. Hanging from the trees, lounging in the sun, iguanas populate the park in the hundreds. How Diego would have loved the sight of them! If a park had that many squirrels in it I'd think twice about entering, as much as I adore squirrels. But iguanas are mellow creatures, and while they'll accept lettuce if you offer it, they won't chase you or mistake your fingers for food. They will, however, pee (or worse) on the unwary, so you need to be on your guard when passing under trees.

Ignacio José quickly won me over with good-natured banter, exciting tales of travel, and descriptions of his work. Whether more artist or *artiste*, I couldn't say, but he was endlessly entertaining. "I adore performance art. Would you like to hear about my Clitoris?" Laughing at his own mischief, he continued, "The clitoris is wise, so in my piece, I was an Oracle. I dressed as a clitoris and answered the burning questions of all the spectators!"

Ignacio José took photos of me with various accommodating iguanas. Handing the camera back with a flourish, he cleared his throat and said, "Well, there's something I have to ask of you, too. Forgive me for being so presumptuous, but I've been having a little, well, *trouble* lately. I was robbed, you see. It was horrible! I was wondering if you could, um, *help* me a bit until I get paid for some work I've done. Perhaps, ten?"

If he knew how many of my friends were struggling actors, writers, or musicians, he wouldn't have looked so sheepish about the request. "I've only got a twenty," I said, scrounging through my wallet.

"That would be just fine!" he smiled.

Starving artists, whether in New York or Bangkok or Guayaquil—God love 'em!

CHAPTER EIGHT

Ideally, I wanted to hold each Austen group late in my visits after getting time to familiarize myself with the place, the accent, the literature. But the Mrs. Gardiner group—so dubbed by Betsy—met every second and fourth week of each month. Since the fourth week of December is generally sacred to family in Latin America, the only option was to meet with them when I'd scarcely been in Guayaquil two weeks.

Catarina was the hostess for the evening. When I arrived, part of the group was already waiting in her spacious living room, accessed from broad carpeted stairs descending at the far end of the foyer. It felt like stepping down into a movie set. As the house was located on one of Guayaquil's many hills this structure no doubt emphasized a gorgeous view from the numerous windows, but darkness had descended and the curtains were closed.

I thrust my hand out in greeting, but Catarina laughingly seized me for a kiss on the cheek. "This is what we do here, *mi amor*!" About fifty, stylishly coiffed and dressed, she was every bit the hostess of the elegant house. There was only one discordant note—a large musical Christmas tree shrilling merry tunes next to the sofa.

"This is Yolanda. Poor thing, look at her arm! She can't stay too late," Catarina introduced a woman of about the same age with a drawn expression, no doubt owing to the cast and sling and attendant pain.

"Catarina was called out to a meeting," Ignacio José apologized, bowing as he presented me with a single red rose. "We've got to hold the group without her." I did a mental double take. Okay—if not Catarina the hostess, then who *was* the elegant woman who'd introduced Yolanda and was now settled onto the sofa, waving a lacey black fan with such grace that her chestnut brown hair billowed without mussing?

"You sit here, my dear," she leaned forward and tapped an armchair commandingly with her fan. "Tell us about yourself."

I gave a nutshell version of my project, while Not-Catarina alternated between nodding at me and raking the noisy Christmas tree with icy looks. "I've done *Pride and Prejudice* once already," I concluded, "with the group in Guatemala."

"Did you have to do it with *a Christmas tree like this around?*" she suddenly burst out, unable to stand one tinny song more. "*Eso es infernal! Somebody*, make it stop!" She punched each syllable of *in-fer-nal*—which translates just like you'd think it would—for emphasis.

Ignacio José pulled a plug to silence the offending tree, and we heaved a collective sigh of relief.

Reseating himself, he patted his pockets and cried out, "Oh, no! They took my keys, too!"

"What do you mean? Were you robbed *again*?" Not-Catarina asked.

"The bus I came on was robbed. They took my money and my cell phone and threw everything else on the floor. Again! Oh, my keys!"

"You'll have to find a girl and go sleep in a hotel, Ignacio José," Not-Catarina teased. She turned to me and explained, "Ignacio José has very bad luck. He gets robbed a lot."

"You need to pass an egg over you!" Yolanda exclaimed.

"A dozen eggs," he said glumly, still searching his pockets.

"It's a folk belief people have here about luck," Not-Catarina offered. "But not where I'm from, in Argentina."

"Here they are, here they are!" Ignacio José exultantly hauled them from the depths of a pocket.

"You're Argentinean?" I asked, trying not to show my excitement.

"Leti's from Buenos Aires," Yolanda contributed as Leti, now properly named, smiled and nodded, fanning herself.

Anybody with a knee-jerk against stereotypes is going to howl, but I've got to say it—*that explained a lot.* Ever since I'd set foot south of the U.S. border, I'd been hearing unsolicited jokes about Argentineans. Here's Luis from Antigua's favorite: "When there's lightning in the sky, what do Argentineans think is happening? They think it's God taking their picture." Mexican and Guatemalan friends told me that what bugs them most about Argentineans is how, no matter where they are, Argentineans behave like they own the place (which sounds like another nationality I can think of…). Hence, my mistake over the hostess identity. How exciting, to meet a real live stereotype! Just as thrilling as the first time I heard a Frenchwoman say, in a Paris bank, "*oooh la laaa!*"

As we got acquainted, new readers arrived—Oscar from Chile and Fernanda, a Uruguayan. I scanned my memory for additional stereotypes I'd picked up on my travels. Chileans, according to Mexicans and Guatemalans, are cultured but cold. Word is that they're "the English of Latin America." Isabel Allende, a

Chilean, has seconded that in print in *My Invented Country*, a memoir about her homeland. The Chilean at hand was a man in his sixties with strong, handsome features, who kept his hair shaved close. Rather than cold, I'd call Oscar reserved, someone who spoke up when he had something worth saying and not much before. He took a seat on the far side of the sofa.

As for Fernanda, well, I'd never heard a single stereotype about Uruguayans, so I was forced to deal with her as a real live individual. Brunette, fiftyish, and friendly, she was somehow either a little melancholy by nature or simply a bit down that night. She seated herself next to Ignacio José, opposite Leti. As the evening progressed, it was clear that this configuration was often ideological as well as literal.

After more introductions and pleasantries, Oscar finally spoke up. "I think we should start," he said quietly.

Ignacio José cleared his throat and called us to order, turning to me. "We work together to decide which books we'll read each month. Normally, we do a formal analysis of a book's plot and we look freely at the moral framework and possible cultural interpretations of the text."

As he spoke, copies of *Orgullo y Prejuicio* were pulled from purses and satchels. Clearly, this was a more structured venture than what I'd done with friends in Antigua and Puerto Vallarta.

"But you're the guest," Ignacio José suddenly reined himself in. "Is there some particular way you'd like to conduct the group?"

"No, I'm fine with however you typically do it. I've only done two groups so far, and with the one in Mexico, we read *Sense and Sensibility* instead of *Pride and Prejudice*."

"They're the same," Leti pronounced with a snap of her fan. Perhaps having it was a change-of-life necessity, but she knew how to *work* that fan. "They're exactly the same, with the focus on two sisters. And all of the obsession with gossip."

"Yes, the social critique," Ignacio José nodded.

"No, it's not critique, it's *gossip*. Everybody here in Guayaquil knows everybody else's business, but it's nothing like the gossip in this novel. And that mother—she's *in-so-por-table*." Once again, she hit every syllable as if to emphasize just how "unbearable" Mrs. Bennet is.

"But she's clever," responded Ignacio José before Leti was quite finished. "She knows how to get what she wants."

"She's a schemer," Fernanda agreed, treading over Ignacio José's words in turn. The cross-talking doubled my difficulties with comprehension but seemed to be good-natured, the rapid flow of conversation among people used to debating ideas together.

"She's got a strong motivation." Oscar, despite not speaking loudly, tended to command attention. The overlap stopped, at least temporarily, as he continued. "They haven't got money, so those girls need good marriages to avoid ending up with nothing."

"This is crucial," Ignacio José agreed. "What do you all think of the social stratification presented in the novel?" His formal tone reminded me suddenly that, according to Betsy, he was actually paid to conduct the reading group and, therefore, determined to earn his salary. "Nobody's on the same rung of the ladder. Some are higher, some lower."

"Darcy's the highest of all," Leti nodded.

"No, it's Lady Catherine," Fernanda corrected. "All the rest are fighting it out on the rungs below them."

A rash of simultaneous talking broke out on this theme until Fernanda changed the subject. "Despite the pettiness and gossip, it's fair to say Austen is a precursor in the fight for women's rights."

"No, no!" Leti leaned forward for emphasis as she spoke. "You're mistaken. Jane Austen wasn't a feminist at all."

The forcefulness of the assertion brought conversation to a halt.

"Well, I think she is," Fernanda countered after a pointed silence. "In some ways, she is."

"She's not a sentimentalist, at least, but she's *not* a feminist," Leti repeated.

Suddenly all eyes turned to me, seeking arbitration.

I took a deep breath. "She's not a feminist by our definition because she never said women should have the same rights as men. She wasn't challenging patriarchy—although she often indicates that certain families need better patriarchs." I struggled with the last word, not one I'd needed to use in conversation up to that point, falling back on the standard "pronounce the vowels like Spanish and put an 'a' on the end" strategy.

Before I could continue with the "but" half of my statement to support Fernanda's view, Leti ran with my comments. "Yes, yes, that's right. There isn't one moment in her work where she shows herself to be a feminist." It was too bad we didn't have Diego to weigh in with his perspective on feminism in Austen.

"Well, it seems to me she is." Fernanda stuck to her guns. "She's writing social critique, she's a well-educated woman, and that in itself was a challenge in her time period."

Ignacio José intervened just as a servant brought over a tray of finger foods. If this Mrs. Gardiner group had domestics, what would Lady Catherine be like? "Remember Lizzy and Mr. Hurst talking, when he says, 'How can a woman dedicate herself to reading and not know how to dance?' Austen's offering different possibilities for women, different visions of what women might be. Yet women do have to adapt themselves to the masculine power structure to get what they want."

"And Austen shows that it shouldn't *be* that way," Fernanda maintained. "We're talking about a village in England here, so of course it's not exactly the type of feminism we'd recognize today. But she had an advanced outlook in general and definitely a progressive outlook on women."

I wanted to jump in and agree but Leti was faster. "No, no! By those standards, Louisa May Alcott is a feminist, too. Jo is a progressive character, but does that make Alcott a feminist? Not a bit!"

"She's not *strictly* a feminist, but she's clearly interested in the cultured women of her time."

"Cultured women are always going to be at least somewhat progressive, that's true." Leti's tone suggested that they were working toward a bit of a middle ground.

"And it was hard for them—they really had to fight!" Fernanda said emphatically. "Look at what George Sand had to do to be taken seriously."

"She even dressed like a man," Leti added.

Ignacio José drew the line at cross-dressing French novelists. "Let's get back to *Pride and Prejudice*," he said firmly. "What do you think of how readerly expectations are established? I believe Austen has a wonderful talent for delicate foreshadowing. She does it from the very first lines—'as we know universally, a young man with money needs to get married.'"

"'*To one of my daughters!*'" Leti's Mrs. Bennet imitation was instantly recognizable; we all burst into laughter.

But Ignacio José, not satisfied with his paraphrase, reached for his copy of the book to verify the line. Even without fluent

Spanish I could tell that the translator's choice, which Ignacio José then read, rang better and came closer to Austen's immortal, oft-parodied opener: "It is a truth universally acknowledged that a single man in possession of a good fortune must be in want of a wife." It's only when you hear a flat rendering of the familiar line that you truly appreciate the flair of the original.

"So you see," he continued, "she likes to hint at things, to set up some intrigue."

"But it's not a book with a lot of surprises, really," Fernanda shook her head, and Leti overlapped her to agree, adding, "It's a very open, obvious book."

Yolanda, protecting her injured arm as she rose from her seat, chimed in for the first and last time. "Well, it's got a happy ending, and that's what I like. But now I'm afraid I've got to go—my ride's outside by now."

Hugged, kissed, and told to take care of herself, she was helped to the door. Conversation drifted into a consideration of the merits of the various cookies and cakes our absent hostess had left for us.

Ignacio José had barely called us back to order and opened a new line of discussion on the shades of distinction between pride and vanity when suddenly we were greeting a late arrival who rushed in with apologies for being held over at work. Meli was the youngest and most animated of the group. In her mid-thirties, she had light brown hair in a short, flattering cut and a dramatically husky voice.

"I have to tell you, I'm in love with Mr. Darcy," she greeted me playfully then shared warm hellos with the other group members. When Ignacio José pointedly raised his voice to continue, Meli hushed like a schoolgirl and settled in next to Leti.

Ignacio José pursued the pride/vanity line of thought further then suddenly stopped himself. "Actually, why don't you share your ideas on the book with us, since we don't always have the chance to talk with a professor? We'd enjoy hearing more from you," he prompted, as all the others nodded agreement.

Shoot—and I was hoping they'd do all the work, especially since I still wasn't feeling so hot.

There were any number of threads in the conversation I could pick up, and I was especially tempted to circle back on the point made about Austen's works being "obvious" in their plotting, to add some shading to that perspective. But rather than haggle, I decided that some context might be more interesting for them. "In British literature prior to Austen, heroines tended to be perfect beings, faultlessly beautiful, and multi-talented. Austen is the first novelist who really lets women be human beings. Her heroines aren't idealized, fairy tale creatures. In fact, when her novels came out, some people assumed they were written by a man, for the realism."

Oscar spoke up again, nodding. "Her style is incredibly clean and frank, something people tend to associate with men. She's direct, concise, with really good judgment. It's very impressive."

Ignacio José agreed. "Yes, Austen writes incredible dialogue, and she really knows how to introduce a character, too—it's very dramatic, the way we meet Mr. Darcy, for instance."

"Oh, I love that character, just love him!" Fernanda, Leti, and Meli layered over each other's cries of enthusiasm.

"And I love to picture him as that actor, the one from the older film, the really long one," Leti said. Meli seconded with lascivious yummy noises as Leti continued: "But I didn't like that new one much, because the balls were totally *de medio pelo*—low brow."

"But they were country families giving the balls," Meli pointed out.

"I don't care about that." Leti dismissed this with a "talk to the fan" flick of her wrist. "That older film had real elegance, real aristocratic magnificence. And Darcy, he's any woman's dream."

Back on common ground, Meli agreed emphatically. "I loved him from the first moment."

"Darcy is detestable," Ignacio José cut in, supported by nods and frowns from Oscar.

"Darcy is *not* detestable!" cried Meli, while Leti and Fernanda rushed to declare him shy with strangers but wonderful, adorable, fabulous.

"Maybe by midway into the book we can see that," Ignacio José conceded. "But in that first scene, he's awful."

"*Es de matarlo a palos,*" Oscar agreed. This is strong stuff, worth giving in the original. Translated literally, Darcy deserves to be beaten to death with a stick or "*palo.*" This phrase, however, is an extreme way of saying somebody deserves a serious beatdown but *not* actual death. Still, the sentiment earned Oscar the prize for "First Reader in Latin America to Want to Manhandle an Austen Character." This was something I'd had my eye out for since leaving the States, given how often Larry and my California students mentioned wanting to shake or dope slap some of Austen's more irritating literary offspring.

The ladies rushed to Darcy's defense and the gender gap widened. Ignacio José tried to mediate, first commuting Darcy's sentence to a less severe beating with a stick—"*Sí, es de darle palos*"—then adding, "But all of his behavior is explained later, when we come to know him better."

"I like him just the way he is," Meli insisted, unintentionally echoing Darcy's literary descendent Mark Darcy of Bridget Jones fame. "I liked him from the first moment."

"But not that Bingley, ugh!" Leti grimaced at the thought of Jane's gentle suitor.

"He's a big nothing," Fernanda agreed.

Wow! I'd never heard Bingley so maligned. I was reminded of the harshness of the women's judgments in Guatemala on men perceived to be weak.

"The one that's really the worst," offered Meli, "is that cousin, Collins."

Leti rolled her eyes and groaned. "All of his pontificating, his tackiness! *Horrrrrriiiiiiible!*"

A colorful list of insults followed. Collins is *un tarado* (a cretin), *un blando* (a coward), *un fofo* (a wimp)—in short, *ridículo*.

"We're in agreement on all of that." Ignacio José put a period to the verbal thrashing. "What about the father, Mr. Bennet?"

"Doesn't even exist." Leti and her fan dismissed him.

"Well, I liked him," Meli countered.

"But that marriage between the Bennets is a nightmare!" Leti continued, raising her voice. "He doesn't just make fun of his wife—I think he actually *hates* her for making all their lives so difficult!" She suddenly gestured toward my tiny digital recorder on the table next to the Christmas goodies. "That thing's right here in front on me, why on earth am I talking so loudly!?" She laughed and set the others off, as well.

Ignacio José took the opportunity to shift the topic. "Leti mentioned earlier that she felt Austen's novels are very similar to each other, with all the concern about getting married. But if you think about it, Herman Melville wrote constantly about sailors, in "The Encantadas," *Benito Cereno*, *Moby Dick*, on and on with sailors, without being criticized for it."

"That's what he knew about, and what Austen knew about

was the whole issue of marriage and competing for husbands," Fernanda said.

"This was precisely the problem for women in that period," Leti observed, "the fact that they didn't have options, they could never live the same as men."

Fernanda pounced. "And *that's* why I say that Austen has feminist concerns, pointing this out."

"But she's not criticizing her culture. It's not a feminist focus," Leti insisted.

"Sometimes it is," Fernanda countered.

"Another way to see it is that she's simply presenting the reality and allowing the readers to use their judgment—like a spokesperson for her era," Ignacio José suggested.

"She did like to write about what she knew, just as Ignacio José points out with the comparison to Melville." I steered us out of the feminist shoals. "In fact, one of Austen's nieces was working on a novel and needed help with a scene she wanted to set in Ireland. Austen basically replied, 'Why take your characters somewhere *you've* never been? Stick with what you know.'"

Oscar weighed in again. "Is there a character in the novel that's like Austen herself?"

Ah, that question again. People really are endlessly curious about the connection between Austen's life and her works. "A lot of people assume that she's Lizzy, but the fact is, we're not sure—any idea like that is speculation."

He took this in with a nod. "I'm not sure if the rest of you had this reaction, but I felt it was Lizzy because we know the most about her. It seems that the author connects best to this character."

"She's the heroine, the protagonist," Fernanda agreed.

"No, there are two protagonists—the two closest sisters," Leti corrected.

"Lizzy's more important," Fernanda responded firmly.

I couldn't tell if this was good-natured sisterly bickering or if there were more behind it. Nobody else seemed uncomfortable with the number of times Uruguay and Argentina were locking horns, so I decided I shouldn't be either. "It's important to keep in mind that during that time period," I said, "you couldn't assume there was a close relation between the author's life and their work. These days, we often think of writing as a way of working out personal issues." I struggled to frame the idea that modern psychology has changed how many writers approach their work, but before I could get this out, the conversation took a different turn.

"I do think Austen was talented," Leti said directly to me, "but this book is really very light. We've read books together that are much more complex."

Ignacio José came to Austen's defense. "We can agree that the basic theme is light, although it was crucially important during her time period. But I must say that I believe Austen's capacity to delineate characters, to enter into their thought processes, to expose the psychology behind their actions is extraordinary. The lightness of her theme contrasts brilliantly with the profundity of her vision."

"That's well said," Fernanda agreed. "Just like *The Unbearable Lightness of Being*."

"Exactly," Ignacio José said, "That's also light yet profound."

"Well, there's *Lolita*; that's an easy book to read, but it's definitely profound psychologically," Leti conceded. "He's a genius, Nabokov." Oscar murmured agreement, nodding emphatically.

"And he loved Austen," I pointed out. "Nabokov said that Austen's works may seem superficial, but that's, um, that's a delusion that changes when you know more about her." Actually, he'd said, "This is a delusion to which the bad reader succumbs." Not only did I have no idea how to say "succumbs" in Spanish, I also didn't want Leti to think I was calling her a "bad reader"—which she wasn't—so I paraphrased.

"Austen's work is marvelous, too, for how it allows us to enter into her time period." Fernanda carefully selected a cookie from the table, passing along the plate as she continued. "We don't have to work at all ourselves to step into the era, this little window into England that she opens for us."

Here was my opportunity to treat the topic we'd arrived at in both Guatemala and Mexico. "Do you believe that this story is particular to its original context, that it could only happen just the way it does in the England of Austen's time? Or could you change the names and relocate it to Guayaquil, for example?"

Ignacio José didn't hesitate. "Impossible. You couldn't set either the people or the places here."

"Or in France or in Spain either," Leti seconded.

Fernanda agreed, joining the cross-talking between Leti and Ignacio José. "Religion is just one of the issues. These people are Protestants. There's the man who doesn't want to be a clergyman and goes into the army, and the other who's a clergyman and is hunting for a wife. It's just like in Agatha Christie's novels—there are things that could only happen in the particular time period in England that she's describing."

"I've got to disagree." Oscar spoke quietly but firmly, again magically silencing the group. "There are values laid out in this novel that you can definitely translate into any culture. She's discussing the end of the eighteenth century, beginning of the nineteenth. When you asked that question just now," Oscar turned to me as he continued, "I found myself thinking of what Chile was like during our time of independence in 1810. There's a Chilean novel called *Martín Rivas*, by Blest Gana. The things that happen in that novel, the problems it examines, like what happens to women without dowries or husbands, all of those things are in Austen. The books aren't identical, but the issues are very similar."

"On that issue, on women's roles, I agree," Fernanda concurred.

Before the feminist debate could flair again, Meli added, "I agree with Fernanda, but I have to say, if you moved the setting to France, for example, I just don't see Mr. Collins fitting in there!"

"There are a lot of specific things that would have to change," Fernanda responded. "Even the countryside they live in, the way land is distributed, and how communities are made up."

"But the real question here," Ignacio José said in his best moderator tone, "is whether or not the book demonstrates universal values."

"Yes, it definitely does." This from Fernanda, firmly.

"On the broadest level, it does," Ignacio José continued, "and from that perspective, it could be moved to whatever situation, not just to our modern day but back to the time of Christ. But I still believe that the specific way these values are examined, the actual cultural configuration in which the values are examined—no. That's specific. These characters are not people I could picture living in Guayaquil, with a house in El Portijo or in San Brandón, with a little cottage nearby."

"No," Oscar responded, "but the psychology of their actions, what's happening under the surface, that really seems the same to me. It's got nothing to do with the landscape or their religion. Not having a dowry in the early nineteenth century, whether in England or in Chile, was a serious matter, so people are going to react more or less the same anywhere that's true. The culture dictates that you've got to get married, and for a woman, you needed money or beauty to do it. Otherwise, you were between *la espada y la pared.*"

In other words, a penniless young Chilean would find herself between the sword and the wall, while her English counterpart would be stuck between a rock and a hard place. Same underlying idea, different detail—rather like the point Oscar was trying to make.

"Europe is one thing," Fernanda took up the line of thought, "but if you're talking about the Americas, it's different. Uruguay and Argentina during this period were very different culturally from Spain or England. The English were much more rigid about class."

"In our countries," Ignacio José directed his comments to me, "things were more free, more fluid."

"The people who came here weren't the real aristocracy. Those people already had what they wanted and stayed put in Spain," Fernanda added, as the others nodded agreement.

Ignacio José carried her point to its logical conclusion: "Some people don't like to admit that. The ones who came were the social climbers, trying to move up the ladder."

"My ancestors came as tax collectors, to make money," Fernanda continued. "Latin America just doesn't have the same history of aristocracy Spain does. Virtually all of the immigrants were from the middle classes on downward."

"They earned their money first," Meli agreed, "then used it to get titles and names."

Ignacio José gestured dramatically. "Exactly! There's a case here in Guayaquil—the illustrious *Conde Caca*" (translation: Count Crap). "He made a fortune collecting crap from Las Peñas, along the Malecón. Thirty-five years collecting crap, if you please, gets you wealth and seven married daughters. Think how happy Mrs. Bennet would have been married to him! He bought a string of names: Don Pedro López de—"

"*Caca!*" Leti sang out, to laughter all around.

After several minutes of small talk, Oscar brought us back to Austen: "If you gave me this book without letting me see the cover and told me it was a modern novel, I'd believe you—I'd have had no idea this was written two hundred years ago. Her prose has such grace, such clean agility. This must be *marvelous* in the original. I've got to buy it in English."

Instant cross-talking rang approval of this statement, with Leti fanning herself and nodding energetically, Ignacio José praising the dialogue, and Fernanda repeating, "She's like a painter—a painter!"

"There's no one quite like her." I was pleased that *they* were pleased, overall, with the book. "Is there any writer with this kind of popularity in Ecuador? Someone focused on customs and relationships from that period?"

Brows were furrowed and heads were scratched.

Oscar finally spoke up. "There weren't any novelists that I know of writing about society in Ecuador during Austen's lifetime."

As the others concurred, Ignacio José added, "Ecuadorian literature didn't establish itself firmly until the beginning of the twentieth century. That's the age of the Guayaquil Group and the Realists, but they were working less with city customs—they consciously wanted to give value to the life of country people, of *campesinos*."

I suddenly remembered the copy of *Cumandá* still in my purse. I pulled it out, curious to have their opinions.

Ignacio José caught sight of the cover first and shrieked (yes, he actually did), "Juan León Mera! She's got *Cumandá*!"

Fernanda, Leti, and Meli reacted as though I'd just pulled a handful of the *Conde Caca's* stock in trade from my purse. If the Christmas tree had still been on, its din would have been drowned out by the universal groan of horror.

"*Dios mío*, what a book!" Leti exclaimed. "It's *fatal, fa-tal*, tacky as can be—don't waste your time on that novel!"

"Give me some paper, something to write with," Ignacio José cried, eager to save me from *Cumandá*.

As the others chipped in titles, he began writing. But silently I resolved to try at least a chapter of *Cumandá*. Any book generating such outrage had to be worth looking into.

While Ignacio José finished up my Approved Reading List, Fernanda asked, "Was this discussion similar to the ones you did in Guatemala and Mexico?"

"Yes and no." My energy level had begun dropping sharply, and that always led to a breakdown in my Spanish. "We talked, we did talk about prejudice, but it was about…not the same types of prejudices."

"The prejudices against women in Guatemala are very strong," Ignacio José offered helpfully.

"No, actually, the issue was indigenous people—about racism and prejudices against people of indigenous origins."

I dug into my purse and pulled out my fancy-pants Dr. Amy

Elizabeth Smith cards from the university, handing them all around after penciling in the phone for the room where I was staying.

"The email there's good, but not the phone number—that's my office in California."

"Oh, you live in California; how nice!" Fernanda studied the card. "Are you married?" All eyes turned, polite but expectant.

"No—I've never been married."

"Jane Austen's situation," Leti said with a smile.

Sometimes I look at it that way. Like Austen, I'd had my proposals, some of them seriously tempting. Did my work stop me? Fear of commitment? Failure to find a man I believed would truly love me 'til death did us part, as it parted my father from my mother? Could Diego be that man? They say that negative parental role models can make relationships hard for people later in life—but I'm here to say that positive ones can be tough to live up to as well.

"I was dating somebody wonderful in Mexico, but long-distance relationships are complicated."

"They're the best thing in the world!" Ignacio José exclaimed. "Somebody there when you want them—but at a distance."

Leti laughed heartily, and somehow, the end of our wonderful talk had been signaled. It was time to stand and stretch, search for purses and bags, say our good-byes. I couldn't believe my luck in having found this wonderful group, thanks to Betsy. They all handed over email addresses and phone numbers, insisting that we needed at least one more get-together before I moved on to Chile.

"Thank you so much, all of you!" I said. "This group has been just *wonderful*!"

Meli led her wagon train of passengers—Leti, Ignacio José,

and me—out to her car. Leti was deposited at her house first, sweeping away in a wave of kisses, kind words, and expensive perfume. By the time we finally reached my part of town, the full weight of my tiredness was hitting me, and all I could muster by way of communication were stupid smiles and nods.

"Fabulous—then it's all settled!" Ignacio José was saying, his head jutting out the window as I shut the car door. "I'll see you Monday at noon." What on earth had I just agreed to?

Damnation. I simply *had* to stop nodding and smiling when I didn't understand what somebody was asking me.

CHAPTER NINE

The lively Austen discussion landed me in bed for two days solid.

"What did they tell you at the clinic?" Emilia, Betsy's sister-in-law, asked over the phone. "Nothing's wrong with you? Well, something's wrong with *them*. I'm making you an appointment with a real doctor."

She called back shortly to tell me it was arranged—after the weekend, I'd be seeing Dr. John Anderson, M.D. Quito, it seemed, was now out of the question. I'd wanted so much to travel to the country's capital, famed for both its natural and architectural beauty, but if a mere book group was enough to lay me out for two days, travel to a city of Quito's dizzying elevation would probably push me into that early foreign grave my mother kept nervously envisioning for me.

Well, at least that gave me time before the next Austen group to brave the horrors of *Cumandá*. Who among us can resist something we've been so emphatically warned away from?

Cumandá, published in 1879, is the most over-the-top novel I'd read in years. It's pure, undiluted schmaltz. One of the more astute characterizations of Austen's work is from Nancy Pannier: "Austen isn't an opera, she's a string quartet." Well, *Cumandá* is an opera. Cumandá and Carlos are the requisite star-crossed lovers—she, a daughter of the jungle and he, a son of Europe. When her father discovers she's given her chaste heart to a *blanco*, he sets her brothers on Carlos. They repeatedly fail to kill him, so her father promises her in marriage to an aged chief who already has six wives. What are the poor young lovers to do?

I could see why Mrs. Gardiner had tried to steer me away from the book. It has about as much to do with the realities of indigenous life in Ecuador as Baz Luhrmann's *Moulin Rouge* has to do with *fin-de-siècle* Paris. But I adored *Cumandá* just as much as I adore *Moulin Rouge*—they're luminous fantasy worlds, pure spectacle, outrageously beautiful.

I did feel obligated, however, to balance things with a group-approved recommendation. *Don Goyo* by Demetrio Aguilera Malta, published in 1933, was first on Ignacio José's Anything-but-*Cumandá* list. The contrast with Mera's novel was night and day. Life in *Don Goyo* ain't opera—it's raw, ugly, intense. The novel is arguably the earliest example of Magical Realism in Spanish-language literature, predating Rulfo's *Pedro Páramo* by decades. On the nationalist level, it's also important for its portrayal of *cholos*, mixed-race Ecuadorians who suffered severe discrimination and economic exploitation by upper-class Ecuadorians and foreign investors.

When I next saw Ignacio José, I kept mum on the forbidden *Cumandá*, but he was happy to hear that I'd enjoyed *Don Goyo*. He arrived with photocopies of several of his published short stories, plus a novel—*El Pintor de Batallas* by Arturo Pérez-Reverte. "You'll love this book, too," he promised. "The author, he's a Spaniard, so talented. It's what we'll discuss with the next group."

I was taken aback. "We're not reading *Pride and Prejudice*?"

He heaved a huge stage sigh. "I'm afraid there's been a

mix-up. *El Pintor de Batallas* was chosen instead. But wait until you see where we're meeting, outside of the city. Our hostess's house is just one step away from that mansion, what's it called—Pemberley!" That sounded like a proper setting, at least, for the group Betsy had dubbed "Lady Catherine."

As for *Pride and Prejudice*, well, so be it. *Así es la vida*. I'd already had one incredible discussion of the novel. If nothing else so far on my journey, I'd learned to stop trying to control everything around me—or, more accurately, I'd learned to *try* to stop trying.

You can never take ethnicity for granted in South America, so I didn't assume Dr. Anderson, who Emilia sent me to for my lingering illness, would be Anglo. It hasn't been too many years since Señor Fujimori was president of Peru, and Chile's homegrown George Washington was named Bernardo O'Higgins. But Dr. Anderson returned my Spanish greeting in brisk U.S. English.

I explained about my fever, the body aches, the pounding head, the persistent weakness, plus that I'd seen a doctor in Mexico who couldn't pin down the problem, ditto the local clinic.

"Did you have any other symptoms that might not have seemed related?" he asked with a frown.

I pondered. "There is one thing. I had a rash. It was weird, too, because—"

He held up one hand like a cop stopping traffic. "Let me guess—bright red, appeared on one part of your body, disappeared, and then reappeared on different parts?"

"That's it exactly! Itchy and painful, too."

He snorted and shook his head in disgust. "Dengue!"

"Dengue?" I had a vague memory of seeing some poster

somewhere about the dangers of mosquito bites. Maybe that had been…in a bus. In Puerto Vallarta.

"There's one disease only that manifests that kind of rash. Dengue. You get it from a mosquito—the *Aedes aegyptus.* How on *earth* could a Mexican doctor in a tropical zone fail to diagnose dengue?" He sounded genuinely angry. "I'll bet he just gave you antibiotics, didn't he?" When I nodded, he went on: "And that's what they did in the clinic here, too?" Double nod at the flashback to that evil injection.

Muttering under his breath, he wrote up a script for blood work. "Let's confirm that this is what you had. You must be in recovery by now or you wouldn't be out of bed, but full recovery takes months. It's a serious illness, and there's no vaccine, no treatment. You just have to ride it out. But since some strains are fatal, consider yourself lucky."

I headed for the door with the lab script, feeling shell-shocked. "It's not contagious," he called out, "so don't worry about giving it to anybody. And one more thing. Take aspirin for the headaches, not ibuprofen. Ibuprofen will make you worse."

Dengue entering the picture somehow made me feel twice as bad as before. Dengue—good god! This was exactly what my mom had been worried about—an evil malady from the tropics that poisons your blood and turns you into a zombie! Should I tell her and give the evil a name, or just leave it be until I was safely back in the United States?

When I returned to the apartment, still reeling from the news, I chucked the almost-empty bottle of ibuprofen I'd been eating ever since the headaches began. So I'd damaged my liver a bit. Maybe I'd grow another.

As stunned as I felt, this was good news on one front: I wasn't a big whiney Austen Loser, after all! There *had* been something wrong with me—I was no carping Mrs. Bennet or mewling Mary Musgrove. Dengue was serious business. Now if only I could find every person I'd been rude to and explain it all to them.

Whatever my disappointment at not reading *Pride and Prejudice* with Lady Catherine, I found Pérez-Reverte's book riveting. But I began worrying about Ignacio José. One day passed, and then another, and no call. I'd have to trust that he'd show up Thursday morning to take me to the group, since I'd lost the contact information Betsy had given me. And even if he'd lost my number, he knew where I lived.

Thursday morning dawned, transformed into afternoon and then evening without a peep from Ignacio José. How dare he go to Pemberley without me! Turning my room upside down and plowing through the scraps in my purse, I finally unearthed the paper with the contact numbers and by evening reached Carmen, one of the group members.

"We're really sorry! We'd been looking forward to meeting you earlier today," she said warmly. "As for Ignacio José," her voice dropped a few degrees colder, "he never showed."

"Do you think something might be wrong with him?"

"Who can ever say? Ignacio José is fascinating, such a talented writer—but he's not reliable. Anyway, we're meeting again in early January and you're welcome to join us. We spent more time this morning exchanging presents than discussing Pérez-Reverte's novel, so we'll cover it again. And maybe we can work in a little Jane Austen discussion."

I happily told her to count me in for January. I fell asleep speculating about Ignacio José, wondering if I could imagine anything half as lively as whatever tale he'd surface with.

In the meantime, Jane Austen's birthday rolled around just like it does every December 16. I decided to celebrate it with the iguanas. I stopped by the grocery store and bought as much lettuce as I could carry.

"Do iguanas like this kind of lettuce?" I asked the clerk. He was the same unfortunate man I'd snarled at earlier about the grocery divider. I wanted to mend fences, but he wasn't buying it; he nodded, still avoiding eye contact. Well, I tried.

Every December when I teach my Austen class, we hold a Jane Austen Night near her birthday to showcase student projects. This December my celebration would be more solitary, but given my sour mood, it was probably for the best. Reaching the park, I settled on a bench, wondering why the iguanas were all still up in the trees.

"It's chilly for them, after the rain," explained the man who had stealthily invited himself to sit next to me, correctly interpreting my tree-ward gaze.

Sheesh. A "Do you mind if I join you?" might have been nice. When I nodded stiffly but remained silent, he settled for a more standard introduction. "I'm Rafael. And you are…?"

"Violeta." It simply popped out.

"Violeta! What a beautiful name!" he smiled.

Why thank you, I just made it up myself.

"Have you been here before?"

"Never. I arrived in Guayaquil today." I capriciously deleted my bookstore trips, talks with Betsy, the Austen reading group, the previous visit to the park with Ignacio José, all with a single sentence.

My students' projects for Austen Night often include recasting her works in fanciful ways, but up until that moment, I'd never been much myself for fantasy improv. What had come over me? But this must have been exactly how Austen felt creating her juvenilia. In those short stories, written between ages twelve and eighteen, she matches, maims, and kills off characters with the zeal of a child improvising scripts for her favorite dolls. The juvenilia is Austen's wildest, most outrageous work. Here's a sample from "Sir William Mountague": "Mr. Brudenell had a beautiful niece with whom Sir William soon fell in love. But Miss Arundel was cruel; she preferred a Mr. Stanhope. Sir William shot Mr. Stanhope; the lady had then no reason to refuse him."

Where else has Austen ever resolved conflicts with such dispatch? On that December morning, I gave in to the birthday spirit of Austen, the wicked little teenager Austen. If that man couldn't leave me in peace with my lettuce, so be it.

"Have you got family here?" he asked. "Children?"

"No, but I've got nieces and nephews. Twenty-eight, in fact." I cavalierly transformed my numerous cousins into my siblings' offspring. "Eighteen of them are my godchildren."

"So you're not married?" If he could tell I was lying shamelessly, he didn't show it.

I lowered my head and sighed. "I was married."

"But now you're divorced?" he pursued, sounding hopeful.

I decided to kill my husband. "Widowed."

"That's terrible!" he exclaimed. His look of genuine concern gave me my first pangs of conscience over lying to a stranger who was, after all, paying me a compliment through his interest. When his hand inched over and stroked my leg—consoling me for my loss, no doubt—the pangs went as dead as my spouse. Let's see, how had he died, my husband Roger? No, wait, Roberto. Car accident? Bank robbery gone bad? Maybe a disease—in honor of Austen's birthday, I could give Roberto a wasting disease.

At that thought, given the slow, difficult nature of Austen's decline into death, all of the fun went out of the game. "Good to meet you, Rafael. Have a nice day." I gathered my lettuce and moved. From the corner of my eye I saw him consider one more run at the Widow Violeta, then leave the park. Well, Rafael could attribute his brush-off to my painful memories of poor, doomed Roberto.

Eventually, the day started its typical climb toward hot weather, and the iguanas descended for their lettuce. Since Ecuadorians don't assume all strangers are out to kidnap their kids, I gave handfuls of greens to several happy children, who were thrilled to feed the prehistoric-looking beasts—no matter whether they realized it was all in honor of Miss Jane Austen.

The Bookstore Mystery had been resolved in Guayaquil, and now, so was the Case of the Cantankerous Professor.

"This is incredible," said Dr. Anderson, staring at the lab results he'd received. "You didn't have dengue when you were in Mexico."

"I didn't?" I felt oddly disappointed at the sudden loss of my exotic disease.

"It's not past tense—you've *got* dengue, *right now*. An acute case." He leaned across the desk to study me, disbelief in his voice. "But you're up doing things! Don't you feel terrible?" His gaze was almost accusing.

Of course I do! That's why I'm here! I wanted to scream. Okay, calm down—this is the nice man who just identified the problem, after all. "I *do* feel terrible. Some days I can make it out of bed; others, I just can't."

"Stop pushing it! Good lord! That's probably why you're still sick." He leaned back hard against his seat, shaking his head in amazement. "Dengue lasts from four to twelve weeks, and from the time it's out of your system, you're still going to be weak for up to three months. Give it a rest!"

The next morning in an Internet café, I called my sister Laurie to consult: tell Mom or not tell Mom about the diagnosis?

"Mom is tougher than you think," she answered. "Bring more peanuts! They're climbing the screen door again! Sorry," she laughed. My call had interrupted one of the daily squirrel-feeding frenzies on her deck. She and her husband live by a woodlot and keep generations of local squirrels in chow, winter and summer. Her enormous, shaggy dog Katie was trained not to chase them, even when sharing the deck with the fearless nut moochers. "Tell Mom the truth," Laurie advised. "I'm sure she'd rather just know."

My sister was right. An illness with a name was more reassuring for my mother than a Mystery Illness, just as it was for me. I could hear the relief in Mom's voice when I called.

"Make sure you do what the doctor tells you," she advised. "You have bug spray, right? And you don't leave your windows open? They say that perfume attracts bugs. You're not using perfume, are you?"

I was glad I'd shared the truth with my mother. But I hadn't told her or my sister the *whole* truth. From sheer embarrassment, I held back the fact that…contracting dengue might well have been my own clueless fault. Leaving Dr. Anderson's office after the first visit, I'd wracked my brain about when a mosquito might have bitten me. It could have happened at any time, given the many long walks I'd taken with Diego, the time we spent on the *azotea*, the lack of glass in the windows. But as I thought back to those happy days in the rambling, work-in-progress house, I unearthed a memory from my first week there.

The memory of a man who'd come to my door. A man with a mask over his face, a plastic cap over his hair, and a tank strapped to his back. A man whose rapid Spanish, muffled by the mask, was beyond me and whose sci-fi get-up alarmed me. He pointed at the house's interior and tried to enter, so I shooed him away and slammed the door. He stood on the landing for a minute or two, gesturing in frustration with the spray nozzle of the tank, then trudged off.

When Diego returned from work I proudly told him how I had saved the house from a sinister invasion. He pondered a moment, then his face lit up with comprehension. "They come to spray for bugs during the rainy season. It's a city program."

"So I should have let him in?" I asked in dismay.

He laughed and kissed me on the tip of my nose. "I'm sure it'll be fine."

And there it was. Thanks to my paranoia about unregulated Mexican chemicals and my panicky failure to ask the man to take off his mask and slow down a bit, I was mosquito bait. Maybe there was an *Aedes aegyptus* out there with my name on it, whatever move I would have made—*¿quién sabe?* But I couldn't help but think that my fears had gotten the best of me. For what it's worth, Mr. Woodhouse, Emma's querulous father, wouldn't have behaved any better. He would have sent a servant out, for good measure, to make sure the masked man hadn't pilfered any of the Woodhouse poultry. But I certainly aspired to higher models of behavior in the Austen world.

Well. Live and learn.

When Christmas Eve arrived, I got an unexpected gift. Perhaps the Dengue Gods thought I had suffered enough. Whatever the case, Ecuadorian TV offered up the most heartwarming and best-est Christmas movie ever—*Die Hard*. I love the Grinch and Charlie Brown and *A Christmas Story*, but nothing says "Merry Christmas!" like John McClane busting up Hans Grüber's yuletide heist, one kill at a time. It's a big Steel Town favorite.

Hearing it dubbed into Spanish was an experience; the biggest loss is Alan Rickman's voice. Janeites who've only seen him mooning after Marianne in Ang Lee's *Sense and Sensibility* need to see him in *Die Hard*. Unfortunately, a lot of the humor drains out of the dialogue in translation. "Yippee ka-yay motherfucker!" naturally has to go, but instead of something lively in Spanish, it becomes "We'll see who's the best!" American John McClane tries to "fire down a 1,000-year-old Twinkie"; Ecuadorian John McClane "eats an old cake." In the fire truck scene, "Come to papa. I'll kiss yer *fuckin'* Dalmatian!!!" becomes a courteous "I've always appreciated you guys!"

Still, it's fun in any language, and I munched my way through a bag of *Galapaguitos*, tiny animal crackers in the shape of tortoises, penguins, iguanas, and other delicious animals from Ecuador's Enchanted Islands. At last, good triumphed at the Nakatomi Plaza, and the credits began to roll.

Suddenly, intensely, I was broadsided by the worst kind of homesickness: holiday homesickness. With the sound of Perry Como's familiar voice, undubbed, singing "Let It Snow," happy Christmas memories overwhelmed me. And there I was, so far from my loved ones, wasting away from a tropical disease. I could just imagine the fake tree in my mother's living room in Pennsylvania *at that very moment*, hung with the ornaments we four kids had loved to unpack each December, some inherited from departed Welsh ancestors, some we'd made in school. Under the tree would be the mechanical Crazy Train my dad treasured from his own childhood—placed all the more lovingly now since he was no longer there to do it himself. The huge, scary string of lights he'd spliced together decades earlier with electrical tape would be glowing in the windows, and my mother's gruesome date-and-nuts bars, made with so much love but still so hopelessly yucky, would have pride of place on a food-laden table.

The credits rolled, Perry crooned, and I burst into noisy, miserable tears.

World travel—what the *hell* was I thinking? Here I was, eating goddamned Galapagos animal crackers in bed while my loved ones half a planet away were enjoying each other's company and dodging the date-and-nut bars. Of course Betsy had invited me to the beach house—she'd practically begged ("Christmas is no time to be alone!"). But wary of my dengue temperament, needing more quiet than the beach house could offer, I'd stayed on my own. And now look at me. Pathetic!

Austen did very little traveling in her lifetime; it's true. She never got to hear a volcano rumble in Guatemala. She never sweated out a crowded Mexican boxing match or fed lettuce to tame iguanas in Ecuador. But there are compensations to being really, truly grounded. There are compensations to living solidly within a family circle, one that contracts with deaths and expands with births but remains, reliably, your family. Reading was a resource Austen valued—but every one of her novels makes clear that the most important resource of all, bar none, is *family*.

I slipped out of bed, ditched the wreckage of the cookies, and stared out the window at the festively lit buildings, at laughing couples and families passing on the streets below. This is a fascinating place, I told myself. How many Americans will ever get the chance to visit Ecuador? I had to make the most of it. Sure I'd need to rest, but there was plenty for me to do here, and I promised myself I'd buck up and do it.

But I also promised myself that next year—I'll be home for Christmas.

New Year's rolled past in a noisy orgy of fireworks screaming off from practically every house and street corner, giving Guayaquil, from the vantage point of my windows, the aspect of a city once more under siege by pirates. Shortly thereafter I met with the final group. The women of Lady Catherine proved infinitely more pleasant than their namesake, although our meeting place did qualify as the Rosings Park of tennis clubs. Located in an upscale development on the edges of greater Guayaquil, this was clearly where the moneyed Ecuadorians came to play. The central gym was designed in the shape of a sailing ship, complementing the riverside location, and the other buildings conveyed a similar sense of movement and modernity.

Carmen introduced me to the other five women, whose names I promptly forgot. I'd met the Mrs. Gardiner group members more or less one at a time, but five women's names at a stroke short-circuited my memory. Only one name stuck with me—because Silvina had brought a large tray of tempting holiday sweets. I mentally dubbed the ones who hadn't come bearing food as Tall, Youngest, Very Nice Necklace, and Short, hoping their names would resurface in conversation so I could avoid having to ask.

"Ignacio José is supposed to join us," Carmen said after ordering a soft drink from a hovering waiter, "but I'm not optimistic."

And I wasn't optimistic about seeing my twenty bucks again, either. Betsy had recently given me the scoop on him. I'd managed to squeeze in one short but very pleasant visit with her and her grandchildren at the beach house, largely spent chasing sand crabs on the shore, enjoying long meals with the family, and reading. Betsy had learned through the telephone extension of the Guayaquil grapevine that Ignacio José was offering a colorful explanation for the missed Pemberley visit. The stairwell entrance of his basement apartment, he claimed, had been blocked by careless construction workers dumping immense piles of concrete—he'd been trapped for two and a half days, forced to survive on canned goods and artistic inspiration. "But he probably just got locked in by his landlord for not paying his rent," Betsy had concluded. Both options were eyebrow-raisers for me.

With Ignacio José and his guidance both AWOL, our poolside conversation ambled from Austen film adaptations to *El Pintor de Batallas* and other random topics and back again. Youngest was the only one who'd actually brought her copy of Pérez-Reverte's novel, and Short leaned over to me and said in a stage whisper, "If she were one of your students, she'd have straight A's every time!" I kept hoping names would surface, but no such luck.

"We're typically better organized than this," Very Nice Necklace explained apologetically after a long sidetrack into family gossip. She was the oldest of the group, approaching seventy, flawlessly coiffed, and poised yet warm and pleasant. "We really can stick to one topic at a time!"

"The holidays have gone to our heads," Tall agreed as she

passed Silvina's sweets over to Short. "We need Ignacio José to keep us honest."

We chatted for a while about California, my travels, the holidays, and Silvina's outrageously good sweets, each member urging the others to take the last of them home. As the sun finally set spectacularly over the water, Very Nice Necklace offered to drive me back—or, more precisely, offered for her driver to drop me off on her way home.

"Oh, thanks, Chela!" Carmen said, suddenly saving me the embarrassment of asking her name so late in the conversation.

"I hope you're not disappointed in us," Chela said as we settled into the backseat of her enormous SUV. "Conversation is harder to maintain during the holidays, but this really is a good group."

As I insisted that I wasn't disappointed at all, I realized, silently, that I kind of *was*. But not with the group. It was clear they were intelligent women whose lack of focus was a combination of hooky-playing holiday spirit and losing Ignacio José's guiding hand. Without him, Mrs. Gardiner might well have devolved into a *melee* between the We Heart Darcy women and the Beat Darcy With Sticks men. I was disappointed, however, not to have gotten Lady Catherine's perspective on Austen. But the first group had gone so well that I simply had to consider this pleasant conversation (plus holiday snacks) as a bonus.

Chela leaned forward to explain something to her driver then turned back to me. "Our group's been going on for more than twenty-five years now, although not with all of the same members, of course. But I've been here since the beginning."

"Have you read any of Alicia Yánez Cossío's novels?"

"Several, yes. *Sé Que Vienen a Matarme*, that novel will stay with you. For our twenty-fifth anniversary celebration we invited her down from Quito. She's an incredible woman, simply incredible." She gazed out the window for a moment then turned to me with a smile full of memories. "This group has been important for me, *really* important for me, over all these years. If you don't fight for space in your life for art and conversation, so much will pass you by—for anybody, but especially for women, since we're always taking care of others. My life is richer because of this group." She patted my hand with a wry smile. "That sounds sentimental, but it's true."

Chela's heartfelt observations stuck with me long after she'd dropped me off. What she shared made me realize how much I'd allowed myself to silently make comparisons between the lives of the Lady Catherine group and those of the teachers in Antigua and my friends in Mexico. I knew what Nora had been up against trying to find time away from the throng living with her, struggling for privacy, and I'd assumed that Lady Catherine—and the ladies of Mrs. Gardiner—had it easy.

And here I was, being a reverse snob. You'd think an Austen lover would be a bit more careful about making assumptions, about giving in to first impressions. But alas, no. Chela's comments made me think twice about the pressure of a woman's role, independent of her finances. Going off in a corner with a book is, on a basic level, a selfish act. It was something Chela had found herself forced to defend, financial comfort notwithstanding.

Thank god for feisty women, rich or poor. Thank god for anyone who'll fight for the right to sit down with a good book— and then, the right to sit down with some good friends and that good book.

My last day in Guayaquil dawned hot. The furnishings that made my temporary home more homey returned to my suitcases— the purple fish blanket, the owl statue, the stuffed chihuahua. Joining them were quite a few more books and some beautiful fabric runners from the indigenous artisans' market. I emailed Diego to let him know that I was about to hit the road again. He'd been shocked when I'd told him about the dengue, blaming himself for not recognizing what had befallen me. "If doctors couldn't identify the problem," I insisted, "why blame yourself?" He promised to protect me from any and all mosquitoes when I finally returned to him.

Would I return to him? I missed him terribly; that I knew. Walking Guayaquil's Malecón, I was always aware of his absence, aware of how, lovely as it was, the Guayas still just wasn't the sea at Puerto Vallarta. I'd spent plenty of time alone when Diego was working, but I'd always felt his presence. I knew that each evening he'd come through the door laughing, asking for a beer, sharing amusing stories about that day's fares in his cab. Could that be my life, what I'd left behind in Mexico? If my biggest complaint was "Gee, he's too cheerful," was I an idiot to hesitate?

But it wasn't just about us; it was about geography, too—and that was something, for the moment, beyond my control.

I spoke briefly with my mother, as well. She urged me to keep coated with bug spray, to avoid perfume ("and strong deodorant— that's like perfume, too"), and to call when I made it to Chile.

Betsy was back from the beach at last, and for our good-bye lunch before my airport run we chose a Polynesian restaurant facing the Malecón, with surfboards for tables. The entire soundtrack of *Pulp Fiction* played as we ate and chatted.

"This visit must not have gone as well as you'd hoped,"

she said with a rueful smile. "But I'm so glad Emilia's doctor helped you!"

"I was sorry not to spend more time with you at the beach and also, that I missed Quito," I admitted. "But even with the dengue problems, I had a good time here." It was true. I'd become familiar with a fascinating, if somewhat rough, city, and I'd read unforgettable Ecuadorian literature. I'd visited museums and spent quiet hours contemplating the broad Guayas river from the Malecón. I'd been disappointed once more in my search for Nancy Drew in Spanish, but hey, I'd cracked the secret on bookstores being organized by publisher. Best of all, I'd enjoyed my visit with Lady Catherine and treasured the Austen discussion with Mrs. Gardiner. We'd even fit in a very pleasant dinner reunion at Oscar's house, minus the still-missing Ignacio José ("I don't understand *how* he could resist free food!" Leti had laughed). My twenty bucks were history—but it would have been nice to have seen that charming, artistic rogue one more time.

"Even though I couldn't be in your book groups," Betsy said, "it's been wonderful for me to talk with you about your traveling Austen project. Reading is *such* an important part of life!"

She asked me how the Guayaquil groups had gone in comparison to the ones I'd already done. I hesitated over how to articulate the differences without sounding critical. Unlike the pickup groups I'd created in Guatemala and Mexico, Mrs. Gardiner had years running as a forum for discussion. They'd become a communal repository of wisdom on dozens of novels, and it was fascinating to see what literary connections Austen evoked for them.

But perhaps *because* of how well read Leti, Yolanda, Oscar, Fernanda, Meli, and Ignacio José were, Austen had been more of a special event for the groups in Guatemala and Mexico. With less time to read, less formal education, and less exposure to a range of authors, Nora and the ladies in Guatemala and Diego and his friends in Mexico seemed much more taken with the novel we'd shared. The Ecuador readers had enjoyed *Pride and Prejudice*, but with less fervor, somehow. Our conversation, rich and rewarding, was more like one I could have had with fellow professors where I teach.

Nora and the ladies had identified with the book on a more personal level, making a smoother transition from Austen's world to their own. It's typically considered a mark of literary sophistication to move beyond seeing your own life reflected in a book, and I suppose that's true, to an extent. But it depends, on the one hand, on the book. Austen creates a world that is simultaneously fact and fiction, one that taps directly into the core problems that confront us as we navigate life and relationships, a world that invites us to make moral self-assessments. On the other hand, the capacity to move beyond seeing your life in a book also depends on your life. The conversation with Chela from the Lady Catherine group was a healthy reminder that, rich or poor, we all have our troubles. But it isn't surprising that the theme of prejudice hit home in Guatemala for women who feel the consequences of discrimination more directly in terms of gender, race, and social class.

There had been one amusing point of entry into Austenland for the Guayaquil readers, however, one subject that really got them going on a personal rather than an intellectual level. Darcy. It was fun to watch the men so willing to give him a good thrashing and the women so eager to bustle in and protect him. With Darcy, they'd all crossed that line from discussing characters within a fictional setting to imagining how they'd interact with them.

But Ignacio José, Leti, and Fernanda were firm about Austen's world having existed in a particular place and time. For them, her characters couldn't step out of the pages of *Pride and Prejudice* and onto the streets of Guayaquil. Smart, careful readers with a broad field of comparison at their disposal, they were able to recognize what's distinctive about Austen. But I was happy with Oscar's compromise. Sure, Austen's characters occupy very specific territory in Regency, pre-Victorian England—but human beings are human beings, and our basic motivations and the challenges we face don't change drastically from one culture or one period to another. Austen's characters seek love and approval and struggle with pride and jealousy, as do we all.

I decided to take Oscar's contribution as an omen that I would have a great discussion with his fellow Chileans on the next go-around with *Sense and Sensibility*. If Chileans really are "the English of Latin America," maybe they'd have a special affinity for Austen? And if smart, contentious, and colorful Leti was any indication, I was going to have a blast in Argentina, further down the road.

Santiago, my next stop, was calling. Betsy and I finished up our Maui burgers, and she helped me haul my grotesquely over-weight suitcases into a taxi, sending me off with hugs and warm wishes. "You've got to take care of yourself!" she urged. "Emilia and I won't be around to help, you know."

I felt a pang at the thought. However little time we'd gotten to share, Betsy had brought sunshine to a cloudy month. I looked forward to exploring a new country, but I was once more jumping off from the familiar and heading to a place where I didn't know a soul.

Then again, I hadn't known Betsy, Lady Catherine, or Mrs. Gardiner when I'd arrived in Guayaquil a month earlier.

CHILE:

AUSTEN IN THE ANDES

In which the author reports for duty at a Chilean university, discovers Used Book Heaven and buys still more books, hangs out with a rooster then flees the police, tries to talk a student out of hitchhiking from Chile to Denver, and, after being asked out by a strange variety of married men, reads Sense and Sensibility *with quirky, insightful Chilean poets (and one bright, bubbly historian).*

CHAPTER TEN

It's got the world's driest desert in the north, ice and penguins in the south—and Chile is more than ten times longer than it is wide.

Sounds very exotic. But I was amazed on the long ride to Santiago from the airport by just how much the landscape reminded me of California's Central Valley. Flat and dry, the wide expanses on either side of the highway were dotted with sparse, scrubby growth. Santiago, Chile's capital, is in the *valle central* of Chile, famous for its wines. California's Central Valley is also wine country. On a clear day, if you climb a levee, you can see the foothills of the Sierra Nevada to the east and the Coastal Range to the west. Santiago proper isn't quite so flat; my new neighborhood hugged the base of one of its largest hills, Cerro (or "Hill") San Cristobal.

On a clear day, without climbing a thing, the striking snow-caps you see belong to the Andes.

The apartment complex where I'd be living straddled the line between two Santiago neighborhoods: Providencia, a pleasant residential/commercial center, and Bella Vista, the funky, lively party center of the city and location of *La Chascona*, one of the houses of fabled Chilean poet Pablo Neruda. I was close to bars and restaurants if I were interested but far enough away that the clubs didn't disgorge noisy drunks under my windows at 3:00 a.m. (so, no *faux* roosters in Santiago, like in Guayaquil). The Río Mapocho flowed by two blocks away, its banks the site of an attractive, well-stocked farmer's market. My mother could eat Chilean fruit in January in nippy Pennsylvania, but now I could get it (and a sunburn)—walking distance.

As I'd done in Ecuador, I promptly decorated my new apartment with the purple blanket, the big-eyed owl, and the stuffed Chihuahua from Diego, along with some brightly colored, woven fabric runners from an artisans' market in Guayaquil. I'd coughed up $100 extra for my overweight baggage on the flight out; not a single book, bright blanket, or big-eyed owl was getting left behind. At the rate I was going, by the time I hit Argentina I'd be able to take an unfurnished hotel room.

The doormen where I lived were a friendly crew, and the day I arrived, I chatted a good hour with Demetrio the Spaniard, Emilio, and Don Alberto. The complex, with a large central courtyard, was composed of three buildings accessed by a gate, beside which stood the doormen's office. At least two were there at any given time, talking together or reading.

"Don" wasn't Alberto's first name; it was the title conferred on him as senior doorman. In his mid-sixties, he and Emilio, a strikingly handsome man in his thirties, were Santiago natives. Slender Demetrio the Spaniard, the youngest, had come to Santiago to study. With Don Alberto and Emilio, I found the "Chileans are cold" stereotype wasn't holding true but another one was: Chileans speak the most difficult version of Spanish in South America. Even more than Guayaquileños, they drop word endings, mash syllables together, and speak quickly. Kind of the

Pittsburghers of the continent, which I found heartwarming—but challenging.

Demetrio the Spaniard, easiest to understand, was also a gold mine; he knew where to find every bookstore, flea market, and weekend book fair.

"You're in luck!" he cried, when I explained my traveling Austen project and desire to learn about Chilean literature. "There's a sale tomorrow outside the Providencia municipal building."

Pursuing books would be just the thing to stave off an attack of new-place-travel-panic, even if I wouldn't be able to show them off proudly to Diego at the end of the day.

The next morning I set off with the map Demetrio had drawn. I am such a book hound that I actually dream about flea markets and thrift stores. My sleeping brain creates dusty, crowded places where, in the midst of old clothing and bric-a-brac, I suddenly discover Nancy Drew mysteries from the 1930s that I never knew existed, despite already owning a complete set. Or I pull leather-bound Dickens novels for a dime apiece from under a stack of warped LPs. Or I stumble over a box marked "Free!" that's stuffed with hardback bodice rippers from the 1920s with titles like *Daughters of Luxury* or *The Barbarian Lover*. I've never had the nerve to ask any of my book-loving friends if they have these nerdy dreams, too.

I hit the *feria de libros*—the book fair—on a mission, since I'd gotten my first reading recommendation before setting foot on Chilean soil. Austen had reminded Oscar from the Ecuador group of Alberto Blest Gana, and finding a copy of his *Martín Rivas* proved easy. My bags grew heavier and heavier with treasures I couldn't live without before I remembered the distance I had to haul them back to my apartment. I was still recovering from dengue and not up to full strength, plus taxis were trickier to catch and more expensive in Santiago—no economical *tuk-tuks* available, like in Antigua.

The walk home was a lot less carefree than the one there. Being passed by a flock of small, screeching green parrots lightened my load for several blocks—wild parrots in the city! But by the time I made it back to the doormen's office I was winded, my back and shoulders on fire.

"You found the sale!" Demetrio the Spaniard greeted me as I staggered up, while Don Alberto hurried to open the security gate.

I emptied my bags onto the counter to display my loot to Demetrio. Don Alberto scooped up the bags as I repacked them and, despite my protests, wouldn't give them back until I was inside the door of my apartment.

"Well, good-bye for now," he said, smiling over his shoulder as he left. Pleasant as he was, Don Alberto was well into his sixties. Still, I was beginning to get the idea that he was, in fact, flirting.

How did a nice guy like *Sense and Sensibility*'s Edward Ferrars get caught up with a sneaky skunk like Lucy Steele in the first place?

"Want of employment," that's how. If he'd had work or studies to keep him busy, he tells Elinor at the novel's end, he never would have entered into an engagement so rashly. Most of us love to gripe about our jobs, but our "employment" often makes us who we are. After all my months of book shopping, hanging out with Diego, doing reading groups, and recovering from dengue, Santiago was where my employment resumed. I'd be teaching two literature courses for U.S. and Canadian students at a Chilean university that offered a special semester on a North

American timetable, January to May; a typical Chilean semester wouldn't start until March.

I'd assumed the miserable slump I'd fallen into in Ecuador was all about the dengue I'd contracted in Mexico and about missing friends and family—and most of all, Diego. Entering the university building in central Santiago and seeing the rooms where I'd be teaching showed me there was more to it. Despite some language difficulties, I immediately felt at home among my new Chilean colleagues. The specialist in American history and culture was Carmen Gloria, an attractive, vivacious woman my age with full, dark hair shot through with striking auburn highlights. She reminded me immediately of Nora—not so much in looks but for her warm, positive, welcoming energy. A friend in the making, I hoped.

School is my element. So yes, I am a nerd. My book orders were in, my handouts were ready to go, and there I was, Dr. Smith again.

The study abroad coordinator, a somewhat timid man in his thirties with large, solemn eyes and dark, curly hair, took me out to lunch to celebrate my reporting for duty and to brief me on the students before classes started. "These are good kids," Ramon said as he led me into the restaurant. "But you need to approach study abroad differently. Trim back your reading just a *bit*. And add some field trips. They love field trips."

Field trips—check.

"Students are often gone on the weekends because they come here to travel," he explained. "It's perfect that you'll be teaching travel literature. And it's one of my favorite genres."

As talk shifted to reading preferences, I realized that Ramon, bright and well read, could be the perfect person to help me with

Austen. The Guatemala, Mexico, and Ecuador groups had all been arranged before my arrivals, but knowing that I had five months in Chile, I'd decided to do the legwork once I got to Santiago. Now, maybe I didn't have much legwork to do.

At the first reasonable opening I asked, "What do you think of Jane Austen?"

Ramon took a sip of wine. "Austen is a classic," he nodded tactfully. "But do you know who I really love?"

Then he did it—he named the author who makes hard core Austen loyalists sigh in distress, the author who wrote, "Every time I read *Pride and Prejudice*, I want to dig her up and beat her over the skull with her own shinbone" and "It seems a great pity that they allowed her to die a natural death." What a contrast with gentle Sir Walter Scott, lamenting that "such a gifted creature died so early!"

Who could contemplate assaulting Austen's corpse with... Austen's corpse? I love to horrify students by sharing these quotes on the first day of my Jane Austen class and asking them to guess the source. Surely the culprit must have been John Wilkes Booth, Jack the Ripper, Charles Manson. Maybe Adolf Hitler?

Nope. Mark Twain.

Why on earth did Twain hate Austen so much? It helps to know the context for his most biting comments. Twain's friend William Dean Howells was an over-the-top Austen fan, and Twain couldn't resist tweaking his nose on this. The "It seems a great pity" comment actually comes from a private letter to Howells, not any polished statement Twain published. The "shinbone" crack was also from a private letter, one to Joseph Twichell.

There's no way a writer as good as Twain could fail to appreciate a master stylist like Austen, so I've got a theory. The cynic in him was galled by all of the happy endings Austen pulled out of her bonnet. Wicked humorist that Twain was, how could he not love great writing like this from *Northanger Abbey*: "A family of ten children will always be called a fine family, when there are heads and arms and legs enough for the number." Or this, from *Persuasion*: "The report of the accident had spread among the workmen and boatmen about the Cobb, and many were collected near them, to be useful if wanted; at any rate, to enjoy the sight of a dead young lady, nay two dead young ladies, for it proved twice as fine as the first report."

So, Ramon's affection for Twain didn't put him on the wrong side of a literary divide for me. My opportunity to pursue Austen came over our decadent dessert, when Ramon asked, "Aside from teaching, what are you hoping to get out of your time here in Chile?"

I explained about the Austen reading groups I'd already done and, by the time the check showed up, I had one committed Austen reader and Ramon's promise to deliver more.

"A number of my friends are poets," he smiled. "That would be appropriate for the land of Neruda, wouldn't it?"

It's a shame how little formal education Austen got to enjoy— only about two years total. What an intimidating student she would have been, no doubt smarter than most of her teachers, taking in lectures with an exacting mind, ready to greet any dullness in her lessons with sharp, sly commentaries. But given how well she turned out, maybe there's something to be said for being more or less self-educated, after all.

For my new students in Chile I was offering versions of two literature courses I do at my home university, one on travel and the other on war. There were five students in the travel class and four in the other, smaller groups than I was used to but good by the standards of the study abroad program. Mine were the only classes taught in English, giving students the chance to speak up without being nervous about sounding like boneheads.

I'd heard that when studying abroad, at least one student per class will seriously go native. This is good if it means they're adapting well, *not* so good if they start missing classes and flunk the semester. I couldn't resist trying to guess which one it might be. In my travel lit course, Alison and Jenny both were open, sunny California girls, and if I hadn't learned that Matt was from Alaska, I'd have assumed he was also from California. All three seemed too classically American to seriously blend in with the rather broody, often black-clad Chilean students thronging the streets outside. There were six other colleges and universities in the neighborhood, located a few metro stops from Santiago's huge, impressive main square, the Plaza de Armas, and close to La Moneda, Chile's equivalent of the White House.

Taylor and Anne, on the other hand, would bear watching. Taylor had an adventurous hippie chick quality to her, and Anne, the only East Coast student, was smart and pleasant but reserved. A Chilean in the making?

From the war literature class, Sarah, who was dating a Colombian and had spent long stretches of time in Latin America, already seemed on her way to going native. I was pleased to discover that Brooke, who also had something of the hippie chick about her, was a fellow Pennsylvanian. Michelle, the most bubbly and cheerful, was a Californian and Emily, sweet and polite, the one Canadian.

Our first field trip, I announced, would be to Santiago's largest cemetery, where we could visit the graves of famous Chileans. "Cemetery" isn't always a word that makes people happy, but as Ramon had predicted, the students knew which part of the sentence really counted:

"Field trip! Yay!"

Two weeks later the anticipated day arrived. The students were especially curious to see the grave of Salvador Allende, since we'd discussed the 1973 coup against Allende in both classes. Despite the CIA's support of the coup, the typical U.S. perspective now is that Augusto Pinochet, who held power until 1989, was a dictator.

Pinochet and company forced the elected president to put a bullet in his own head and tortured and killed thousands of Allende's supporters in 1973, among them musician Victor Jara, Chile's Bob Dylan (picture Nixon having Bob Dylan tortured and killed, and you get the idea). Given that thousands more Chileans were kidnapped, tortured, and killed over the next decades, it's hard to see how anybody could call Pinochet anything but a dictator. I'd warned my students, however, not to make assumptions. A considerable percentage of Chileans felt that Pinochet saved their country from becoming another Cuba. Today Chile has a strong, stable economy, and some credit this to Pinochet (while others point out that Chile *always* had a strong, stable economy, in comparison with its neighbors).

Basically, it's best not to discuss the coup unless somebody brings it up. It's a raw, painful subject, one that can surface unexpectedly. The day before the cemetery trip I'd casually mentioned to the doormen how much I enjoyed walking along the banks above the Río Mapocho when, suddenly, Emilio fixed me with a hard stare.

"After the coup, that river is where people went to look for their brothers, their children. Their mothers." His voice cracked. "The banks were stained with blood because that's where those bastards would throw the people they'd murdered." He spoke slowly, deliberately, wanting to make sure I understood every word.

I could only nod. Two things were clear: that some terrible, terrible story lay behind this pain and that any response I made would sound trite. Demetrio the Spaniard, seated next to him at the counter, put an arm around his shoulder. After a moment, Emilio gave a short, uncomfortable laugh. "But you're right; it's nice to walk along the river now."

Standing at Allende's grave with my students, I recalled that exchange as a solemn silence descended among the students, typically so animated and talkative. It was one of those moments that *never* could have happened in the classroom. On the granite wall above the crypt are inscribed the words of Allende's final speech to the Chilean public during the bombardment to wrench him from La Moneda, the Chilean White House. Two of the students slowly sounded the words out in Spanish, touching the stone gently as if reading Braille.

For anyone wondering if Salvador Allende and novelist Isabel Allende are related, they are. He was her cousin, and his overthrow sent her into exile in Venezuela, where she wrote *La Casa de los Espíritus* (The House of the Spirits), her best-known novel. But most Chileans I asked said, "Her newest novel is better, *Inés del Alma Mía*—Inés of My Soul—about the Spanish settlement of Chile."

Shortly after our field trip I hunted for *Inés* near the University of Chile, an area Carmen Gloria told me was a used book heaven. In the block closest to the metro stop Universidad de Chile are dozens of small used books stalls, along with an extensive indoor book mall and several independent bookshops. On the right days of the week you can also find a large book fair several blocks south of the metro, near the Parque Almagro.

This sort of book commerce has all but disappeared from the States, a fact that truly makes me sad. A person simply can't earn a living in a major city with a bookstall of the size operated by many people in Santiago. Large chains and Internet businesses are efficient, but for real booklovers, there's nothing to replace the pleasure of browsing used bookshelves and visiting with people who know every title they have for sale. I quickly found *Inés* there at a good price (although, alas, still no Nancy Drew in Spanish).

Austen never wrote historical fiction, but given her complaint that history is "dull, with the men all so good for nothing and hardly any women," she would have approved of Allende's giving us an important female perspective, although she would have been scandalized by the story itself. Born in Spain in 1507, Inés Suárez sailed to Peru in search of her husband, who had followed Pizarro to the "New World." By the time she arrived he was dead, but the dashing Pedro de Valdivia was very much alive. They became lovers, despite Valdivia's having a wife in Spain. Inés joined the party of *conquistadores* heading south to claim the territories that would become Chile—if only they could subdue the Mapuche, the indigenous people already living there.

Inés saved Valdivia from attempts by subordinates to hijack the expedition, nursed men in battle, and even donned armor and fought. Eventually Valdivia, now considered the founder of Chile, died gruesomely at the hands of the *Mapuche* whose land he had invaded; Inés married one of his young captains and lived to a ripe old age.

The book dealer who'd sold me Allende's historical novel had it right when he'd handed the volume over with a smile: "If you haven't heard this story before, you're going to love it!"

Who knows if Inés and Valdivia were the cause, but Chileans seem to have had an odd spin on marriage and extramarital hanky panky ever since. Affairs don't raise too many eyebrows, perhaps since divorce only became legal in Chile in—I am *not* making this up—2004. Previously, people with enough money and influence could get an annulment, although it's hard to imagine how they did so with a straight face when they had children. To this day average Chileans settle for separation and on-the-side arrangements. Affairs just-for-the-heck-of-it happen, too.

For instance. Every time I spoke with the tall, handsome security guard at the university building, he kept me updated on his wife's extended stay in Spain with their daughter. Late one afternoon he shifted the topic from his wife's absence to my being all alone in Chile, far away from my family—surely I was lonely, too, and surely it would be nice for us to be lonely together, yes?

I'm no expert, but I'd like to think that in the United States, cheating still carries some sense of shame. Don't married American men on the prowl sneak their rings off and fake bachelorhood? In Chileans' defense, they're very up-front about things; the guard had made clear he was off the marriage market. When I turned him down he shrugged and smiled but didn't seem too put out. Thank god, since I'd now have to see him every day I taught.

This little encounter forced me to rethink a decision I'd made only the day before. Don Alberto, the friendly doorman at the apartment, had asked me out to dinner. I usually don't date men in the "old enough to be my father" category, and of course there was Diego. But given our current separation and my uncertainty about the long-distance situation, keeping our options open was only reasonable. And yes, I was lonely. Don Alberto was attractive for his age and had a kindly, patient air. He could be just the man to help me adjust to a new city. In a moment of weakness, I'd agreed to meet Don Alberto that upcoming weekend at a nearby restaurant.

Then in a moment of clarity, after the brush with the amorous security guard, it dawned on me that Don Alberto probably wasn't single. Marriage was the norm in Chile, and newly legal divorce was out of the reach of a doorman's salary.

"There's something I need to know," I said to Don Alberto the day before our date, as he abandoned his post yet again to walk me to my apartment. "Are you married?"

I watched the painful struggle on his face between "I don't want to lie" and "I don't want to blow this date." To his credit, honesty won out. "Well, yes. I am. But things with my wife are—"

I gently stopped him. "Thank you for being honest. But I can't go out with you if you're married." Not only would Jane Austen have approved—if it had happened to her, no doubt she would have written something scathing about him in a letter to Cassandra (a letter Cassandra would then have dutifully burned upon her sister's death). But Austen's good judgment would probably have kept her from getting into this type of situation in the first place. What had possessed me to agree to a date with a man I'd now have to see multiple times every day?

Don Alberto eyed me wistfully for the next week but didn't

say a word. Then one morning as I was in the basement loading the dryer, I turned to find him watching me from the doorway.

"Won't you reconsider?" he said without preamble. "Can't we just have coffee, just as friends?"

"Well, if you mean it—just as friends." Coffee was innocent enough.

"Really?" he said, smiling brightly. "That's wonderful!" Then he grabbed my face with both hands and laid a great big kiss on me, tongue and all.

I shoved him backward, too stunned to speak. Had he been younger, I would have socked him on the jaw. Given that he was married, he probably had kids, and given his age, *they* had kids. I couldn't go around punching somebody's granddad even if he had frenched me, uninvited.

"Forgive me! Forgive me!" he sputtered. "I thought that you—I mean I—" Then he turned and dashed out of the laundry room.

Flabbergasted, I scanned the room for a security camera. God forbid Demetrio the Spaniard and Emilio had witnessed that outrageous scene, me in my "everything's dirty" laundry clothes and early morning bed-head, and Don Alberto acting like a teenager. No camera in sight. At least I was spared that embarrassment.

I decided to debrief the episode with Carmen Gloria. Smart, well read, and endlessly curious about American culture, she was a huge fan of *Sex and the City* and adored girl talk. In my five months in Chile I never once saw her when she wasn't dressed to the nines, looking fabulous.

We met up at Santiago's Central Market. Built at the end of the nineteenth century to shelter the traditional seafood and produce markets, it was eventually converted into shops and restaurants. Santigueños (and clever tourists) flock there for the high-quality food and lively atmosphere.

After we'd caught up on the latest gossip at the university, I shared my Don Alberto story. Carmen Gloria shook her head most of the time I was talking.

"*Puchas!*" she exclaimed when I'd finished. A softening of the ever-popular word "*puta*" (whore), "*puchas*" means anything from "Oh, boy" to "Holy crap!" depending on how you inflect it. "You're pretty dumb for a smart woman, *sabes?* First of all, don't *ever* tell this story to anybody at the university. Promise me."

"I promise, Carmen Gloria."

"Good. You can tell me this kind of thing because I'm open-minded, you know." Suddenly, I got the sense that there was more to this story than I'd realized. I'd been wondering how I'd managed to send the wrong signals, but clearly, it went beyond that.

"Okay," she continued. "First of all, you can't be friends with Chilean men. Period. Any Chilean man asking you *anywhere*, unless it's strictly work related, is coming on to you. Telling a man you'll have coffee with him means you're giving him the okay to try for more. Second—and here's the real reason you can't tell *anybody* else this story—you're a university professor."

Since I already knew that, I waited to see where she was heading.

"University professors do *not* date doormen," she said, giving my hand a squeeze across the table. "I'm not saying this is *right*— I'm just telling you how it is. This Alberto *knows* that university professors don't date doormen, so he naturally assumed that if you were willing to go out with him, it's because you were look-ing for some *fun*. You know—something *physical*. You're not offended that I'm telling you this, are you, *querida?*"

I wasn't offended, but my sense of order was—this was

Emma territory, and Chile was supposed to be about *Sense and Sensibility*! Class is an issue in all of Austen's novels, but the precise ranking of who is above whom (and how far) and who can be matched with whom is more appropriate for a conversation between Emma and Mr. Elton or Emma and Mr. Knightley. Apparently, if I magically landed in *Emma*, my being a professor means that Robert Martin, the kind farmer who loved Emma's protégé Harriet, would be off limits—except for a roll in the hay.

"I guess I need every bit of help I can get with the Chilean dating scene, Carmen Gloria. So no, I'm not offended!"

She laughed and patted my arm. "What a sweetheart you are! Now let's go walk off some of this big lunch, so that we have room for ice cream at *La Rosa*!"

Blundering into class issues made me decide that it was time to try *Martín Rivas*. In Guatemala, practically everybody I'd spoken to had read José Milla's *Historia de un Pepe* as a student. *Martín Rivas* is the book Chileans tend to remember from school. The author, Alberto Blest Gana, was born in Santiago in 1830 to an Irish father and a Chilean mother, which makes the Father of the Chilean Novel half Irish, just like Bernardo O'Higgins, the Father of Modern Chile.

I could see right away why *Orgullo y Prejuicio* brought *Martín Rivas* to mind for Oscar. I wish I had the book in electronic form, to search the number of times the word *orgullo* is used. "*Lo que predomina en el Santiago es el orgullo*," proclaims a major character: "What rules in Santiago is pride." Martín arrives in the capital seeking help from his father's former business partner. Naturally, the wealthy man has a daughter worth falling in love with, who is pride itself—the lovely Leonor. Every man in Santiago pursues her, but she decides that nothing would be quite so pleasurable as bending poor but proud Martín to her will. When her flirting gives way to real affection for him, she is mortified.

Lady Catherine in *Pride and Prejudice* wasn't crass enough to mention money in her plan that Darcy should marry her daughter Anne, but Lady Catherine wanted business as usual—the rich marry the rich. What keeps Austen's novels from being preachy or predictable is how she shows that pride isn't restricted to the wealthy and also that some forms of pride can be a real strength. Lizzy's pride in herself and her family is what keeps her from backing down in the face of Lady Catherine's demands that Lizzy leave Darcy be. Blest Gana's work is equally subtle on the subject of pride.

While he acknowledged Balzac as his biggest literary influence, I couldn't help but wonder if Blest Gana hadn't gotten a peek at an Austen novel or two, somewhere along the line. I emailed Oscar in Ecuador with two big thumbs up for his recommendation.

Dating blunders aside, I'd passed some happy months so far in Chile by the time the evening of March 28 rolled around. Dengue was in my past. Missing Diego had settled into a dull ache, rather than the daily sadness I'd felt in Ecuador. My students had adapted well to their studies and their new cultural environment, fortified with the occasional field trip. One of Carmen Gloria's students, in fact, had jumped in with both feet and joined a local reggae band, so we braved the chain-smoking crowd in a Bella Vista bar to go and hear him. I still had my eye on my own students to see if any would "go native." Ramon, the study abroad coordinator, had delivered copies of *Sentido y Sensibilidad* to four of his friends, all poets. Carmen Gloria, although not a poet, had promised to join us for a mid-April group. So, all was going smoothly. After an evening spent reading a vintage Chilean children's magazine I'd found called *El Peneca*, I fell asleep, content that things should turn out well in April for Austen.

Two hours later, the *bomba* jolted me awake. The second (and third and fourth) kept me awake for hours.

Late-night explosions weren't a common occurrence in Santiago; they're more like a biannual occurrence. Chile is politically stable, student protests aside, but twice a year like clockwork, Santiago bursts dramatically into riots. September 11, the date of the coup against Allende, is rung in with illegal fireworks and *bombas*, making the city as noisy (but not as festive) as Antigua at Christmastime. The other date is March 29, known as "*el día del joven combatiente*," the day of the young combatant.

I lay awake for hours, nervous about the intermittent explosions, fretting over whether things would get bad enough to hit the U.S. news and, therefore, my mother's living room/kitchen/bedroom TV sets. Best to call her tomorrow and see if she brought it up first.

Ramon had warned me and the students to avoid the city center on the 29th, and since I'm a big chicken, I did. But I couldn't resist getting out in my own neighborhood, so I headed to a nearby mall of secondhand booksellers. I'd already spent plenty of Chilean pesos there over the last few months, so I figured that the sellers, accommodating with questions about local literature, would fill me in on the background to the disturbances.

I figured wrong. One after another said, "Oh, it's about some boys who were killed," and when I asked who killed them, one after another said, "Well, they were killed on the streets. Have I shown you this nice book yet?"

At last I entered a stall packed from floor to ceiling. Enrique, the owner, always gave me a wink with my purchases, so he might be more forthcoming. He fetched us both coffee from a tiny hot pot. "So," I began, after we'd talked books for a bit, "why do they call this *el día del joven combatiente?*"

"Because of two young men killed on March 29, 1985."

"Who killed them?"

"The police," he said evenly. "They weren't armed, but who knows what they were doing. Maybe nothing. You didn't have to do much during the military regime to get in trouble."

There I was, breaking my own rule—don't bring up the coup. I hadn't thought of an event twelve years after as connected, but of course it was. No wonder I'd been getting the cold shoulder from the other booksellers. Would I *ever* learn to stop putting my foot in it, one way or another?

Apparently not. Unable to resist, I continued: "*Carabineros* killed them?"

He nodded. *Carabineros* are Chile's police force, famous for their discipline. According to world corruption indexes, Chile has less corruption than any other Latin American country (and less than France and Japan). Bribing a policeman in Mexico or Ecuador is not only smart, it's often expected. Try bribing a *carabinero*, and you might land in jail. The *carabineros* joined the military in the coup, so while many people respect them, others see them as government enforcers.

"Read this," Enrique said, handing me a report by the *Agrupación de Familiares de Detenidos y Desaparecidos*—the Group of Families of the Detained and Disappeared.

When I pulled out my wallet, he frowned. "Just bring it back when you're done. And stay out of the city center today."

As I tucked it in a bag with some earlier purchases, his smile returned. And I got my wink. He was definitely attractive—but ten bucks said he was married, too. I'd better just read the book, bring it back, and stay clear of men in Santiago. With Diego still on my mind, surely that was the best course?

At our next session of the travel lit class I saw there was no chance we'd be able to talk about our upcoming exam until we'd swapped *día del joven combatiente* stories. Quiet Anne, a "most likely to go native" candidate, was looking suspiciously red of skin.

"Did you get soaked?" asked Taylor, the good-natured hippie chick, my other prime candidate. She was alluding to the tank-mounted police water cannons known to Chileans by the ironically affectionate nickname, *El Guanaco*. A guanaco is a shaggy Andean beastie that shares the talent of its cousins the llama and alpaca for spitting vengefully (and accurately).

Anne confessed that she'd ventured into the middle of the mess and couldn't escape a patrolling *Guanaco*. Apparently the *carabineros* put something in the water so that along with the punishing pressure, anybody hit comes away with burned skin.

"I hear they use acid," somebody offered.

Anne shook her head. "It's probably just pepper spray. The whole thing was crazy. It was *crazy*."

All the news reports had concurred—this was the worst "celebration" of the anniversary so far. Amazingly, nobody was killed, but real chaos had erupted. All public transport, including the metro, had to be shut down, and shops, cars, buses, and police vehicles citywide were attacked and burned. Nearly thirty *carabineros* had been injured, several seriously, and over nine hundred people arrested. Aside from my short trip to the book mall, I'd stayed put in my apartment, watching the coverage on TV. It felt surreal to know that the social breakdown unfolding on the screen was less than a mile away.

When things had settled back to normal a week later and my mother had been assured that order was restored, I went to visit the church of San Francisco, the oldest in Santiago, its original portions dating back to the 1580s. The adjacent Franciscan monastery houses a museum where you can see the Nobel Prize for Literature won in 1945 by the poet Gabriela Mistral, the first Latin American to receive this honor—Chile truly is a land of extraordinary poets, male and female.

The monastery gardens were my retreat from big city tension. I spent many happy hours there reading, relaxing, and visiting with the tiny resident rooster, Uriel. Every time I arrived, he courted me with a charming rooster dance, spinning and trailing one wing seductively along the ground. If I ignored him for too long, he would peck my feet possessively.

That day, after quality time with Uriel and some Chilean literature, I was surprised to find the doors locked as I tried to leave the monastery. "I can let you out now if you want," the guard said, "but something's going on. The *carabineros* are gathering again."

Curious, I decided to take my chances; he immediately locked the enormous wooden doors behind me.

There must be a height requirement for *carabineros*, judging by their looks. The only thing more intimidating than a towering *carabinero* is a row of towering *carabineros* mounted on horses—the sight that confronted me as I stepped out of the sixteenth century and back into the twenty-first. An armored vehicle pulled up in front of the church, and out spilled more *carabineros* in full riot gear, shields and all. Although the air was thick with tension, nobody was burning or breaking anything, so maybe the *carabineros* had been called out on a preemptive basis.

Heading for the metro, I hit the eye of the storm one block westward. A large group of young Chileans, many with scarves hiding their features, were converging on another armored vehicle, but this one had a mounted water cannon. The infamous *Guanaco*!

I thought back to my class, to Anne's angry red skin after her encounter, and decided it would be best to keep my distance. But then again…it wouldn't hurt to get one photo or maybe a bit of video footage. How fast could this thing move, anyway? And the water canon was pointed in the other direction, so I was safe.

I waded into the group of shouting, jostling students, some of whom were darting forward to throw things, more a gesture than a menace. Rocks and bits of brick were no match for plated steel. The people on the opposite side of *El Guanaco* were the ones in trouble, anyway, as the punishing spray disbursed them, squealing and dodging. Then, through the lens of my camera, I saw the swell of bodies that had been surging toward the tank abruptly change course. Realization dawned at that precise moment: although the tank couldn't turn on a dime, the water canon could. And did.

So much for my photo op. I was swept back in the opposite direction by the panicked crowd, unintentionally catching footage of my own pounding feet for half a block. I couldn't remember the last time I'd run so fast. I'd certainly never done so dreading I was about to get soaked with high-pressure, riot-strength pepper spray.

What was the scariest thing that ever happened to Jane Austen? I couldn't help but wonder. Stephanie Barron's fabulous mystery series assigns Austen numerous adventures, but if she had any in real life, she kept them to herself (or dutiful Cassandra burned the evidence). Certainly she'd never had to flee a *guanaco*, but she probably managed at some point to fall out of an apple tree or anger a neighbor's bull while crossing a field. Come to think of it, I got myself into hot water with British livestock when I climbed the fence into the field next to St. Nicholas Church at Steventon, hoping for a photo of the illusive well pump, supposedly the only surviving trace of the house where Austen was born. Angry cows appeared out of nowhere and chased me right back over the fence for my shameful incursion.

You'd think I would have learned my lesson about chancy photo ops.

CHAPTER ELEVEN

As the evening set for the Austen group drew closer, Ramon would periodically tell me, "My friends are all enjoying the novel!" When I asked if *he* were, he'd dodge. "I'm just about to start it…" The day before we'd arranged to meet at my apartment, he called me aside after one of my classes. "Amy, I'm so sorry. I can't make it to the group. But the others are still excited about it."

I was sorry, too. There went my chance to win the Twain lover over to Austen's camp! But *así es la vida.*

We planned the meeting at my place for 7:00 p.m., which I assumed meant that folks would begin to arrive around 7:30. To my surprise, the first eager Austen reader arrived early. Fernando was soft-spoken and pleasant and, like all the readers Ramon had invited, a poet by nature with a day job. He was tall, with light brown hair and an apple-cheeked aspect that made him look youthful, despite being about my own age.

Elvira arrived next. She was a fascinating woman, quiet and composed. We'd barely made introductions when our small talk turned to literature, and at my request, she recommended several Chilean authors: Antonio Gil, Marta Brunet, and Cristian Barros. If I had to match Elvira up with a U.S. writer, I'd say she was the Emily Dickenson of the group, solemn, intense, and passionate about literature.

Silvia, Marcia, and my friend Carmen Gloria arrived more or less at the same time. Silvia, tall and slender with enormous dark eyes, had an elegant air, without the hauteur. In another era I could see her gracing a Paris café, poet and muse all in one. Marcia, smiling and cheerful, reminded me quite a lot of Carmen Gloria. A Bolivian who had transplanted herself to Chile, she was smart and energetic and, somehow, the least "poet-y" of Ramon's friends, taking stereotypes into account. I wasn't surprised to learn that her creative writing branched out into prose as well.

The odd-person-out was Carmen Gloria. While a writer, her genre was history. She published frequently on the mining trade between Chile and Bolivia, exploring, among other themes, the exploitation of workers.

"I've got a lot of things to say about *Sentido y Sensibilidad*, although I'm a bit out of your literary environment," Carmen Gloria commented as we jumped into the discussion. "But what surprises me are the absences."

Registering our curious looks, she continued. "They talk about servants, for example, but they don't even name them. I tried to think about other works from this time period that address social class issues, like works on the French Revolution. But this novel just doesn't seem to *have* a historical context. I read it, thinking that if I didn't already *know* what period it was written in, I wouldn't have been able to figure it out." Oscar in Ecuador had also noted the timelessness of the text, but I don't believe Carmen Gloria, as a committed historian, meant it as a compliment.

"That's what makes it so timely now," Fernando offered. "That's what they say in the book itself in the opening materials."

"It's so lacking in context, *that* becomes the context." Carmen Gloria gestured for a moment as she struggled to articulate her thoughts. "It's another way to see history, because basically what she's showing is that there are coexisting worlds that *don't touch* each other."

Marcia joined in. "The bourgeois life they live *is* the context. They've got so much leisure, so much time on their hands to do the stupidest things. Their whole lives are centered around social activities—their own lives, and nothing else. That little nucleus of upper-class people was disconnected from the social events and the politics of the period."

"Unfortunately, there are people just like that today," Carmen Gloria added, to general consensus. I was curious to see how far she might pursue this connection with contemporary Chile, but talk quickly swung back to Austen's original context.

"There's a part in the novel," Marcia said, "when Elinor says that the men always enrich the conversation, specifically because they talk about politics. Just think about it—how cut off they were from life."

"It wasn't until I got to page 182 that I found a reference to somebody actually working," Carmen Gloria pursued. "I kept asking myself, what part of the year is this, anyway? Are they all on vacation? Surely by December or January somebody was going to have to get moving with *something*!"

With a smile I thought back to Juan in Puerto Vallarta, so put out by Austen's shiftless male characters.

"Well, things in general aren't represented in much detail," Silvia joined in. "There's very little concrete detail, even about things like what they eat. It's all very distancing, somehow."

As the others concurred, Carmen Gloria directed a glance at

me. "I realize this is your specialization and that this is the only Austen novel I've read, but I have to say that it doesn't seem like there's much detail on the characters either. I've read lots of Russian novelists that I adore, who really leave me stunned with the depth of their descriptions, but with Austen I feel like something's left hanging."

Silvia, eager to agree, overlapped with Carmen Gloria's thoughts: "I feel the same way. The sisters themselves can't even ask each other things directly. I haven't read any other Austen novels either, but maybe it's the English character, to distance themselves from profound emotions. Supposedly, to this day that's a notable difference between our cultures."

Isabel Allende's comments about how Chileans are "the English of Latin America" came to mind, but before I could form a sentence to share the idea, Carmen Gloria added, "There's also a difference in reading between Latin Americans and North Americans here, too. I don't feel like I identify with the characters, and I'd actually be ashamed to say, 'Hey, my brother is just like that character.' When we were talking about Austen before this meeting, it surprised me when you mentioned that in the United States it's common to do that."

"Look," Marcia interrupted, "I agree on the issue of distance in the novel. Also, I see a real poverty in this world, in spite of the reading they discuss, the painting and music—although actually, I'd love to have one tenth of the free time they've got to dedicate myself like crazy to those things! But how horrible to be subjected to such controlled relationships. I really find that Austen's got a very broad understanding of female psychology within this framework, the sort of tricks women play on themselves to keep up the illusion of being in love, or the attitudes about how to handle commitments. I found it really contemporary—it works for any context."

"Does that mean, then, that you identified with a particular character or recognized one as familiar?" Carmen Gloria asked.

"No," responded Marcia, "I recognize our gender, in general. Both men and women, actually."

That led to a line of discussion about Austen's style as a woman. I took a moment to explain her anonymous publication and the fact that some readers, owing to her clean style, assumed her to be a man.

"A cold style, even flat," Marcia said. "Especially with respect to emotions, very flat. It interested me, it really grabbed me. It's very precise, clean, and distant. Austen's distant from her own story."

"She uses very precise words." Silvia picked up the line of thought. "But it's as if she's not involved. She describes, she shows, but doesn't put herself in there."

"Personally, I think she really does," Fernando contradicted politely. "What she does—and this has to do with the English character, I think—is use a screen of humor between what she says and how she says it."

I was struck by how often these readers were commenting on the techniques Austen used to delineate the characters more than on the actual characters. But they were writers themselves, after all.

"It's irony, yes," he continued, as someone raised this point. "That makes the story colder, but it also makes it less obvious from what perspective the story is told, although I'd say Elinor emerges as the heroine. But one thing that really struck me was how cut short the end of the book feels, as if at some point she just got tired of writing," Fernando finished, to nods all around.

No doubt they could all identify with the desire to wrap up a work, but not at the expense of quality.

"Yes, because Marianne spent most of the book saying that Brandon was a *pichiruchi*—there you go, Amy, there's some good Chilean slang for you!" Carmen Gloria laughed over the word that, as far as I could make out, best translated in that context to something like "geezer." "And Elinor wasn't as perceptive about Edward in some ways as she should have been."

Elvira, silent up to this point, finally joined in. "Not about Edward, but with her sister and with herself, she was. Elinor is very perceptive—either Elinor or it's the narrator who's perceptive. The irony and the criticism of their social environment are very important."

"I looked for that sort of criticism," Carmen Gloria countered. "I really looked, but I didn't find it."

"I did," Silvia responded, "but it's subtle."

"There's actually a passage that's not even irony, because it's so direct," Fernando pointed out. "Lady Middleton feels discomfort around Elinor and Marianne because they read books that are satirical. She doesn't know what satire *is*, but it makes her feel offended and suspicious all the same. There are lots of criticisms in the book, but that one is the most direct, because it has to do with the very act of writing and of reading."

"There's also the situation of how dependent women are and the issue of the first born inheriting," Elvira said. "The first born is supposed to improve the family fortunes by marrying well, but when the money is taken from Edward, it's given to the brother who won't spend it wisely, since he's a reckless type and he married Lucy. That's satire."

Elvira paused for a moment but with the air of having more

to say. She hadn't spoken up much, so the others waited for her to continue—a striking contrast with the lively verbal dog-piles of the Ecuador group.

"Austen's narrative style is distant," she added, "but the characters communicate their world. The physical world of the novel isn't very concrete, but there's an internal world you enter. There's the Colonel, for example, and the nature of the love he feels for Marianne, one that seems somehow diluted and might even be closer to what we'd call friendship here. And there's all of the busywork that defines the women, embroidering, making comforters. The whole world of the novel is very rigid, very closed. The richness of it all for me is the analysis Austen provides of their feelings."

Elvira spoke slow, clear Spanish, but I still struggled a bit, mostly because I was trying to pull together the threads on Austen's depiction of feelings. If I understood correctly, the consensus seemed to move in the direction of Austen not showing her character's feelings directly but rather filtering them through an interesting narrative voice.

"I have to say that Elinor seems to me to be a lot older than she's described as being in the book," Carmen Gloria said suddenly.

"And just think," Silvia added, "the Colonel says he's old and he's only thirty-five or so." Thirty-five was at least a few birthdays back for all of us in the room that evening, and a wave of laughter and agreement met her comment.

"Death's approaching!" exclaimed Marcia.

"Oh, my back hurts!" Carmen Gloria cried, pretending to be an ailing old Brandon. Then she turned to me and said, "And what led you to choose Austen as a specialization? What drew you to her?"

"To be honest, in part it has to do with the entire cult of Austen we've got in the States. It's fascinating to see how many people are crazy about her."

"But I read a criticism by Mark Twain that was incredibly harsh!" Carmen Gloria countered. "Something like, 'if you've got a library with a book in it by Austen, then it's not worth much.'"

We could certainly have used Ramon right about then—chances are he'd have known the exact quote, which runs as follows: "Jane Austen's books, too, are absent from this library. Just that one omission alone would make a fairly good library out of a library that hadn't a book in it."

"There are writers who hate her and writers who love her," I said.

"Supposedly Rudyard Kipling loved her," Carmen Gloria returned, nodding.

"Virginia Woolf, as well. And so did Vladimir Nabokov, especially for her clean, pure style. But Charlotte Brontë, the author of *Jane Eyre*, didn't like her at all. She thought her world was cold and her characters, insignificant. She was very hard on Austen for the distance she maintained."

"Well, I see it as a criticism of that world," Marcia interjected, "and anyway, it's what makes it interesting. If she had been too involved, it would have been harder to criticize the trivialities."

"Comparing how tall the kids are," Fernando offered, hitting directly on one of Austen's best eye-rolling scenes from the book, one that makes clear how little the lesser characters have going on in their heads.

"And that opening dialogue, when the brother keeps lowering the amount he'll give his sisters," Marcia added, as Silvia joined in: "So ridiculous!" I wasn't surprised that this scene came to mind so readily for them, as well; Diego had loved it, although it had really made Salvador angry.

"That was impressive," Fernando agreed. "That woman really bargained him down."

"I think it was only half ironic," Marcia said. "The text is really current because that kind of thing still happens, but now, with the people who've got economic power, it's better hidden, better disguised."

"And marriages of convenience, for money," Silvia put in.

Carmen Gloria shifted slightly in her seat, smoothing her skirt. "I've always said that culture imposes so much on relations, especially for women. That imposition of 'maternal instinct,' all of the cultural impositions on women's behavior."

"And to think how a woman born so long ago wrote a novel exposing that," Marcia said. "There was so much pressure for women trying to find husbands with a certain amount of money to be a certain way. If you didn't draw or have this skill or that, you might not find anybody."

After pursuing this line of conversation for a while we lapsed into a comfortable group silence, during which people reached for their drinks or flipped through their copies of the novel.

Carmen Gloria drew us back together again, returning to a point Fernando had made earlier. "This book makes me think of the old custom of publishing novels in magazines, with chapters coming out one at a time, where you're moving toward a happy ending, but the action is drawn out to get you there and then *suddenly*," she leaned forward then threw her hands in the air, "here it is!"

"I didn't like the end either," Silvia said. "It wasn't consistent with the earlier level of the language, the descriptions of the characters, and most of all, their feelings. Everything was lost, and the actions weren't consistent with where the characters really were, psychologically. How did it all happen so fast with Marianne?"

"In two or three lines we've got a change that runs against what Austen was narrating for three hundred pages!" Carmen Gloria agreed.

"A lot of critics agree about the abrupt end of this novel," I offered. "It's the first one she published, and it's not as polished. There are lots of people in the U.S. and U.K. who write their own sequels, and when they don't like how things turned out, they change them. There's a sequel where Marianne decides she's made a mistake and runs off with Willoughby instead, and they—"

A crowing rooster cut me off. What the heck?! Fernando leaped up, with apologies and sheepish looks at the rest of us, to grab the book bag he'd set on my desk in the living room. Since I doubted he'd smuggled in tiny Uriel from the Franciscan monastery gardens, I had to assume he was hunting for his cell phone.

As we all laughed, Marcia picked up the sequel topic. "I had no idea people did that. If I don't like the end of a book, I might think about how I'd do it differently, but it seems really funny to me to write a whole new novel."

"That's bizarre," Silvia concurred.

"Well, there's Borges," Elvira pointed out. "He encouraged writers to take some of his characters and work with them, and he did the same with characters from other fiction."

Jorge Luis Borges, an Argentinean (so, more about him later), is arguably the most important writer in Latin America. Surely if Borges did it, it was legit?

"But to take a novel and write another ending to it," Silvia intervened with a dubious look, "that really surprises me."

"It's rewriting," Elvira said.

"Yes, but with Borges it had to do with admiration," Carmen Gloria countered.

"For me, I'd *think* about how I might end a novel differently," Marcia added. "But to write, publish, and put my name on a sequel, that would be kind of embarrassing."

"In a society of mass communication, it's not surprising this sort of thing happens," Fernando suggested.

As the line of conversation turned toward the "cult" aspect of Austen's fame, I opened my computer to show the group a photo that summed up the level of adoration certain folks feel for Austen.

"*Tell me* that's not a picture of you!" Carmen Gloria glanced at me with horror then turned her gaze back to the close-up of a tattoo on a woman's arm.

"I took this at a conference held in England. It's a quote from one of Austen's first novels, *Northanger Abbey*." It read, "Alas! If the heroine of one novel be not patronized by the heroine of another, from whom can she expect protection and regard?" The text wound around her upper arm in the shape of the symbol for woman. Someone who takes her Jane seriously—I loved it!

"Are there other authors people are this fanatical about?" Carmen Gloria asked, as the group all exchanged wondering looks. "Like Mark Twain?"

"There are fan groups for lots of different authors, but none as large or as widespread," I responded.

Before we moved too far away from the ending of *Sense and Sensibility*, I couldn't resist checking in about something. Most of the Mexico readers had opposed the match between Marianne and Brandon on grounds of the age difference—especially Josefa and Juan, thinking about their own daughter's marriage. Was a mismatch what these readers didn't like?

"Many of my students in the States feel disappointed with the end of the novel, like you are," I began. "Some even say that it seems like a punishment for Marianne to end up with a husband so much older than she is."

"I don't think it's bad in that sense—that seems pretty common for the period," Silvia replied quickly. "My problem is with how poorly the narration works in comparison with the rest of the novel."

"In fact, it's not even 'narrated,' really, it's just mentioned," agreed Fernando.

"I also got the impression," added Carmen Gloria, "that Austen created one character at the beginning, but didn't quite stick with that character for the ending."

Again, I couldn't help but notice how "writerly" their reactions were compared to those of the other groups. Nobody was focusing on how they felt about the characters—nobody was taking Fanny Dashwood's greed personally or worrying that Marianne won't really be happy with Brandon. Given their interest in Austen's technique over her subject matter, I decided to share a bit about her juvenilia, assuming they'd be interested in her development as a writer. We discussed the wild stories of Austen's youth as I refreshed people's drinks.

"Was Austen very religious?" Carmen Gloria asked during an opening in the conversation. "It surprises me that the theme doesn't come up, given the time period when she was writing. Since her father was a clergyman, it seems like she would have spent more time on that subject."

"She was religious in her private life," I answered. "We know she wrote some prayers. But while morality is important in her works—keeping your word, being loyal—morality's not tied with observing a specific faith. That makes it easy to adapt her novels. There's even a Bollywood version called *Bride and Prejudice*. It's set in modern India, but the plot's essentially the same."

"Has she been translated into many languages?" Carmen Gloria asked. "Because I think Austen's really not known in Chile. I've mentioned her to a few people here, and they have some idea who she is but only because of the film versions of her novels."

"People just know her by name," Fernando said.

"Very few people have read her," Silvia agreed. "Maybe it has to do with people not reading much from that time, but they *do* read Russian novels from that period."

"What about Emily Dickinson?" Fernando said, raising the subject of the group's preferred genre. "I don't think people here know about her poetry."

"I think they do," Marcia countered mildly.

"But where can you get translations of her poetry? I really don't think they exist."

"I believe she's been translated," Elvira offered.

"Do you mean it's hard to find translations of Dickenson in particular or poetry in general?" I asked.

"I think that poetry's translated less, in general," Silvia responded.

"I really don't like to read translations of poetry," Carmen Gloria said with a shake of her head. "I just feel like I'm not really connecting with the writer when I do."

"Well, I think it would be practically impossible to translate poetry from German or French," Carmen Gloria continued. I could see the others poised to pick up this line of conversation, so I cut in.

"We've got a reservation at a restaurant nearby," I said half apologetically, knowing how they'd love to talk poetry but not wanting to miss our table at the popular nightspot I'd selected. Our two hours had flown by in no time.

"Okay, but one more thing." Carmen Gloria gestured dramatically with one hand for attention. "I've got a recommendation, because I was just going crazy trying to contextualize Austen, and I found somebody on the Web. Read Mary Wollstonecraft," she said.

Wollstonecraft's major works came out in the 1790s, when Austen was drafting early versions of some of her novels. Wollstonecraft lived a life radically different from Austen's; she traveled widely, had multiple lovers, and bore a child out of wedlock. Near the end of her life she married and gave birth to Mary Shelley, author of *Frankenstein*. But the two writers shared many ideas about women, including that mutual respect is the best foundation for a good couple.

Carmen Gloria knew that a laid-back attitude toward timing still got my knickers in a twist, despite my best attempts at assimilation. Saying a bit more about Wollstonecraft, she winked at me and reached for her purse to move things along. But suddenly getting a naughty look on her face, she pulled out her cell phone and dialed.

"Hello, Ramon?" Carmen Gloria said, adopting that instantly recognizable answering machine voice when she didn't reach the study abroad director himself. "We're waiting for you. We haven't even started the discussion yet!" Wow, that was *very* naughty of her! "It's nine o'clock at night already! Should we start without you? Well, give me a call. *Chao!*" Even a Twain lover who'd slighted Austen didn't deserve to think he'd held up the entire reading group. But I had to assume they'd work it out, since Carmen Gloria and Ramon had known each other a lot longer than I'd known either of them.

Just as we seemed poised to leave, another exchange about how critical Austen actually was of her culture flared up again. Then Fernando raised yet another topic. Would other happy diners be enjoying our table by this point? Well, so be it. I had to chill out and let the night happen.

"It's just fabulous when Willoughby and Colonel Brandon have that duel," Fernando said, laughing, "and they *both* manage to walk away satisfied. It's like magic. They've done the right thing, there's nothing more to be said!"

Elvira agreed: "The role of manners and customs is something I liked about the book. Compare it to things today. Our relations are often so fraught, so harsh, especially from the point of view of language."

Silvia nodded vigorously. "Such a fault of courtesy—that's the word. I also liked that about the book. It's something worth recovering, something worth teaching."

I was surprised to see this somewhat more sentimental side of the readers, who'd been so focused on the critical and technical aspects of Austen's novel. North, Central, and South America weren't so far apart after all. The teachers in Guatemala were definitely taken with Austen's emphasis on courtesy, and it's a common subject of conversation with my California students. They often find themselves pleasantly surprised by a world where people treat each other with a certain courtliness (the irony being that they're precisely the generation so often accused of completely lacking manners themselves—but what's a discussion of Austen without a little irony?).

On that note, copies of the book were stowed, and purses and jackets gathered for the walk to the restaurant. I waved at the doormen on the way out, who looked curious at the size of the group I was hosting; I'd been a very private tenant. Don Alberto, fortunately, was off duty. Most of the readers began lighting cigarettes, and Carmen Gloria and Marcia discussed the small-world discovery that Marcia's mother had been one of Carmen Gloria's favorite high school teachers. Suddenly, Fernando caught me by the arm and allowed the others to move on ahead of us.

"There's something I have to tell you," he said, looking vaguely embarrassed. What on earth was he about to confess? Sending one more glance in the direction of the smoking, chatting cluster ahead of us, he fixed me with an urgent gaze. "It's about Elinor. When I was reading the book I…I fell in love with her. I really did. I fell in love with Elinor!"

Too surprised to answer, I stared at him for a moment then smiled. Here was a Chilean who liked more than Austen's narrative technique!

He smiled back, sighed with relief that his secret was out, and changed the subject.

"404" wasn't a highway. It was an edgy, fusion-style restaurant featuring live music. Clean lines, metal, and glass dominated the décor; the contrast with the Guatemalan restaurant where I'd dined with the ladies, cheerfully cluttered with wooden furniture, photos of happy diners, and enormous plants, couldn't have been greater. Despite my fussy fears, the hostess was happy to find us a table well past our reservation time. The smokers in our group, respectful of the nonsmokers, agreed to seating on the first floor. This made conversation a good bit easier since the musicians, also fusion oriented in a bluesy rock sort of way, were on the upper level surrounded by an immense cloud of smoke.

After settling in at our table, we quickly found ourselves back on the topic of Austen, as Silvia suggested that the translator appeared to be Chilean.

"There really are a lot of Chilean phrases in the book," Marcia agreed.

"The language seems really contemporary, too," Elvira added.

"Speaking of contemporary—" This was a great opening to ask my standard question about whether Austen could be transposed neatly into their contemporary culture.

The group pondered for a moment, then Fernando responded first. "As far as I'm concerned, yes, I think Austen could be transposed here to Chile."

Feeling a little wicked, I pursued, "So, you'd say there are Chilean women like Elinor?"

He studied his hands resting on the table for a moment, looking a little nervous that I'd expose his Elinor secret. Then he smiled. "I think so. Certainly among the big landowners of the countryside, I'd say so."

"I think so too," Silvia said. "The politics, the social classes, all of those marriages of convenience, those things seem universal."

"But one important difference here," Fernando said, "is that, instead of titles being so important, family names are what establish a person's social status."

"Very good point," Elvira said, while Marcia added, "I think that's true of Latin American countries in general."

"Names here," Fernando continued, "actually function like a barrier against race mixing. Clarifying that I'm from, let's say, the Undurraga family of Concepción, and not the Undurraga family of some other place, since we're the ones who are—"

"White," Silvia finished his thought. "As in, we haven't got any indigenous blood."

"This really is a 'whitened' country," Marcia explained. "The nature of the conquest was different, and more indigenous people survived in places like Bolivia and Peru. But here they deliberately tried to 'whiten' things up, to the point that you hardly see indigenous features in the streets like you do in Brazil and other countries."

"Not pure indigenous," Fernando clarified. "But the fact is that all of us here are mixed race."

If there were a good Spanish equivalent I'd use it, but since there isn't, I'll go for the French: *déjà vu*. Somehow I hadn't expected this theme to surface in the Chile group, but while it took longer than it had in Guatemala, here was the race question once again.

"There's even a kind of pride people have in not being indigenous," Fernando added with a sad shake of his head.

As good Chilean wine arrived and then, eventually, our food, we talked about the difficulties of getting poetry published in Chile (conclusion: very difficult). As the talk moved further away from Austen, I also couldn't resist verifying if we, as a group, were an enormous statistical anomaly—six childless people over forty. I already knew Carmen Gloria didn't have children, but since the subject had never come up, I'd assumed the others didn't either.

Lo and behold, both Marcia and Silvia were mothers, proud to say so when asked. I was struck by the difference with the Mexican readers of *Sense and Sensibility*—children were front and center in the discussions with both groups, especially with

Salvador and Soledad. Then again, readers in Mexico had been much more focused on drawing connections between their own lives and the novel. That merited some thought when I had less wine in my system.

At the hour when the staff in any self-respecting American restaurant would be upending chairs onto vacated tables and sending pointed glances at lingering diners, we talked on, and 404's hostess was busier than ever ferrying in new arrivals. Oscar, the Chilean from the Ecuador *Pride and Prejudice* group, had hosted a dinner for the book club shortly before I left Guayaquil. He'd invited us to his place for 9:00 p.m. While he had plenty of appetizers, the first course didn't hit the table until 11:58 p.m. Still weak from dengue, I was nearly fainting with fatigue by the time the mousse topped off the six-course menu at 1:00 a.m. Clearly, Chileans loved their late dinners, even on a weekday.

Dengue-free, I could completely enjoy this dinner and wonderful *sobremesa*, that warm, fitting *latino* tribute to lingering over good food and good company.

"Well, *amiga*," Carmen Gloria said, sipping her wine then gesturing toward my tiny little recorder on the table, silently taking in our conversation amid the glasses, dishes, and rumpled napkins. "With this group, I think you've got enough material for five books. We've covered *everything*!"

Although Austen faltered somewhat at the end of *Sense and Sensibility*, as the readers had pointed out, the beautiful pacing of the rest of her novels shows that she was an admirer of good timing. Slowly but surely, I myself was spending more time responding to local rhythms and less trying to impose my own. To smiles and laughter all around, I dramatically hit the off button and picked up my wine glass.

Chapter Twelve

For pretty much any day of the year, my mother can name at least two birthdays. She has the entire extended family down—aunts, cousins, nephews, great-grandkids, and all. This is no mean feat, since my German grandmother was the youngest of fourteen. One of my aunts hoped to top that number until my uncle, happy with eight, snuck out and got a vasectomy (my poor aunt cried for a month). I have twenty-eight first cousins, and once they got to reproducing, we quickly hit triple digits. My mother knows *all* their birthdays, along with those of her four children's friends, coworkers, and coworkers' children (plus most of my ex-boyfriends' birthdays, although at my request she finally stopped mentioning those).

Knowing her affinity for dates, when the anniversary of my father's death comes around in April, we all call—my oldest brother David from Pittsburgh; Laurie from Gettysburg; and Shawn and I from wherever on the planet we happen to be. You'd think Chile would win me the long-distance prize, but that year Shawn beat me again: he called from Bangkok, Thailand. He's dubbed the anniversary Welshman Day, in honor of our father's ancestry.

My mother and I were able to enjoy longer, more comfortable calls from Santiago since I had a home phone and didn't need to hunt down a booth on a dog-filled street or in a noisy Internet café.

"Now that your group is done," she asked when I reported in for Welshman Day, "what else are you working on?"

"I'm reading a lot of Chilean literature. I'm also giving a talk on Austen at one of the other universities here. In Spanish. I'm pretty nervous about it."

She and my father had supported me through every band concert, every role in every play, every recital in college during my music years, and through doctoral exams when I switched to English. "You'll do just fine," she said confidently.

"I'm keeping an eye on my students, too. One of them has started to miss a lot of class, and I'm concerned about her."

While Mom commiserated over my student, the word "concern" set off her maternal alarm bells.

"You haven't had any new problems with your health, have you? Nothing since you've been in Chile?"

I could only hope the Gods of Travel would forgive me a lie of omission. While my dengue was finally gone, I hadn't told my mother about the ringworm incident. The secretary for the study abroad program was also a registered nurse, and when I'd reported for duty in January she'd greeted me, handed over orientation materials, and pointed at the large, puffy purple circle on my right calf visible below the line of my Capri pants.

"You know that's ringworm, right?" she asked dryly.

Hell's *bells*. I'd noticed the circle growing on my leg midway through my time in Ecuador, but I'd decided that if I ignored it, it would certainly go away. *Ringworm?* I bolted off to a clinic, freaked that I'd brought a stowaway to Chile. Once I named it Pepe, however, I started to feel better about the whole situation.

By the time the doctor told me ringworm was a fungus and not an actual worm, I felt kind of cheated.

I vacillated over my mother's question, since she'd been so direct. But technically Pepe wasn't a Chilean problem, because I'd smuggled him from Ecuador.

I settled for a downplay. "Nothing major. Just a skin thing on my leg way back in January, and that was easy to get rid of. Oh, you know what! My friend Cheryl will be coming down in the beginning of May!" No, I was also not above the change-the-subject dodge. "We're renting a car and touring around once classes finish up."

"I'm so glad that you're getting this opportunity," she said. Her voice took on a wistful tone. There were two closets in her bedroom, and I was willing to bet that right then, she was looking at the one that still held some of my father's clothes. And his reading glasses.

"I know. Dad would have loved to have heard about it," I answered. Ringworm and all, in fact.

The *Mansfield Park* talk was my academic debut in Spanish, so naturally I got the worst cold I'd had in years two days before. If only Diego were there to help nurse me and laugh my nervousness back into perspective!

I'd scripted the talk, fearing I'd freeze up in front of the audience, so with enough tissues the delivery itself was manageable. I spoke on how Patricia Rozema's very liberal film adaptation explores issues of race and class. I'm partial to the film for the excellent directing and the way it challenges just how the rich get rich. But it's also a catalogue of every sexual subject Austen delicately ignores, from girl-on-girl to incest to rape. There's even a scene that prompted one of my students back in the States to blurt out, during a class viewing, "Lady, get your hands off that PUG!" When I spoke on it years earlier at a conference in England— the same one where I spotted the fabulous *Northanger* tattoo—I spent twenty minutes afterward calming an important Australian scholar who was literally shaking with rage over Rozema's liberties with Miss Austen's most morally profound novel.

A bit of sneezing aside, I made it through the talk just fine. But the Q&A with smart, competitive graduate students and professors was another matter. I have enough trouble deciphering what certain academic types are saying in English, let alone a second language, and some of the questions that night left me slack-jawed.

Thank god for Carmen Gloria. She'd arranged the invitation for the talk in the first place and was a huge help, fielding questions for me and helping translate. But there must have been a few folks who went home shaking their heads over the stuttering, sniffly *estado unidense*. Well, I did my best. I just had to pray I hadn't soured anybody on Austen!

Maybe I wasn't up to academic jargon in Spanish, but I was certainly doing better than when I'd arrived and had my first conversations with the doormen. Ever since the laundry room liplock I'd been slipping past the post quickly when Don Alberto was around, but now there seemed to be several new faces. The handsome Emilio, who'd become so agitated over the subject of the coup, hadn't been there for more than a month. Curious, I finally asked Demetrio the Spaniard if he knew why.

His expression turned deeply sad. "His mother committed

suicide last month. Apparently, not long after the coup she went to get milk one evening and didn't come back." I'd read enough Chilean history about "detentions" to know where this story was heading. "Some neighbors found her months later, lying in an alley. She'd been tortured and also—well, she wasn't the same. I guess she couldn't take it anymore, even after all these years. Emilio's helping out with his family right now."

Good god. I thought back to how I'd stood there early in my visit, chirping on about how pretty it was to walk along the river. No wonder Emilio couldn't look at it without thinking about the bodies dumped there, about people hunting for their loved ones. I was glad that I could see the beauty of Santiago—I couldn't be sorry for that. But this was one of those reminders that I was only skimming the surface there. Even months of familiarity couldn't make me or my students, for that matter, capable of seeing the city the way Chileans do.

Still, that's no reason not to *try* to see the world through another perspective—and this is exactly what good students do when they study abroad. Over the course of the semester my students went through a powerful range of experiences in Santiago, which they bonded over—relationships with Chileans, spiritual awakenings, increased political awareness.

As predicted, one did go native. It wasn't Anne, the smart, reserved young woman who already seemed half Chilean; it wasn't sharp, slender Brooke, the fellow Pennsylvanian; it wasn't even Sarah with the Colombian boyfriend. It was adventurous hippie chick Taylor. She'd fallen in love with Valparaiso, about an hour and a half away on the coast, Chile's funkiest student town and the San Francisco of South America. So much in love that she didn't make it back to Santiago too often for class. I'd noticed her increasingly long absences, and her fellow students were also concerned.

Immersion in a new culture can inspire huge changes, but so can reading. Any bookworm knows how a truly powerful book can motivate us toward major change. Give a woman an Austen novel and, if she takes it to heart, *seriously* takes it to heart, how will she behave? She'll soul search about what she wants in a partner; she'll evaluate how well she behaves toward her family; she'll consider her role within her community and how well she treats people, no matter what their status in life; she'll acknowledge the value of being true to herself, while being respectful of others; she'll go out dancing once in a while; maybe she'll even learn to sew.

But as a teacher, as a mentor, I hadn't given Taylor *Sense and Sensibility*. I'd handed over Che Guevara's *The Motorcycle Diaries*, the record of his youthful adventures exploring South America, a trip that spurred his political awakening. When Taylor finally resurfaced and I sat her down for a talk, she was apologetic for the missed classes but brimming over with enthusiasm for her summer plans: hitchhiking from Valparaiso, Chile, to Denver, Colorado.

All of the students in the travel literature class had read Guevara, but Taylor was the one who took his narrative to heart, *seriously* took it to heart. She wanted to explore more of Latin America, like Guevara. She wanted to put her faith in the kindness of strangers, like Guevara. She wanted to see if she had the fortitude to survive a lengthy, uncertain, wandering existence, like Guevara.

I was extremely impressed. And alarmed. Reading that particular book was only one part of what was driving Taylor to want a richer, more personal travel experience than what a well-run study abroad program could provide. Her time in Chile was central, as well as her own inquisitive, passionate nature. But clearly, the book was a catalyst. How could I explain the difference between Guevara's world and ours? Guevara was a man in a *machista* culture, traveling with a trusted friend, using his native language. Taylor was an attractive young woman wanting to travel alone, using earnest but weak Spanish, and heading slowly home toward the country that—in some measure thanks to Che Guevara himself, after the Cuban Revolution—many *latinos* and *latinas* view as Public Enemy Number One.

"I really think I can do it," Taylor said, her eyes bright with imagined adventure. Reading the skepticism on my face, she nodded vigorously. "I can do it!"

I consulted with well-traveled Sarah on the subject shortly before classes ended. "It scares the hell out of me just thinking about it," she said, shaking her head. "I've been around Colombia with my boyfriend, and I'm no coward, but hitchhiking through that country would be *suicide*."

"Please tell Taylor that, okay?" I urged. It's not my job to discourage intrepid students from learning experiences, but I was feeling responsible for having introduced her, so to speak, to Guevara.

As classes wound up, Ramon hosted a farewell pizza party for the students at a Santiago restaurant, where we colonized the entire outdoor seating section. This was exactly the sort of gathering of noisy Americans (plus one Canadian) that I avoid like the plague while traveling. But we had a lot to celebrate—a wonderful semester, new friendships, and for the students, an imminent return home to their loved ones. I ditched my squeamishness about offending the locals for one night and joined the party, happy for the opportunity for personal good-byes. Matt the friendly Alaskan took a lot of ribbing as the student Most Frequently Robbed in Chile (grand total: three times). The poor guy really seemed to have had a sheet of paper saying "Mug me!" taped to his back, despite being tall and sturdy.

I made a point, as the revelry began to wind down, of taking Taylor aside again.

"I've got addresses of people in Ecuador you could probably stay with," I told her. "If you email me, I'll give them to you." I'd recommended an abbreviated tour up the Pacific coast through Peru then back down to Santiago, to pick up the return airfare she had already paid for. Whether she would take that suggestion, *¿quién sabe?* But I wanted to make sure she would take the initiative and pursue the contacts. The ball was in her court. Reading the right book at the right time can be a life-changing experience—so I had to hope for the best for her.

Saying good-bye to students is something you get used to as a teacher, comforted by the knowledge that the ones you've really influenced have a tendency to pop back up again, one way or another. Saying good-bye to Carmen Gloria was harder. She'd been a rock for me in Santiago, a warm, loving, hilarious, smartly dressed rock. She'd shown me around Santiago, she opened her home to me, and she'd even opened her parents' beach house to me, as well. One of my nicest trips had been a long weekend of sight-seeing and gossiping at their home just south of *Isla Negra*, the site of Pablo Neruda's fanciful shoreside home.

"You can't leave Chile without seeing *Isla Negra*," Carmen Gloria had insisted.

We stopped in a seafood restaurant the first evening there. Our middle-aged waiter, discovering I was from the United States, became extra attentive. When Carmen Gloria went off to find a restroom, he hovered near the table speaking Spanish so rapid I only caught every third or fourth word. Was he enthusing over the local sights or some dessert I should try? Stumped, I nodded and smiled. Smiling in return, he pulled a slip of paper from his pad, wrote something, and held it out to me.

"*Puchas!*" Carmen Gloria, back from the bathroom, intercepted the paper and shooed the man away. She read it, rolled her eyes, and wagged it at me accusingly like a traffic ticket—the waiter had written down his name and phone number. "What did I *tell* you about Chilean men, Amy?!" She shook her head in amazement, then we both burst out laughing. I sure am a slow learner.

I was also surprised that *Isla Negra* is not, in fact, an island, but that was the only disappointment. While Neruda's home in Santiago was sacked by the military when he died twelve days after the 1973 coup, *Isla Negra* was left alone, so his quirky collections of bottles, seashells, pipes, and nautical figureheads remained intact.

Apparently timid about actual sailing, Neruda nonetheless loved the ocean, and his grave, overlooking the pounding Pacific, is subtly designed to look like a ship heading out to sea. It's a beautiful, dramatic spot, and I couldn't help but feel the contrast with Austen's simple grave—a worn paving stone on the floor of Winchester Cathedral. When I'd made my pilgrimage there, I'd crouched at one side to read the inscription, wincing to see less attentive visitors treading directly across it. The solemnity of the occasion had been further impaired by the fact that I couldn't get that cheesy 1960s song "Winchester Cathedral" out of my head.

After touring Neruda's house and hiking the grounds of *Isla Negra*, Carmen Gloria and I lingered in the outdoor café over our favorite cocktail, the famous Chilean *pisco sour*.

"You've got to come to the States and visit me," I urged her. "You can't really teach American culture until you dive into the middle of it, you know."

"I know, I know!" she laughed and raised her glass. "So here's to our next visit—in the USA!"

Cheryl, one of the close friends who attended my "Happy Fortieth" in Las Vegas, flew down for a visit shortly before I left. She was the first American friend I'd laid eyes on in nearly a year. It felt ridiculously good to see her and catch up on stateside news. As kind and patient as my new Chilean friends were, my uneven Spanish made every conversation challenging. Cheryl was a little bit of home. There's nothing like relaxing into your own language with an old friend who knows you well and has seen you at your worst—and is *still* willing to travel thousands of miles to hang out.

"So what exactly is up with this man in Mexico?" she asked shortly after arriving.

"Boy do I wish I could answer that question." I wasn't holding back; we'd been in the dating trenches together. I honestly didn't know what I should do about Diego, as close as we'd grown during our months together.

Cheryl, a second-degree black belt in Tae Kwon Do with energy to burn, hauled my nerdy butt out for tourist activities I'd been meaning to get around to for months. We started with the San Cristobal funicular, scaling the summit to join the daring crowds taking the cable gondolas from one peak to another for the best views of Santiago.

After several days exploring the city we rented a car and headed west, then south. We braved the steep streets of Valparaiso, laughed over questionable accommodations in tiny towns, dodged Chileans herding animals on narrow rural roads, hunted down the famous murals in Chillán by Mexican painter David Alfaro Siqueiros, soaked in the idyllic hot springs of Pucón. I was thrilled to share a portion of my travels with such a good friend, and very sorry to see her go.

But my own departure loomed. There's a mathematics to nesting, I'm sure, that explains how length of stay + space available = accumulating way too much stuff. Shortly before leaving I shipped six boxes of books to the States, along with various touristy tidbits. Cheryl had arrived with one suitcase and left with two, generously lugging back for me still more books, plus movies, Chilean board games, and summer clothing I'd no longer need.

I gave Diego the heads up that I was poised to move yet again. "Please, *princesa*, please be careful!" he wrote back. What little he'd heard about Paraguay had to do with their crime rate and government instability. How long it had been since we'd seen each other! Half a year had passed since I'd left sunny Puerto Vallarta and his cheerful company. It hardly seemed possible.

Since Diego knew I'd read *Sense and Sensibility* with the Chilean group, as we'd done together in Mexico, he was curious about the outcome. I was happy with both groups, but the differences were dramatic. The Chilean readers had taken a much less personal approach to the novel. Not surprisingly for a group of writers, they'd focused on Austen's narrative voice, her use of irony, her social critique, and her capacity to wrap up a plot. I couldn't help but think that the Mexican readers' more personal reaction had been influenced by their tendency to connect literature with the Bible—to look for personal applications via parables and positive role models. Then again, there had been that wonderful private moment with Fernando, when he confessed that Elinor had lured him across the life/literature divide. Still waters, as I'd so often found in Chile, run deep.

I'd been thrilled with all four of the *Pride and Prejudice* and *Sense and Sensibility* groups, but now I was eager to branch into new territory at last in Paraguay—with *Emma*.

On my final day in Santiago I took a turn around the enormous central square, still present but already nostalgic. As I headed down a nearby pedestrian street, a bustling group of young Chileans hauling a video camera and sound equipment approached.

"Excuse me!" one of them asked, "Would you mind being interviewed for a student project?"

Normally I'd run like hell from strangers with a camera, but I had free time—and they were students, after all. It was my "employment," as Edward Ferrars would say, to help students. "I'm an *estado unidense*, and my Spanish isn't the world's best," I warned them. "Will that still work for you?"

Looking surprised, they went into a quick huddle, which resulted in a unanimous "Why not?"

"We're doing a project about ethics and values," the student with the camera explained, slowing his speech down noticeably. A microphone appeared in front of my face. "Do you think Chileans these days have good ethics and values? And if so, which ones?"

Puchas! What an enormous question. My months in Chile ran on fast-forward through my mind.

"Patience and kindness," I found myself saying. "Chileans have been very patient with me—with the way I use the language, with all the cultural differences I had to negotiate. I've lived here for five months, and I've definitely benefited from people's patience and kindness." There was Ramon at the university, the doormen at my building (unsolicited frenching aside), Carmen Gloria and her endless generosity, the poets who'd shared their time and their insights—and even this young stranger himself, who had slowed down his rapid-fire Chilean Spanish to help me out.

I was tempted to dive into an explanation of Jane Austen, my reason for being in Chile in the first place, and the role that "good ethics and values" play in her novels.

"Will that do?" I asked instead, deciding not to be a camera hog.

"Super!"

No way of knowing, in the end, if my little speech would make it into their film or wind up on the cutting room floor. But I do know that they all set off after their next subject looking content. Energized by some positive feedback, they had carried on with their project; a new country and a new Austen novel on the horizon, I was ready to carry on with mine.

PARAGUAY:

Assumptions and Asunción

In which the author makes a few more bad assumptions, gives a talk on Austen for some inquisitive Paraguayan middle-schoolers, rides a rocking horse, buys still more books, follows the footsteps of some Nazis, and finally, enjoys a film adaptation of Emma *with the lively friends and family of her hosts and then gets an* Emma *reading group surprise.*

CHAPTER THIRTEEN

People who haven't read Austen often assume that her novels are all the same. There's some dancing, some dialogue, some mix-ups, then a happy ending. My students in California once organized a debate over this very question, *à la* Cher in *Clueless*: "Are, like, all of Jane Austen's novels totally *the same*, or what?" Arguments raged back and forth for close to an hour until Rickie the baseball player silenced the room with the cry "TOP RAMEN!"

Rickie liked my teaching style and signed up for something with me every semester. That fall, the only course that fit his schedule was Jane Austen. He'd sighed and registered, braving the taunts of his teammates the entire semester for reading "chick lit" (getting drafted by the Cleveland Indians shortly thereafter no doubt dulled the pain).

He'd listened to the opposition's points, frowning with concentration until that moment when he literally threw his hands in the air like a preacher who's seen the light and shouted the name of the cheap packaged noodles so many students survive on. "That's *it*! She's Top Ramen!" Dumbstruck, we all waited for him to work through the thought because clearly, from the startled expressions of his debate partners, this was not part of their plan. "There's chicken, and there's shrimp," Rickie said, scanning our faces urgently, leaning forward and clutching his desk. "There's vegetarian. And there's beef. But they're *all* Top Ramen! Chicken and shrimp and beef *aren't* the same, but they're *all* Top Ramen!"

Indeed. A nice analogy for how Austen's works fit within a genre—they're all comic romances—yet each remains distinctive. People who assume "read one, you've read them all" are missing out on the wonderful differences between chicken and shrimp and beef.

Austen readers should be particularly sensitive to avoiding assumptions, since that's one of Austen's most important lessons. I'd known this when I set out from the United States yet had to relearn the lesson in various colorful ways throughout my travels. And now I'd reached country number five-out-of-six, still making an "ass" out of "u" and "me"—but mostly out of me.

I'd assumed that a plane ticket and a passport were enough to get me out of Chile and into Paraguay. Wrong. I made it through Chilean customs and was about to board the flight when the man taking boarding passes noticed that I had no visa in my passport. "You can't buy it at the Asunción airport," he said, shooting down my next assumption and hustling me out of the line. "Go to the embassy here in Santiago."

The folks in the hotel where I'd spent my (intended) final night in Chile had assumed they'd already seen the last of me, but they were wrong, too. The Paraguayan embassy didn't open again until the next day so, too embarrassed to let Carmen Gloria or anybody else know I'd failed to make my exit, I holed up in my room reading until I could get my visa and secure another flight.

"Don't worry about it!" Martín assured me the next night as I apologized yet again to my hosts for my day-late arrival, finally seated in their comfortable living room in the correct country. Dorrie smiled and added, "You see how close we are to the airport! The joke around here is that you just have to listen for the plane to land then get in the car."

Coquetta, the family boxer, was ecstatic at the appearance of another person to spoil her. She had the barest stump of a tail, and wagging it in greeting set her entire back end into rapid, comic motion. Then she flopped onto her back, confident that no one could see her belly without wanting to rub it.

Dorrie and Martín are alumni of the university where I teach—Martín is a Paraguayan and Dorrie, a central California girl. They met while he was studying abroad in the eighties, fell in love, and now, three children and twenty-six years of marriage later, there they were in Asunción, welcoming me into their home for the month. Dark-haired, dark-eyed, and boyishly handsome, Martín had energy to burn; he somehow managed to convey a constant sense of motion, even when sitting still. Dorrie, blond, blue-eyed, and beautiful in a classic, unostentatious way, was soothingly calm, practical, and centered—the perfect complement for Martín.

Located on the outer edges of Paraguay's capital, their house was large and tastefully decorated yet welcoming, with a lived-in feel. A high stone wall surrounded the grounds outside, and when I wandered out before dinner, I was surprised to catch sight of two immense turtles on the lawn. How on earth had they gotten in? I bolted inside for my camera, wanting a photo before they escaped, then returned to find the turtles had each moved an entire centimeter. Pets, I discovered, not Paraguayan wildlife.

I emailed later that day to assure Diego I had finally made it in one piece, and I called my mother.

"I was looking at your dad's globe, and I see that Paraguay doesn't have a coast," she said, as I gave her a briefing on that month's new country. "Does that mean there are fewer mosquitoes?"

I wanted to say yes, but I was finally getting the idea, especially after talking with my sister Laurie, that fudging reality for my mom when she asked a straight question was disrespectful, even if I did it out of good intentions. She was no Mr. Woodhouse; she wouldn't use information to twist my arm with guilt.

"No, I'm afraid it doesn't. But I'm soaking myself with bug spray all the time, so don't worry. I'll be careful!" That was no lie—I'd done a little checking on the Internet and discovered that if you catch a different strain of dengue after you've already had one, the infection is distinctly worse. Or fatal. I'd noticed signs in the airport about protecting against dengue, and Martín and Dorrie, knowing I'd already suffered a case, warned me to be very careful. Several people in rural zones outside of Asunción had died of dengue earlier that month.

No need to tell me twice. I'd learned my lesson the hard way. My dad always claimed that he got bit more often by mosquitoes because of his tasty Welsh blood. Even if I drove off locals with my personal chemical cloud, I wasn't leaving an inch of temptation exposed.

The morning after my arrival I got a troubling email from Lili, the staff member at the Paraguayan cultural foundation that was sponsoring me for talks on Austen at two local libraries. Martín had asked her to take charge of finding readers for the *Emma*

group. "Check with Martín," her latest note said. "I've got the copies of *Emma* in English, but he's getting your readers."

Uh-oh. We needed the novel in Spanish—but then again, maybe he'd invited readers who could handle it in English. I scanned back through my mails and found the one, cc'd to both Lili and me more than a month earlier, where Martín explained that he wanted *her* to invite the members. Then I found the one where I'd asked for copies of the book in Spanish.

Nervous but not wanting to stampede, I waited until after dinner to raise the subject. Dorrie headed off to her office on the ground floor to work. The local representative for an international nonprofit organization, she had the advantage of working at home but the drawback of very long hours. As Martín and I cleared the table and loaded the dishwasher, I found an opening to ask about the readers, desperately hoping he and Lili had discussed some change of plans that hadn't made it into the email exchange.

"Lili's taking care of getting the readers," he reassured me, bustling around the kitchen's central island with his usual animation.

"She emailed this morning and told me you were doing it. I think this means there's no group arranged," I said, crestfallen.

Martín stopped in his tracks at my distressed expression. "We can fix this," he assured me, giving my shoulder a pat then pulling out his cell phone.

Despite my controlling nature and tendency to panic, I was immediately relieved. Martín was a problem solver. Like Dorrie, he worked for a nonprofit organization, but as the director. Prior to that, he was the mayor of Asunción. A progressive reformer in a country that had lived under an ultraconservative dictatorship for more than thirty years, Martín had run the capital while dodging assassination attempts and keeping his children from being kidnapped (a not uncommon strong-arm tactic in Paraguay). When the vice president was assassinated during Martín's term in office, all hell broke loose. Numerous students were killed in the ensuing demonstrations, and opposition forces attempted to take over the congress building.

Lacking military vehicles to defend it, Martín called in all of the city's garbage trucks and construction vehicles to surround the congress and shelter the demonstrators, preventing further casualties. The man who could think on his feet with such creativity in the midst of a genuine life-or-death crisis could surely solve my little Jane Austen problem.

Cell phone cradled between his ear and shoulder, speaking rapid-fire Spanish, Martín reached into the refrigerator, offered me a bottle of beer, then opened one for himself. It was a thing of beauty to watch him in action, pacing the kitchen, talking and laughing into the phone while smiling at me reassuringly.

"Okay, here's the deal," he began, three calls later. "I found a group of women who are going to be talking about *Pride and Prejudice* together two weeks from now, and you're welcome to join them. Will that work?"

I didn't want to look a gift-group in the mouth, but it really was time to move on to *Emma*. "I'd love to join them—I really appreciate it! But since I've read that novel with groups in Guatemala and Ecuador already, I was also hoping to discuss *Emma*…"

He nodded thoughtfully, took a pull on his beer, then asked, "What about a film viewing? There's time for that. Did you bring the movie with you?"

Fortunately, I'd brought along the Gwyneth Paltrow and Jeremy Northam version. "Great!" Martín responded. The dialing and pacing recommenced. Five calls later, he was smiling more broadly than ever. "Done!" he cried. "Right before you meet with the *Pride and Prejudice* group, we'll watch *Emma* together here!"

No liberties or lives had been saved, but I was certainly grateful—crisis averted. Still, I was disappointed that reading *Emma* would have to wait until Argentina. Unless maybe I could think of another plan myself? I was *so* ready to move on to *Emma*. Something would come to me. I'd have to sleep on it.

In Austen's day libraries weren't public; they were private businesses, like movie rental stores. You paid a membership fee and a charge per book. This is one of the reasons novels of the period were often published in multivolume format—booksellers and libraries charged per volume. *Sense and Sensibility*, for instance, came out in three separate volumes, as did *Pride and Prejudice* (so the next time you read one of the ubiquitous time-travel Austen adaptations and somebody picks up a single-volume first edition, you can hit your nerd buzzer and say "*wrong!*"). The unwashed masses of England didn't get free, regular access to books until later in the nineteenth century.

These days, Americans take libraries for granted. Pretty much every town, no matter how small, has one. And if you can't find what you want in your town, you can request it from your county library, right? Not in Latin America. From Guatemala onward, I was saddened by the poor state of public libraries in places where buying books was also out of the reach of many people. If Antigua had a public library, I never found it, and the library in Puerto Vallarta, a city of 250,000, was smaller than the one where my mother had worked in Donora, Pennsylvania, population 6,000. I'd located a privately funded library in Guayaquil, but you needed to read the books on-site, and—I *swear* I'm not making this up—the books were organized by publisher just like in the bookstores, despite someone having hand painted Dewey Decimal numbers onto the edges of the wooden shelves.

Paraguay was by far the poorest country I was visiting during my year, and given what I'd seen in more prosperous places, I braced myself for my visit to the school/library complex where I'd been invited to give a talk on Austen shortly after my arrival. But I'd allowed assumptions to set up shop again and thus was pleasantly surprised at the attractive, well-stocked Roosevelt Library, housed within a public school sponsored by the *Centro Cultural Paraguayo Americano*. And it warmed my heart to see a photo of good old FDR himself above the circulation desk. You can say all you like about cultural domination from the north— but, along with classics from around the world, the shelves were stocked with Latin American authors.

One of the teachers took me around for a tour and showed me the auditorium where I'd be speaking. While I had a library talk in Spanish planned for later in the month at San Lorenzo, a small town nearby, this one would be in English, since the students needed practice listening to native speakers.

"They're going to be shy," the teacher warned me, "so don't be offended when they don't ask questions. They're always like that with foreigner visitors."

Sound check checked, I sat down in the front row and waited, trying not to feel too anxious as the noisy crowd of more than a hundred filled the auditorium behind me. I'm not used to addressing middle and high school kids, but I'd done my best to plan the talk toward their interests, while getting in my pitch for Austen.

"This," I began, reining in my rapid Pittsburghese when I took the stage, "is where Jane Austen was born." The house itself no longer exists, unfortunately, but I showed them PowerPoint photos of St. Nicholas Church at Steventon, where her father served (I left out the part about getting chased by cows in the adjoining field). I briefly explained who Austen was and why she was important, assuming that most of them would have no idea. That turned out to be a legitimate assumption, for a change.

I also explained my book group project and spoke a bit about each country, showing photos of the readers from Guatemala, Mexico, Ecuador, and Chile. I was not above pandering to keep them awake, so I worked in a few cheesy shots—one of a noisy rooster outside my house in Puerto Vallarta, another of me petting an iguana in Guayaquil, which struck them as thunderously funny (laughing with me or *at* me? *Quién sabe...*).

They especially liked selections from my graffiti collection, and that was where I let the cows out. I explained that Chileans were very political on many levels and offered up photos of two spray-painted approaches to vegetarianism. The first was a sweet, big-eyed cow saying, "*No me coma*"—don't eat me!—and the second, a fierce cow draped with an ammo belt, Pancho Villa style, armed and ready to defend herself from carnivores.

From my vantage point on the stage I could see that I had put some of them straight to sleep, iguanas and killer cows notwithstanding. There were also some decidedly sullen expressions out there. But many students looked alert and interested, so with any luck I was winning over some Janeites or, at the very least, piquing their interest in reading groups.

I asked if there were any questions as I wrapped up, but remembering the teacher's warning, assumed there wouldn't be any. Wrong again.

"Why do you think so many people like Jane Austen?"

"Why didn't Jane Austen have babies?"

"Can we get Jane Austen books in Spanish?"

"Why on earth did you come to Paraguay?"

This last question raised an enormous howl of laughter—they didn't think of their homeland as being on the typical *gringa* tourist beat.

"Your country has a very interesting history," I told them. "And I was invited here by my host." A dead silence hit the chattering students when I referred to Martín by name. Then they erupted into whispers and gasps, repeating his name. Any high-profile politician has both friends and enemies, I suppose; no way to know if they were impressed or taken aback.

"That was really wonderful!" One of the teachers approached the stage as the multitude, many questions later, finally headed back to their classes (perhaps they'd cottoned on to the equation more questions = less class time?). She shook my hand and said, "A book group would be a great way to get some of our shy students to talk more to each other."

Another teacher joined us and introduced himself as Tony. "Have you already got an Austen group arranged for Paraguay?" he asked. A number of students had followed him up. With a hopeful smile, he added, "We would love to be in an Austen book group with you."

Talk about luck! "That would be fabulous," I said quickly, as pleased as could be. "I'd love for us to read *Emma* together. How does that sound?"

He looked to the students for approval, and one of them answered in slow, careful English, "We would like that very much!" The boy smiled broadly when the sentence came out the way he'd planned. My previous groups had been heavy on women, but here was a male teacher and six teenagers, half of them boys. This would be interesting.

"I'll deliver copies of *Emma* tomorrow, in Spanish," I promised, "then we can set a date for the end of the month." After my initial panic over Lili getting the book in English, I'd remembered that I already had the copies I'd planned to use in Argentina. Well, I needed them *now*, so I'd just have to hope I could get my hands on more Austen next month in Buenos Aires.

Emma was back on!

I wasn't pandering to the students when I'd said that Paraguay has a very interesting history. Fascinating is more like it. Once upon a time, Paraguay was one of the most prosperous, advanced countries in South America. With a range of geographic features and climates within its borders, it had solid agriculture and industry, strong education, and the best rail system on the continent. Then in 1864, apparently anticipating an invasion by Brazil over long-standing disputes related to Brazil's relations with Great Britain, President Francisco Solano López sent troops across Argentinean territory to avoid being caught in a pincher move, not realizing that Argentina had already signed an alliance treaty with Brazil and Uruguay. López suddenly found himself at war with more than half the continent.

Paraguay held out for five bloody years then succumbed to its enemies, who made off with a high percentage of the country's original territory. While U.S. intervention has been a source of grief in many Latin American countries, in this case, it was a major reason Brazil and Argentina didn't swallow Paraguay whole in the decades after the war. During my visit several Paraguayans brought up the important man responsible, very surprised I hadn't heard of him: President Ay-yeas. Ay-yeas? I was at a loss as to who the heck this could be until I saw his name on a road sign, since quite a number of things are now named for him: Hayes. As in, Rutherford B. Not a chart-topping president in the United States, but fondly remembered in Paraguay.

The war also devastated the population, military and civilian. The prewar count of Paraguayans was nearly a million. By the end of the war the figure was closer to 200,000—fewer than 29,000 of them men. That's a lot fewer guys than you'll find on a crisp fall weekend at my *alma mater* at a West Virginia University football game, to give a little perspective. Poland was steamrolled by Germany in WWII, but that massacre pales in comparison to what happened to Paraguay.

The country has never really recovered. A tragedy on that level leaves its mark on a nation's literature, and Paraguay's best writers have dedicated themselves to the subject, directly or indirectly. When I visited bookstores in Asunción and asked about women writers, every bookseller gave me the same name: Josefina Plá. With a bit of research I learned that she was actually born in Spain, but she moved to Paraguay young, married a Paraguayan, and lived there until her death in 1998 at age ninety-five. She claimed Paraguay, and it claims her.

I was bowled over by her novel *Alguien Muere en San Onofre de Cuarumí* (*Someone Is Dying in San Onofre de Cuarumí*, cowritten with Angel Pardella). The main narrative thread is the slow death of one of the village women, but the backdrop is the War of the Triple Alliance, just ended. There's not even a coffin maker left in San Onofre, so when one of the few surviving men dies, he's squeezed into a trunk. Two young boys drag him to a shallow grave then accidentally drop him in face first. "*El día de juicio le va costar para salirse*," opines a local woman dryly—"He won't get out of there easily on Judgment Day."

Despite the heaviness of the theme and the dark humor, the novel is surprisingly positive. The women it focuses on are survivors. In the face of destruction, starvation, the loss of their husbands and sons, and attacks by thieves and rapists who pass through their village in the postwar chaos, they stick together as a community. They keep their pillaged church clean, and, as they reminisce about their lives before and during the war, comfort their dying friend. War has disrupted every facet of their lives, but it can't break their spirits. Austen would no doubt admire these women, but she never would have dreamed of putting horrors like what they experienced on paper.

Shortly after my school talk, Martín and Dorrie took me on a Sunday drive to see some of the most important battlefields of the war. We also visited the pretty little town of San Bernardino, where moneyed folks go for a lakeside getaway from Asunción. Before we left I booked a room in the *Hotel del Lago* for the next weekend, partially because of how charming it was, partially to fulfill a Morbid Tourism Wish—to stay in the room where Bernhard Förster committed suicide in 1889.

If the average person knows anything about Paraguay, it tends to be, unfortunately, the Nazi connection. Förster is one of the reasons that link was forged. He was a raging anti-Semite married to philosopher Friedrich Nietzsche's sister Elisabeth. Nietzsche, despite the Nazi appropriation of his concepts, was no anti-Semite. He loathed his brother-in-law and wanted no part of Förster's plans to found a pure "*Nueva Germania*" in Paraguay. When the colony failed, Förster checked himself into the *Hotel del Lago*, drank for six weeks, then poisoned himself. Nietzsche's sister apparently had to sign away most of the colony land to pay his hotel bill and have him buried. In the 1930s, Hitler sent a delegation to spread some German soil on Förster's grave, walking distance from the hotel.

"I've asked about that room myself," Martín said as we toured the enormous, turreted nineteenth-century building. "They've shown me a different one each time, so I'm not even sure they know which one it is." When I returned a week later, the room they led me to was so attractive I was willing to take it on faith Förster had met his end there.

Places where people are born or die hold an intensity, a profound kind of energy. Austen fans have the misfortune to lack access to both of these places for her. Steventon Rectory no longer exists, and the house where Austen died in Winchester, her head on big sister Cassandra's lap, is privately owned. As Austen's health declined rapidly, the family had moved her there from Chawton to seek the help of a medical specialist, but in vain. I located the house on a visit to England in 2003 but joined the ranks of the disappointed when I saw the handwritten sign taped to a downstairs window: "THIS IS A PRIVATE HOUSE AND NOT OPEN TO THE GENERAL PUBLIC." No doubt an attempt to stop devoted Janeites from knocking and pleading to be let upstairs, to see the sacred ground.

There was nothing sacred for me about a racist like Förster; staying in his room was more akin to the impulse to watch horror films. I had to wonder, however, if Paraguayans knew anything about him, because it was clear that my sunny, balconied room with the adjoining turret adapted as the shower was a favorite honeymoon spot. The large antique armoire was full of lovers' graffiti on its inside panels, some as old as I was:

Entre estas cuatro paredes
Y en esta cama de bronce chillona
Hemos pasado nuestros tres primeros maravillosos
Días de casados
Oscar y Josefina, 7/5/64

"Between these four walls, and in this squeaky bronze bed, we've spent our first three wonderful days as a married couple." Jali and Folfi, equally poetic, left their own contribution: "*Muchas veces la cama se convierte en cuna cuando se trata de felicidad, ella es testigo y es la única que puede relatar la inmensa dicha que experimentamos en ella.*" Or in other words, "Often happiness can convert a bed into a cradle; this bed is the witness and the only one that can tell about the immense happiness we experienced here."

Numerous other messages filled the armoire. There was nothing especially romantic about the anatomically correct heart someone carved into the back panel (valves and all), but I enjoyed the thought of all this happy love energy exorcising the spirit of Förster.

With Diego thousands of miles away, however, I'd have to make the best of the room on my own, so I decided to dig into more local literature. The most important, internationally known Paraguayan author, Martín and Dorrie had assured me, was Augusto Roa Bastos, and his most important novel, *Yo el Supremo*. Based on the life of Dr. Francia, a dictator who ruled Paraguay from 1814 to 1840, the book is a complicated combination of novel, essay, and poetic reflection on history and power. I quickly realized it was *too* complicated for me. As with Asturias back in Guatemala, I'd need much better Spanish to tackle Roa Bastos.

Fortunately I'd also brought along *La Babosa*, published in 1952 by Gabriel Casaccia. In *La Babosa* (literally *The Slug* but in this context, *The Gossip*), the world Casaccia depicts is like the evil flipside of Highbury, the setting of Austen's *Emma*. While Austen's small town is cozy and friendly, Casaccia's is the embodiment of a harsh Spanish saying: "*Pueblo chico, infierno grande.*" Small town, big hell.

Austen offers the best face of rural life, but she doesn't sentimentalize it. She shows how problematic gossip can be, for instance, and through the Miss Bates and the Mr. Elton storylines, she illustrates how we've got to treat our neighbors well, even if they're irritating or rude. But her world is rosy indeed compared to what Casaccia dishes up. What if Miss Bates, instead of merely being a nuisance, were actually *malevolent?* What if she had it in for the Reverend Mr. Elton, trashed his reputation publicly, and hounded him to an early death? Angela, the gossipy "*babosa*" old maid, does just that with the local priest. And what if Emma, instead of loving her older sister, *hated her* because Mr. Woodhouse had preferred Isabella? What if Emma found every possible way to torment her, finally driving her to suicide? Angela the *babosa* manages that feat, too. And what if Emma, instead of having loving patience for her father's quirks and weaknesses, exploited them at every turn to get what she wanted? That's what pretty much every character in *La Babosa* does with pretty much every other character.

Greed is a major theme as well. Ralph Waldo Emerson, not an Austen fan, once wrote, "I am at a loss to understand why people hold Miss Austen's novels at so high a rate. Never was life so pinched and narrow. All that interests any character is, has he or she money to marry with? Suicide is more respectable." Well, Casaccia would have given Ralph W. an instant coronary. I enjoyed how well written the novel is but was stunned by its fierceness. Could small town Paraguay really be that brutal? Plá's novel shows the ugliness of war, but also, unity and compassion in the face of adversity. Austen shines things up a bit to show us the best a small town is capable of; perhaps Casaccia was deliberately darkening things to expose the worst.

But I was certainly getting the fish-eye from the local women working at the hotel. I'd popped out on the balcony my second morning there to find three of the maids on the lawn, looking up at my window. They fell silent and scattered in three directions when they saw me. Something similar had happened over dinner the previous evening on the huge outdoor patio of the hotel. I got the feeling that a woman my age traveling alone, with no children or grandchildren in tow, was distinctly suspect.

Maybe my stay in Honeymoon Central was beginning to work on me, or maybe feeling like an unmarried oddball factored in. Either way, after I'd settled back in with Martín and Dorrie again, I found myself thinking more and more about Diego's desire for me to return to Puerto Vallarta. Living there, he'd pointed out, would certainly cost me less than being in California. The problem was I wouldn't have my California salary in Puerto Vallarta.

It dawned on me that I should think of this the way Emma

and Mr. Knightley tackled their own "where to live?" dilemma. First things first—did I really want to be with Diego, regardless of location? Although Mr. Knightley lacks Darcy's sex appeal, he has endeared himself to generations of Austen fans by declaring that what mattered to him most was being with Emma, even if that meant leaving his own home to humor Mr. Woodhouse. Love first, lodging second. So there was the question: did I love Diego?

I knew I missed him. I missed his perpetual cheerfulness, his playful temperament, his sweet, dark eyes. I missed our long walks in the mountains outside the city, our lazy afternoon swims in the sea, our nights out listening to music and dancing. But there was only one way to know how much I was missing Diego versus how much I was missing being *with* Diego in a beautiful Mexican seaside town—and that was to invite him to visit California. We could get to know each other better, he could see how I lived, and I could see how he would fit in with my friends.

He answered my email the same day: "*¡Claro que sí!*" Yes, of course!

Diego had been to Arizona years ago but never California, and he liked the idea of seeing where I taught. "Maybe I can sneak into one of your Jane Austen classes," he joked. There was no way of knowing quite how long it would take him to get a tourist visa, so we'd have to leave the plans open-ended, but if all went well, we could finally see each other again that upcoming fall. My home was no tropical paradise. If we got along just as well in California's hot, flat Central Valley, well, that really *would* be love.

CHAPTER FOURTEEN

Emma movie night rolled around fast. The first guest to arrive was Erna, a close friend of Dorrie and Martín. The couple had spoken about her earlier with admiration, given that, among other talents, she was equally fluent in English, Spanish, and German. She was, in fact, a simultaneous translator. The only thing more impressive than a person who speaks three languages equally well is one who translates at the speed of normal conversation. In 1993, when Jimmy Carter served as an independent observer of Paraguay's first democratic election since the 1940s, Erna swapped his English into Spanish for the entire country (and the world) to hear.

I assumed she'd be intimidating. Wrong again. I should have known that any friend of Dorrie and Martín would be just as pleasant as they were. She was, however, a little more…brash. With short, stylish hair and a huge winning smile, Erna was the kind of wisecracking woman people in the 1950s called "a pistol!" Think Rosalind Russell in *His Girl Friday*, but prettier and with a fouler mouth. I adored her immediately and couldn't wait to hear what she'd have to say about *Emma*.

The rest of the Austen party arrived soon after. There was Lili from the school, accompanied by a young German friend who smiled silently the whole evening; Victoria, a dark-haired, delicately pretty cousin of Martín's who looked to be about my age; Paula, one of Martín's nieces, a smart, pleasant woman in her early twenties who also was more of an observer than a participant; and finally Alicia, an elegant, well-dressed family friend in her fifties who swept in on a wave of delicious perfume once we'd already started the film.

Dorrie and Martín bustled around making sure everybody had drinks and snacks until the others urged them to sit down and enjoy the movie. "Enjoy the movie" with this group meant livening it up with chat. Hardly an action passed without commentary, and Erna took the cake for candor. When Emma archly comments to Harriet Smith that she hadn't noticed Mr. Martin in one scene, Erna blurted out, "Oh, right, deny it! You were hot for him the second you saw him!" Various comments erupted when Frank Churchill runs off for a haircut, and Erna cut through them all: "He's gone off to chase *whores*, that's all!"

Austen would surely have been shocked, but the authors of *Pride and Promiscuity*, the so-called "lost sex scenes" of Austen, could have taken a few notes for a sequel.

As the movie swept to a close with dancing, merriment, and marriages, the group began to clap and laugh. Lili called out, "Oh, I want to marry Mr. Knightley!"

"You do?" Erna responded, raising an eyebrow. Mr. Knightley was, I suspected, pretty stuffy for her taste.

"So was this book famous when it first came out?" Victoria asked, as Martín returned with another round of drinks.

"Well, I can't believe what Mark Twain said about Austen," Erna said. "I read it on the Internet. Something like, 'I wouldn't have Austen on my shelf if there were no other books left in the world!'"

"Was it because of the aristocracy?" Martín asked. "Twain was really a populist, so he probably objected to the decadence of their lives."

Surprised that Twain had surfaced again, as he had in Chile, I explained about the context of the private letters to his friends, who he'd been razzing about Austen.

"And was *Emma* scandalous for its time?" Victoria asked, pursuing the original reception of the novel.

"I don't see why it would have been," Lili answered.

"But it seems to me that breaking the social barriers like she does must have been scandalous," Victoria continued. "Look at that party at the end, where the classes are mixed."

"That's how the movie ends but not the book," I explained. Hollywood was basically making Austen more palatable, because the novel actually clarifies that Emma and Harriet *can't* stay friends once she marries Mr. Martin:

> *Harriet, necessarily drawn away by her engagements with the Martins, was less and less at Hartfield; which was not to be regretted. The intimacy between her and Emma must sink; their friendship must change into a calmer sort of goodwill; and, fortunately, what ought to be, and must be, seemed already beginning, and in the most gradual, natural manner.*

Students in California who've only seen the film are always surprised and disappointed when we discuss this passage since they like to think of Austen as revolutionary. But in this sense, she wasn't. Separate spheres were the order of the day.

"But that separation exists to this day here, too." Dorrie said.

Martín agreed: "There's a *very* strong separation among the social classes."

"There's no idea here, unfortunately, of a community that's for everyone," Victoria agreed. "With the arts, too. I'm sure there are a lot of people who've never heard of Jane Austen or even the movies."

"Or haven't heard about *any* books," Alicia added.

"People here really don't read much," Lili said ruefully.

Victoria nodded. "But it's also *so* hard for people to get access to books here with everything that's happened over the last thirty years."

Massive cross-talking broke out at once, and the consensus was clear: books were expensive and hard to get for most Paraguayans.

"And aside from the Roosevelt, it isn't like having the public library 'down the street' in the United States, where you can go and read what you want," Erna pointed out, switching into English for "down the street."

"For really poor Paraguayans," Lili added, "it's not just about buying the books or borrowing them. You also have to worry about whether you can afford shelves to put them on or a place the books can be without getting dusty or dirty."

"Okay, who wants to eat 'Happy'?" Martín suddenly called out, switching to a more cheerful subject: food. "That's what's left of Dorrie's birthday cake."

"Who wants a piece of happiness?" Dorrie seconded, laughing. As drinks were refreshed and more food was shared, the talk became general for a stretch.

Alicia was the one who brought us back around to Austen. "I liked *Sense and Sensibility* much better."

"You did?" I encouraged her, curious.

"Much more profound, a lot more honest feelings all around. In *Emma* everybody's covering, covering, covering," Alicia continued. "There's cover-up in *Sense and Sensibility*, too, even from one's self, at times, but those people are really feeling *deeply*. *Emma* was just…sheeeeesh." Her sentence turned into a sigh of frustration.

"That's what one of those Brontës said about her; I mean, it was scathing," Erna offered. "No passion, she's not capable of it, blah blah blah."

"Well, I liked *Emma* better than *Sense and Sensibility*," Dorrie said. "Just marrying your daughters off, that's not very interesting to me. But this is very romantic, because Knightley was suffering the whole time. And Emma couldn't see it."

Martín tried to make a comment, but because he had a mouth full of "Happy," it came out as a sound that set the group laughing.

"I don't think he was out there being honest either," Erna dissented. "I didn't see him suffering; I didn't see him in love."

Two camps quickly formed on the issue, everyone talking at once. I struggled to keep up with the contest, half in English, half Spanish.

"Well, look at the movie again!" Dorrie insisted. "The next time you'll see that there are all these takes of him sighing."

Victoria agreed. "Why do you think that he keeps getting so mad at her?"

"It's because he cares," Dorrie continued. "Why else would he send her to hell all the time?"

"Well"—Erna leaned forward on the couch to take them both on at once—"he's mad because she's an *ass*, and that's why *I* would send her to hell!" She punctuated the sentence by lifting her drink.

"He sees her as someone who's just immature, that's all, but he cares!" Dorrie responded.

"Then why the hell doesn't he just *jump* her?!" Erna shouted in mock frustration.

"Because he *loves* her!" Dorrie and Victoria cried in unison.

The friendly dispute set the whole room laughing again. The conversation then moved into territory I had covered with the other groups, as people wondered, among other things, whether Austen had published under her own name and was famous in her lifetime.

"What a time that was!" Martín, a history lover, interjected. "You've got Admiral Nelson; the English were at the point of defeating Napoleon; they were beginning their real period as a world power. They were accumulating money at such a rate that they could maintain a Navy with 1,500 ships and, not too much later, send ships like the *Beagle* around the world."

Dorrie nodded agreement, then picked up the thread of Austen's fame. "So if Austen was successful during her lifetime, more or less, and always has been, what is the attraction?"

"Nothing has changed," Alicia offered. "Jealousy, pettiness, all of those things. Somebody wants to hear some gossip about somebody else or to trick them. Well, it's just the same today—nothing has changed."

"Definitely." Several of the others agreed.

"What's appealing is that people can identify with these situations and the human emotions here," Martín pursued, "and that's why a novel of manners like this can manage to survive. It's a portrait of its time, but it also goes beyond that, to basic human elements, so people now can read it and say, hey, these people are familiar."

While Dorrie and several others agreed, Alicia frowned and offered a dissenting opinion. "Well, there are values here that translate, but it really feels to me very much a story of its time. *Anna Karenina* is more about intense human emotions across time, but *Emma* seems, well, *muy costumbrista*, about their customs and manners."

"There's a lot about the dances," Lili assented, "the specific types of gatherings they have—"

"But this movie deals with love, impossible love," Victoria cut in, "love that encounters different types of obstacles. You've got the secret engagement of Jane Fairfax—"

She was cut off in turn at the mention of Jane's name, which provoked a storm of contrary opinions about The Jane Fairfax Situation.

"Well, maybe the book makes clearer what's going on," Lili broke through.

"What it shows is the social class tension," Martín offered. "Jane doesn't have many options. It's almost like trafficking in women, shipping her off to work."

"Yeah, that whole governess thing, boy…" Erna agreed.

"And it comes up again when Emma made fun of that older woman," Victoria pointed out. "And Mr. Knightley says, 'Hey, she used to be rich. You never know how things might turn around for someone.'"

"Oh, he's the one who's perfect, with perfect values." Erna rolled her eyes, and the others laughed.

Alicia took up the point. "It's like he's Emma's conscience, pointing out what she should do."

"For me, the themes of conversation were completely of that time period," Dorrie said. "But the human feelings, the psychology, what was happening—that really did seem universal, something that translates across time."

"Like the father's fear that he'd be left alone," Victoria offered, while several others immediately chipped in, "Yes, that's right!"

"When I got here twenty-six years ago," Dorrie said, "I actually heard of women who'd say, 'My mother wouldn't let me get married.'"

Talking over the end of her sentence, the other women rushed to point out that this wasn't a thing of the past. "It's true to this day," Alicia said, "that there are women here who don't get to marry because of their parents wanting them to stay and take care of them."

"When it comes to high school girls," Lili explained, "it's hard to get parents to agree to let them study the regular material, because they only want the girls to learn to sew. 'Girls don't need those other subjects!' And they won't let them study. Even when people at the school advocate for them, the parents won't agree."

I wondered how Diego, Josefina, and her family would feel to know that this same point we'd discussed in Puerto Vallarta had surfaced here, too. The entire group fell silent over the depressing implications of girls being denied education.

To pull us out of the slump, Alicia threw down the gauntlet. "Okay, can any of you figure out what Knightley sees in Emma?"

"But I *love* Emma!" Dorrie cried in surprise.

"I know, I know," Erna sighed and patted Dorrie's leg.

"Seriously, I adore Emma!"

"Oh, Dorrie!" Several of the others laughed, while Erna stuck her tongue out, emitting an eloquent "bleeech" sound.

I could hardly keep up with who was slinging which insult:

"She's causing trouble with everybody, she speaks badly about everybody!" "She's a loser!" "What a pain!"

According to Austen's nephew James Austen-Leigh, Austen knew she had a controversy on her hands prior to the publication of *Emma* in 1815. For the subject of her book, she told her family, "I am going to take a heroine whom no one but myself will much like." Readers have been arguing about Emma ever since.

"Maybe it's clearer in the book why she acts the way she does," Alicia suggested, "but here in the movie, I just don't see it."

"She's a spoiled rich girl," Martín agreed, using an expressive word in Spanish that we lack in English: *ricachona*.

"She's adorable!" Dorrie insisted.

"She's boring," Lili said bluntly, "and she's not even a good matchmaker."

"She's childish," Martín added, an observation several of the others echoed. Then he gestured toward me. "But now I want to introduce you all to Amy Smart!" The original announcements for my Austen talk had gone out with the wrong name on them, and Martín couldn't resist teasing Lili as he transitioned away from the Emma debate.

"I know, that was all my fault!" Lili apologized. "How could I forget the name 'Smith?'"

"Hey! Are you related to Harriet Smith?" Dorrie asked suddenly, and the group burst into laughter yet again.

"She's got a fascinating project, and we're very glad that she joined us in Paraguay," Martín continued. "And we all want to know when *your* book will come out!"

"Yes, tell us more about your project," Alicia prompted, so I gave the best short version I could of the previous reading groups and having taught in Chile prior to arriving in Asunción.

"But is what we did here worthwhile for you, since we didn't get to read the book?" Victoria asked.

"I always love to hear people's reactions, whether to the books or the films," I assured them. "And I'm going to do a reading group with people from the school where I gave the talk, because they asked me if I would." The strong anti-Emma sentiment that evening had me more curious than ever now about how the teachers and students would react to Austen's pampered heroine.

"What an HP, that Frank Churchill, don't you think?" Dorrie said suddenly, plunging us back into *Emma*.

"Why?" Martín wondered, while I was wondering instead, what's an HP?

"Oh, definitely an *hijo de puta*!" Erna said, answering my question: son of a whore.

The insult opened the floodgates, and another wave of cross-talking broke out as the group wrangled over who was the most unpleasant: Frank Churchill ("HP!"), Mr. Elton ("He's a bigger HP than Churchill!"), or Mrs. Elton ("What a bitch! She's the worst!"). I was on the alert for somebody to threaten violence, but they stuck to verbal abuse. No dope slaps from that group so far.

Dorrie switched to English to defend her position firmly: "I'll tell you what. Frank Churchill could have kept his engagement a secret—"

"Without flirting with anybody," Erna cut in.

"—without flirting with Emma!" Dorrie concluded.

"That was all part of the theater," Martín argued. "His girl-friend Jane understood that they had to stage a whole play to keep people distracted from their secret."

"So he wouldn't lose his money," Alicia agreed. "Well, I've

got a theory. They had to throw people off the scent, and here's Emma, this matchmaker, who's *so* naïve about what was going on with Elton and other people that Frank thought, 'I can use her now to keep people off my track!'"

The group fell back into good-natured wrangling over the level of Jane's complicity and over just how big a skunk Frank Churchill was (or wasn't). Jane, most seemed to think, was forced into the deception by circumstances beyond her control and was actually quite likeable.

"So maybe Jane wins out over Emma in terms of the quality of her character," Martín suggested.

"*Yeeeeeeeessssss!*" Erna cried out triumphantly.

"In good human qualities—" he continued.

"Yes, yes, yes, yes, yes!" Erna punctuated.

"No, no, *no!*" Dorrie countered while the others burst into laughter over the revival of the Emma thrashing. "She's just not adorable like Emma's adorable!"

"Emma's *not* adorable!" Lili said. In the midst of all the talking, the subject of Mr. Martin and Emma's meddling surfaced. "All he wanted was a nice, good-natured woman to marry."

"Mr. Martin isn't worried about money like all these other people," Victoria agreed. "He just wants a good life."

"He's the one real man around that place!" Erna said with a laugh, and the others heartily agreed.

"Mr. Knightley definitely thinks very little of Frank Churchill," Dorrie said.

"Well, he's jealous, that's why," Alicia offered.

"That makes him more human," Martín said. "He's the richest of all of them, the most powerful; he's the one who can help the others."

Victoria picked up this point: "He defends Harriet; he defends Miss Bates."

"He's the one who can make them listen without trouble for it," Lili suggested.

Dorrie shook her head. "It isn't just about his power. He's also a gentleman."

"Well, he's not the only gentleman around," Erna added. "But the others don't want to risk their social standing by stepping in to help Harriet at that dance."

"When that Elton won't even dance with her." Alicia looked disgusted.

"I can't stand that guy," Martín said to approving nods all around.

"He needs to be *squooshed*." Erna laughed.

Aha! That definitely sounded like violence. But although Erna was a Paraguayan now, she'd been born in the States, so maybe it didn't count.

"Well, I liked his wife," Dorrie said, and the others howled in protest until Erna finally said, "Okay, now you're just *trying* to provoke us!"

As we laughed over the character debates, Dorrie turned to me and asked, "Amy, are there continuations of this story?"

"Not by Austen, but there are sequels by other people. One even has a lesbian twist. There are people who think Knightley is too old or too stuffy for her—like some of you did—so they change the outcome. There's one where Emma, feeling bored, is eyeing a French governess who shows up in the neighborhood."

"Not a French maid?" Martín said in mock disappointment. "But what about *Bridget Jones's Diary*? That's a great update of Austen!"

Most of them had seen the film, although not all had realized it was an adaptation of *Pride and Prejudice*. I was about to bring up *Clueless* when Dorrie and Martín's son Tommy arrived home for the evening.

"You can take our picture!" Dorrie said, greeting him with a kiss on the cheek.

"Okay, people, let's get this right, because she's writing a book about us, after all!" Erna teased as we scrambled around the sofa, trying to fit everyone in.

"Emma!" Dorrie called out, and the others took up the cry, posing and smiling. "Emma!"

"Sorry," Tommy said in frustration. "The camera just died! I don't think I got the picture."

Shoot—my battery problem again, just like in Mexico. But now I was prepared. "I've got some batteries upstairs. I'll be right back!" After rummaging around in my bags for several minutes, I found the batteries, rushed back down to the living room, and handed them over to Tommy.

"Party!" Erna shouted, putting a big happy smile on every face in the photo.

Later, as I listened to the recording of the discussion, I reflected with pleasure on the film viewing. There'd been no need to ask if the *Emma* viewers felt a connection with Austen. They'd quickly transitioned back and forth between Highbury and Asunción on romance, parents controlling their children, and basic human emotions.

But there was a surprise in store for me near the end of the recording—because when I'd left the room to get my batteries, I'd also left the recorder running…

And so, seated at my computer, I listened to the sound of

my feet pounding up the stairs and heard a silence fall over the group. Then soft laughter, a comment, and Erna saying in a theatrical Mrs. Elton voice, "All right now, if we talk while she's gone, we've got to tell her everything!"

"Listen to us, gossiping!" Alicia laughed.

"Let's tell her I'll match her up with someone!" Dorrie's suggestion was greeted with laughter and teasing, as they discussed my single status and the pros and cons of the plan.

"Well, I'm good at this!" Dorrie insisted. "I introduced Peter and Mike, after all!"

"Who are Peter and Mike?" asked Lili.

"And are they still *together*?" Alicia, cutting to the chase, set off another wave of merriment.

Wow. I was barely out of the room, and there was Emma casting her matchmaking spell over the group! And better still, she'd adapted to gay matchmaking, if I was interpreting the names correctly. Very heartwarming. No doubt about it: Austen was alive and well in Asunción.

Señor Guapo the Chihuahua and my big-eyed Mexican owl, the decorations that helped each new country feel like home, had traveled with me to Paraguay, along with my fish blanket and some colorful Ecuadorian table runners. They'd been joined in Chile by a fanciful troupe of wooden llamas and a delicate copper alpaca inlaid with *lapis lazuli*. I accommodated my animal retinue in Dorrie and Martín's daughter's room in a spot where I didn't have to move any of her belongings.

Shortly after the movie group, I noticed the maid had carefully dusted and rearranged them.

This polite act set me brooding. How much of Asunción was I *really* seeing, here in a house with servants where, happy as I was, the surrounding walls were so high I couldn't see the neighbors? A house where, coming home late after my San Lorenzo talk on Austen in Spanish, I was confronted by an armed guard who, I was later told, patrolled there every night? I had no doubt that every precaution the family took was reasonable for their political situation, but I couldn't help but feel that I was a bit too sheltered there.

When I announced over dinner that I wanted to take a hotel room downtown for a few days, I was greeted with skepticism and concern. Martín was the only one who thought it was a good plan.

"You know you're welcome here as long as you want to stay," he added. "But some time in the center will give you a better sense of the city."

"Please be careful!" Dorrie urged. "This isn't California!"

According to my new policy of being more open with my mother, I called and let her know about the move, reassuring her that I'd still load up on bug spray and promising not to venture out alone at night.

Because of my fondness for morbid historical spots, I chose a hotel converted from the home of one of Francisco Solano López's brothers. When the War of the Triple Alliance ground closer to a total defeat, López turned viciously on his own family. Among other atrocities, he had his brothers shot and mother and sisters publicly flogged.

Much of Asunción was burned during the war, but some beautiful, well-maintained colonial architecture survives today. Decades of economic struggles, however, have also taken their toll. There are attractive newer structures, but many of the oldest buildings have damaged or deteriorating façades. The interior of the city's striking central cathedral has also fallen into disrepair, although when I visited, it was brightened by the arrival of a truckload of flowers and the happy banter of a wedding party preparing for an upcoming ceremony.

Many major cities in South America are ringed by what Old Hollywood referred to as "shanty towns," but their reach is much more extended in Asunción, with some dwellings near the river built onto the city sidewalks. While the downtown parks and squares are pleasant and nicely laid out, one was completely occupied by tents. The tenants there cooked, did their laundry, and generally went about their business as a form of protest against the unequal access to the country's land: about 77 percent of the land in Paraguay is owned by 1 percent of the population.

There were fewer bookstores than I'd found in Santiago, although more than in Guayaquil. I was surprised to see that a number of them opened at 7:00 a.m. One owner told me it was a holdover from the days of the dictatorship. Frequently, lengthy curfews made evening hours impossible, so enterprising book dealers added hours to the earlier part of the day. Another told me instead, "We just like to get up with the sun around here!"

I'm an early bird myself, but now that I was downtown, it was easier to take advantage of the nightlife. Since the *Emma* film gathering, I'd been eager to get to know Erna better, and we made plans for dinner at a Brazilian restaurant. It was a veritable meat marathon, with waiters cruising the tables offering cuts of beef, lamb, chicken, and whatever other animals the cooks could lay their hands on. Each diner had a small wooden device painted half red, half green. When you displayed the green half, that meant "More meat, please!" while the red signaled "I'm about to burst, thank you!" After tasting the chicken hearts (yes, I love chickens, but I love to eat them, too), I decided to pack it in.

"I'm *stuffed*!" Erna groaned in agreement. "Now we'll be able to soak up plenty of alcohol!" Sated, we set off for a downtown bar to attend a "*Cuentería*." A "*cuento*" is a story, and a *Cuentería*, a public storytelling event. A sexy vampire tale was in progress when we entered. We ordered some beers then scanned the crowded, colorful locale, full of Asunción's artistic set, for a place to sit. In the press around the storyteller there were two seats left, one on a bench and the other on a wooden rocking horse.

"Guest of honor gets the pony!" Erna said, raising her glass for a toast. This could work out well; when I couldn't hold the horse upright, it would be time to cut me off.

The featured storyteller was a handsome Colombian touring South America to share stories, and I was thrilled that I could follow his tales without trouble. I'd been told that Colombians speak the clearest Spanish on the continent. I was also impressed that this group of people, drinking heavily, was up for an experience that took some concentration. I'd certainly never attended anything similar in the United States.

Several nights later, Erna and I headed out for more cultural diversion. The same school that had hosted my talk on Austen was, I'd been pleased to learn, staging a version of Casaccia's *La Babosa*. When the curtain rose, however, Erna and I could only gawk and giggle like schoolgirls. The announcements had failed to note that the play was in *Jopará*, a mix of Spanish and *Guaraní*, the local indigenous language. Even Erna, linguist that she is, was at a loss. We stuck it out, however, trading whispered quips throughout. "Well, now I can still read the novel without having the ending spoiled," she said as we left, "since I have no idea what the hell just happened!"

Paraguay is the only South American country with two official languages—Spanish and *Guaraní*, spoken by more than half of the population. Before I'd arrived, I'd assumed that the attitude toward indigenous cultures in Paraguay would be the same as in the other countries I'd visited. Yet another bad assumption. *Guaranís* face social and economic discrimination, but their culture and language aren't marginalized the way the *Mapuche*, for instance, are in Chile. Pinochet, Chile's dictator between 1973 and 1989, would never have addressed the public in *Mapuche*, even if he'd known the language (which he didn't). Alfredo Stroessner, Paraguay's strongman from 1954 to 1989, was bilingual and frequently made political speeches in *Guaraní*.

Cruising the local bookstores, I found many titles in *Guaraní*, including an important children's series sponsored by the novelist Roa Bastos that contained dual-language titles. I'd picked up a volume called *Folklore Paraguayo* to get a better sense for the indigenous literature. Many of the stories promote respect for the environment and local wildlife by illustrating what happens to greedy hunters who kill mothers raising babies or people who deplete resources thoughtlessly.

Knowing that children were the intended audience, however, I was taken aback by the violence. One specific message for kids was loud and clear: don't go into the jungle alone. You might, for one thing, get treed by the *Aó Aó*. It's like a sheep, except *evil*. It'll dance around the tree on its hind legs bleating, "*aóaó aóaó aóaó!*" after which it will dig up the roots, shake you to the ground, then eat you. Or there's the *Jasyjatere*, which disguises itself as a bird.

It'll lead you into the jungle and show you how to enjoy honey without getting stung. Problem is, when it decides to kiss you on the lips (and yes, it *will* want to kiss you on the lips), it will scorch your mouth, leaving you mute and simpleminded, at which point it'll abandon you in the swamps and seek its next victim.

The originals of European fairy tales are certainly bloodier than the versions kids in the United States now enjoy, but somehow, I still couldn't picture the Reverend or Mrs. Austen reading Jane and Cassandra or their brothers anything like these *Guaraní* stories at bedtime. Presumably, the stakes were higher in Paraguay for children straying off, hence the heavier scare tactics. Had little Jane wandered too far from the rectory, at worst she could have gotten nipped by a badger or a neighbor's dog (or chased by a cow). Paraguayan jungles hold greater dangers.

Still, some of the stories are downright lurid—especially that of the *Curupí*, whose penis is so long, he wraps it around his waist like a belt (if you'd like that last bit in *Guaraní*: "*Tuichaiterei ndaje hapi'a. Péva ipukutereígui chugui ndaje, olia iku'áre, pono oikupy lia mba'e chupe*"). Any girl foolish enough to range beyond shouting distance from Mom and Dad will get lassoed by his freakish male member—the book actually has an illustration of this—and raped. If she manages to survive, she'll be stark raving mad.

In *Letters to Alice on First Reading Jane Austen*, Fay Weldon suggests that single women in Austen's time could find some comfort in celibacy, knowing that any married woman had a good chance of dying from childbirth; two of Austen's sisters-in-law did. Even with this possibility severely reduced by the mid-twentieth century, if I'd heard the story of the *Curupí* as a little girl, I'd probably still be a virgin.

CHAPTER FIFTEEN

I had one more literary activity before the *Emma* reading night: the *Pride and Prejudice* gathering with *Las Amigas*. While guests like me were welcome, the key to official *Amiga* membership was being an ex-patriot. Kitty, the hostess, was an American married to a Paraguayan, as were the other women, so this conversation, for a change, was in English. When Erna and I arrived, we were greeted by Kitty's pack of ten leaping, friendly dogs who were lured off into the central courtyard when lunch was served, more delicious food than all of us, including the dogs, could have managed. Like Dorrie and Martín, these were people living toward the high end of Asunción's social ladder, yet they were warm and unpretentious.

Las Amigas had read *Pride and Prejudice* and now were gathering to watch the Knightley/Macfadyen film. Erna naturally livened up the viewing with snarky commentaries. During Mr. Collins's inept preaching she cried out, "Oh *lord*, he's not even good at *that*!" with such a combination of disbelief, outrage, and disgust that our laughter drowned out the rest of the scene.

While I was interested in their opinions on *Pride and Prejudice*, the fact that I'd already discussed the novel both in Guatemala and Ecuador led me to focus more once we made the (apparently inevitable) shift from Austen's world to Asunción.

An attractive woman in her forties named Susan made the leap first: "All of this concern about dances, marriage, about domestic life, it's really still the same for many women here today." I soon discovered that she was married to the grandson of novelist Gabriel Casaccia, author of *La Babosa*. Asunción's cultural circles are small enough that there aren't many degrees of separation. A week or two there and you know someone who knows someone who knows Roa Bastos or Josefina Plá or, in this case, Casaccia.

The fact that Asunción can be a small world, socially speaking, surfaced again when the conversation turned to several books that had come out recently on Paraguay. "There's one you've got to read on Madame Lynch called *The News from Paraguay*," Kitty the hostess told me. "She's a controversial figure from our history." Madame Lynch was President López's lover and *de facto* first lady. Irish by birth and a known courtesan, she was scorned by his family. She scorned them right back. Lily Tuck's novel recounts how Madame Lynch invited López's family and friends for a sumptuous dinner on a river barge. When they crowded the buffet but spurned the hostess, Lynch had the feast, plates and all, dumped into the river. She ate alone and let them watch, increasingly hungry and panicked as she held them hostage for a full day. Lesson: don't mess with the Irish!

"I've already read a bit about her," I answered. "And some other things on Paraguay, too."

"Well, not all the writers who come here for research are very polite," Linda, another of the *Amigas*, added. "Many of us have opened our homes to people who've turned around and written some unflattering things. That one woman, you know who I mean—" she gave the group a meaningful look "—she certainly won't get invited back."

The others nodded in agreement. Since they knew I was working on a book, I suddenly found myself the subject of some speculative looks.

"I'd never abuse anybody's hospitality!" I assured them.

I can see why *Las Amigas* were concerned on the subject. Who would want to find themselves insulted or turned into a caricature in print? Once the cat was out of the bag that those fabulous novels "By a Lady" were actually by humble Jane Austen, her friends and neighbors must have thought twice about exposing any silliness in front of her, lest they turn into a Mr. Woodhouse, a Reverend Elton, or a Miss Bates.

But while many people suspect that Mrs. Bennet is based on Austen's own mother, I think that's selling Austen's creativity short. She was writing novels, not memoirs. Either way, Austen was discreet enough in her fiction that if she were skewering friends and family members, we're not sure which ones. No doubt her sharpest comments were saved for her private letters anyway, which Cassandra knew better than to share with outsiders. The history lover in me mourns the loss of those letters profoundly—but discretion does have its virtues.

When *Las Amigas* learned I was staying downtown in a hotel on the fringe of the city's red light district, they'd assumed I'd be murdered by muggers before I could hold my *Emma* group. Fortunately, they were wrong. But I did get a few surprises when I showed up at the classroom in the Roosevelt Library to meet with the *Emma* readers. Tony, the teacher who'd requested the group, had been enthusiastic, and so were the students, half of them boys, to whom I'd given the copies of the novel. So I assumed they'd all be there, ready to go.

Wrong again. What I found instead were three women who looked so young I assumed they were students. They weren't. They were all teachers from the school who'd attended the talk but whom I hadn't met.

"We don't know what happened to the others," laughed a pretty girl with long, thick dark hair who introduced herself as Ana María. She didn't look a day over sixteen. "But here we are, anyway!"

Lorena, at twenty-two the oldest of the group, reminded me of the saucy, gum-cracking Italian girls from my junior high I'd tried so hard to imitate when I hit my Billy Joel phase. With shortish brown hair and a sardonic gleam in her eye, Lorena, I suspected, would have some strong opinions on Austen. About that, I was right. Alicia was the final reader. Barely twenty, with a heart-shaped face and a gentle smile, she was not as poised and elegant as Martín's friend Alicia from the *Emma* movie night. Still, though dressed in a simple blouse and jeans, this younger Alicia was just as pretty. As the night went on I could see that, although a bit shy, she was just as insightful, as well.

We waited in the nearly empty classroom a few minutes to see if anybody else would show, chatting about how my digital recorder worked and about their English studies (albeit in Spanish). Lorena finally turned the conversation to Austen. "So, what did you want to talk about with this book?" I couldn't help but remember Mercedes in Guatemala, so ready to get the ball rolling.

When I replied that I wanted to leave it open to their interests, they smiled, exchanged looks, and again, Lorena jumped in.

"Well, I couldn't help but think about how Austen creates

characters just like people I know here—especially Emma and her father."

I hadn't exactly clocked any of the other groups to see how long it took us to get around to this point, but I didn't need a stopwatch to know that this was certainly the fastest that anybody had discussed the connection between Austen and their own life and culture.

"Emma's father, how do you say his name?" Lorena continued. "Woodhow? Woodhouse? He's very sweet; he loves Emma, but to be honest, there's something about him, something not good, something that's…"

"Selfish?" I offered.

"Well, we all have our points of view, you know? And he just wanted everybody to have the same one he does. His daughters are perfect. They can't do anything wrong. That's the way Emma grew up, thinking the same thing and *definitely* not wanting any criticism."

Lorena's volume had risen as she spoke, and her final statement reverberated strongly in the large, uncarpeted room.

"There a lot of echo here." Alicia smiled wryly. Especially with only four of us in a space that could easily have accommodated fifty.

I nodded and pursued Lorena's point. "So, Emma's spoiled?"

"That's putting it mildly." Alicia laughed. "She's really a very observant person, but she uses that to manipulate people. I don't like her." She shook her head. "At first I did—because she knows what's going on around her, but from the moment she got that other girl to reject the marriage proposal, I stopped liking her."

"The way she manipulated her," Lorena agreed, while Ana María, clearly the quiet one of the group, nodded as well on behalf of poor little Harriet Smith. "Making her think that she was *helping* her!"

"Very selfish!" Alicia burst out. "My god, that girl thinks she's some kind of *goddess*. I really identified with the friend because to be honest, my mother's just like that, just as manipulative. I was okay with her up to that point, but after that, forget it!"

Lorena smiled and took up the challenge. "*I* liked her!"

"Oh, you liked her, eh?" Alicia raised her eyebrows and gave her friend a comic look.

"She knew what she wanted and she knew how to get it. She had a lot of confidence." While Alicia and Ana María continued to look dubious, Lorena continued: "She was really sure of herself, and I can identify with that."

"She's certainly a product of her environment," Alicia conceded. "But what about that man, that Kini, Kina—"

"Knightley," I chipped in. This was a stumper, just as Willoughby had been in Mexico and Chile. So many unpronounced letters.

"Yes, him," Alicia continued. "I could see right away he was interested in her, but somehow it was, well…"

"Kind of strange." Ana María joined the conversation at last with a firm pronouncement.

"Yes," Lorena agreed, "he was constantly criticizing her."

"Well, I don't know how that turned out because I didn't make it too far," Alicia confessed, and the others exchanged a conspiratorial look. Had they not finished the book either? I was tempted to ask but didn't want to interrupt. Alicia continued on about Emma, comparing her own family situation to Emma's machinations with Harriet, her father, and with "poor Miss Taylor" as well. I prompted them a bit to consider the question of intention—pushy as she was, didn't Emma often have other's good in mind? Nope—not good enough.

"And the father, pretending to care about Miss Taylor," Lorena said, shaking her head in disgust. "He just didn't want to admit he was going to miss her, so he had to act like it was bad for her to get married. So selfish!"

As Lorena and Alicia overlapped each other's harsh words on Mr. Woodhouse's behavior, Ana María speculated quietly, with a knowing look: "Well, maybe that's *why* she got married—to get *away* from that house!" The spacious room rang with our laughter.

When the subject of whether or not Miss Taylor and Emma could actually have been considered friends came up next, I explained English governesses to the little group. But when I used Jane Fairfax to illustrate how women of good family backgrounds became governesses, I was greeted with blank stares. Oh dear—did that mean they hadn't made it to Jane? Could pique with Emma and her fussy dad have kept them from getting very far in the novel?

Alicia drew us back to Austen's controversial heroine.

"When it comes to learning, well, I can really identify with Emma. I'm just the same way about starting something then dropping it, starting something else then dropping it. I've started learning Italian, I've started this and that, I learn a bit, then I drop it."

"The beginning is usually the best part of something," I said, empathetic. I think a lot of people today can see ourselves in this quality of Emma's. No doubt it shocked moralists when the novel came out in late 1815, but it makes her more human today.

"Identifying with her made me like her at first," Alicia

continued, "but once she made her friend reject that proposal, to do a thing like that to somebody—"

Lorena cut her off. "You know what? I thought 'what a dummy!' about Harriet. How could she let herself be manipulated that way? That was really *stupid*."

I couldn't help but glance at Ana María to see if she'd weigh in to tip the scales on the dispute. She smiled innocently and kept her thoughts to herself. Alicia and Lorena talked their way away from the question of *how* Emma behaved and settled instead on *why* she felt the need to direct the lives of others.

"Maybe it's because she feels lonely," Lorena speculated.

"She's a lonely person," Ana María nodded.

"But she's really self-sufficient," Alicia disagreed, the frustration in her voice mounting as she spoke. "Or at least she thinks she is. I just don't know! Why is she such a busybody? I've got to finish the book to figure it out, because I don't understand! What did she *get* out of her interfering?"

There was no disagreement on this point—Lorena and Ana María seconded the sentiment as Alicia continued: "Was she jealous of Harriet? Was it because she liked to have power over others? The psychology of it all is very complicated, because she's also a good person in some ways."

Although I understood their sentiments, I felt the need to weigh in on the social context. "Emma was important in her village. It wasn't unusual for a woman of her social class to be looked on as the person who dictates taste and guides the lives of others 'below' her."

"She felt it was her right?" Ana María asked.

As I answered yes, Lorena burst out, "But all the same, she thought she was better than other people. And when she'd step in and make decisions for somebody, she'd say, 'What a great thing I just did! That was wonderful! That was my good action of the day!'" Alicia and Ana María broke into laughter at Lorena's mincing Emma imitation: "'Boy am I great!' But she always had to feel like she was doing something good because what she was *really* doing was nothing, she did *nothing*!"

"She couldn't work, though," Ana María pointed out, reining in her laughter. "So what could she do?"

"Run other people's lives, I guess!" Lorena shrugged and smiled.

"There's a great job for you!" Alicia gave Lorena a pointed look, breaking into laughter again.

"Just like *La Babosa*," I offered.

"Yes!" they all cried at once. Apparently everybody reads Casaccia's novel in school—they knew it well. "And that's just what we're like here, to this day!" Lorena added. "We all know each other in this city. My cousin always turns out to be the friend of somebody else's cousin, and so on."

We spent a while discussing Casaccia and other Paraguayan authors, and they unanimously agreed that the most important woman author was Josefina Plá.

"Her son is a high school teacher somewhere around here," Alicia shared. Eventually, we circled back around to Austen, and I asked them to all 'fess up about how far they'd made it in the book.

They exchanged guilty looks, and Lorena admitted, "I didn't get much past the point when Emma talked Harriet out of marrying that farmer." The others nodded ruefully.

"So you did read scenes with Mr. Knightley. What did you think of him?" I probed.

Another exchange of looks, and this time Alicia stepped up. "He was a dummy."

"Definitely," Lorena seconded. "He was really thick."

"I didn't like him." Ana María shook her head, making the thumbs down unanimous. Ouch! Poor dull, respectable Mr. Knightley!

"He was a dummy for wanting to be with Emma," Alicia added, and I was reminded of the earlier conversation at Martín's house where the sentiment was the same, Dorrie excepted. "I'm not in very far, but you can see where that's going."

"Maybe he sees something in her we haven't seen yet," Lorena suggested.

On that hopeful note I said, "Will you all send me an email when you do finish? I really want to know what you think of how things turn out!" I passed around a sheet and got their email addresses, giving them my own on slips of paper; back in Chile I'd run out of my snazzy official "Dr. Amy Elizabeth Smith" cards from the university.

I invited the three of them out for dinner to thank them for their time, but they all had family waiting at home. We spent another twenty minutes in pleasant gossip then prepared to go our separate ways—but not before I got them to promise that they'd email me when they finished *Emma*.

"Now that we've talked about the book, I *am* more curious about the ending," Alicia assured me as we made our way out to the street. "This was fun!" The others agreed.

"We'll have to do book groups with our own students," Ana María added as we exchanged hugs and promises to stay in touch. "Thank you for the inspiration!"

I was happy to provide inspiration, but I wanted to do more than that. On the taxi ride home it dawned on me that a bit of cash could help that inspiration along and cover the price of some books for their students. But I knew I'd never get them to accept cash, so how could I manage this?

The next morning I got my answer. Despite the fact that I would have done my Austen talk for free, the school was paying me for the event. Lili emailed to ask if I wanted the money in U.S. dollars or Paraguayan *guaranís*.

"Neither," I answered. "Sign it over to Ana María, Alicia, and Lorena." That would cover some books—and chips and soda for their first meetings. A good book is its own reward, but I suspected that Paraguayan teenagers, just like Americans, would find a little extra inspiration in any event that included snacks.

Once again, my time in a fascinating new country was rushing to a close. On the positive side, every passing day brought me closer to seeing Diego back in the United States, closer to the visit that would help us decide what we wanted out of our relationship. But I regretted not having more time to explore Paraguay, and I couldn't leave without seeing the Jesuit missions.

Beginning in the early seventeenth century, Jesuits established extensive missions on land now divided across Brazil, Argentina, and Paraguay. The Jesuits sheltered *Guaraní* Indians from Brazilian slave traders, educating them and teaching them trades. When other Spanish colonizers envied their economic success, the missions were attacked (with a nod from the Spanish crown, which expelled the Jesuits). By the 1770s any *Guaraní* who couldn't escape were enslaved. The extensive ruins, those within Paraguay's borders mostly falling within a hundred-mile radius, were now one of the country's prime tourist attractions.

I arranged for a two-day tour with an overnight hotel stay

in between. The driver was a brusque, burly man named José, who spoke fluent *Guaraní*. But I couldn't seem to retain a single word he tried to teach me, even the entertaining insult for Argentineans that means "bloated-pigskin-that's-good-for-nothing" (could my experiences in country number six *ever* live up to all of this anti-Argentinean buildup?). We arrived at *Jesús de Tavarangüe* to find the employees had all gone off to lunch, leaving the site unguarded.

"Let's go in anyway," José said with a shrug. "If they show up, we can pay."

A pair of adventurous young Germans had made the same call. They were teetering along the west wall of the ruined cathedral, completely roofless, with a three-story drop in either direction. "*Idiotas*," José snorted, studying them for so long I got the nasty feeling he was hoping to see them fall.

Daredevils aside, *Jesús de Tavarangüe* was breathtaking. A rural site, its isolation allows you to experience how that mission became the whole world to the generations of people who spent their lives there. Fields stretch for miles around the crumbling church structures. Just as in Antigua, Catherine Morland would have adored exploring the picturesque ruins. Where stained glass had once been located, beautiful vistas of the nearby countryside were now framed. Only traces of statuary and relief carvings had survived; stone faces, arms, sometimes torsos, softened by time and exposure to the elements, appeared randomly like spirits trapped in the walls of the church that had seen so much life and death pass through.

Several hours later the same Germans appeared at our next stop, *Trinidad del Paraná*. Since a guard was on duty, they were scolded down from their balancing act before they could provide any entertainment *à la* "two dead young ladies" on the Cobb at Lyme Regis. The buildings that made up the compound of *Trinidad del Paraná* were more structurally intact, but the site had less luck avoiding encroaching modernity. Someone had decided that visitors to a richly historic religious site would like nothing better than to cap off their day with a few hours at an amusement park; build it next to the mission, and folks can use the same parking lot! Ferociously chipper Paraguayan polka music from the carousel (or maybe it was the food court) provided the jarring soundtrack for the entire visit.

The tourist agency had assured me that José was knowledge-able about the Jesuit sites. He wasn't. The only subject he showed any enthusiasm for was *Guaraní*, and when that hadn't panned out, he brooded. He wasn't a bad teacher, I assured him as we set off again in the car—I simply can't learn new words unless I see them written down. By the time I'd left the States nearly a year earlier, I'd made so many Spanish flash cards that I organized them in a twenty-four-drawer tool shop unit intended for nuts and bolts and screws.

Night finally rolled around. There'd been several hotels I could choose from through the agency. In keeping with my Morbid Tourism Theme in Paraguay, I'd selected the sprawling jungle complex outside of Encarnación that supposedly harbored escaped Nazi Josef Mengele for years. I didn't ask which room he'd favored—that was going way too far—but I did insist on my *own* room when we discovered that the agency had booked José and me into the same one.

The guide's humor was no better the next morning. I couldn't bear to spend one of my last Paraguayan days in silence, so I began scraping the bottom of the conversational barrel, asking what kinds of tourists he liked best ("They're all the same to me") and what roadkill he sees most often ("Dogs"). Jane Austen's name produced a shrug, but he did perk up briefly when I asked him if he had pets.

"When my dad died he left me three birds, four dogs, a hamster, and a monkey. Very nice birds. But the monkey, he played with his organ in front of my guests. *Muy grosero*, that monkey. Very rude. I got rid of him."

He punctuated this last sentence with a satisfied grunt. I pondered the monkey's fate for a few moments, finally deciding that maybe silence was okay for a while. We visited two more missions, *San Cosme y San Damian* and *San Ignacio*, both beautiful and, fortunately, both with guides on duty to share details about their history and architecture (and no amusement parks in sight or sound).

On the long drive back to Asunción, ready to give conversation one more try, I threw caution to the winds and broached politics.

"This country used to be safe, you know," José gave me a hard stare before returning his eyes to the road. "We had order around here." He didn't have to add "when Stroessner was in power"—that was understood. "You could walk the streets. Now there are criminals everywhere. And all this talk about 'human rights.'" He spat out the last phrase as if it were something filthy. "Democracy. It just doesn't work."

"Don't you think there's room for something between dictatorship and too much freedom? Some kind of middle ground?" I asked.

He eyed me again. "Maybe," he shrugged, but his tone said, "*Hell, no.*" Two feet away from each other in the front seat of the car, dusk settling around us, we were worlds apart. José looked about my age, which would make his birth date 1964-ish. At that point Stroessner had been in power for ten years and would stay there for another twenty-five—most of José's life. Could he really imagine a different system, especially if he had suffered no firsthand experience of what it took to maintain "order?" Maybe if his mother had been kidnapped and tortured the way Emilio's had in Chile, he might feel differently about things.

But order of a kind does have its advantages—just ask Austen. My students in the United States often skim past that very important paragraph at the end of *Emma* with the comment about Harriet returning to her place since "the intimacy between her and Emma must sink; their friendship must change into a calmer sort of goodwill." Film adaptations gloss over this, implying that of course Emma and Harriet will remain chums. But that's not what Austen herself tells us. Emma is Harriet's superior; she can't be her friend. She can't hang around with the wife of a farmer, certainly not one dependent on her own husband. She just can't.

I've had various students over the years try to argue that the separation the book calls for has nothing to do with social class. Surely it's something else—maybe Emma and Harriet will just be too busy to hang out? Or maybe they're worried about those gypsies and don't want to get caught too far away from home? We love to think of Austen as our contemporary, and in the United States, that means she's not supposed to be a "snob." Isn't this what Emma has to learn?

Actually, it's not—and I never felt the message as sharply as I had in Paraguay. Emma learns that she's got to read situations and people more carefully and that she should be kinder to her inferiors, like Harriet and Miss Bates. Cher in *Clueless* may learn that her buddies should be free to date stoners from the grassy knoll (especially ones willing to donate a bong to a good cause), but that's 1995. In Regency England, Emma is near the top of the social order, and the only way for her to stay there is to *stay* there. Order has its advantages, but mostly for the people at the upper end or for those more afraid of change than they are of oppression.

I didn't debate José, because I wasn't naïve enough to believe I understood a complex land like Paraguay after only a month's stay. But I know that Martín or Dorrie could have taken him on. A cause dear to their hearts was Martín's self-sustaining agricultural school, which I had visited before my reading groups. Instead of focusing on top-down order, they believed in bottom-up growth.

"The point here isn't to teach poor children how to farm. They're not stupid—they already learn that from their families. What they *don't* learn," Martín had explained, "is how to make money at farming. Not just how to raise chickens, but how to make a profit from chickens. That's what's going to make the difference in the end."

Although I thought I'd confronted the classism of *Emma* head-on back in the States, its full implications didn't sink in until I read the novel in Paraguay, with Paraguayans—until I could talk to a man like José and visit a school like Martín's. Democracy means freedom, and freedom always means risks. But if you really want to combat crime, the progressive theory goes, you don't need to call out the army, impose curfews, and shoot anybody who disagrees with you—just give more people a fighting chance to make ends meet. To be self-sufficient.

The system under which Austen's characters lived, with its lack of social mobility, doesn't look so sinister when the people at the top are compassionate landowners like Emma and Mr.

Knightley or Mr. Darcy and Lizzy, just as patriarchy doesn't seem
so bad when you've got kind, responsible brothers to care for you
as Austen's did for her, Cassandra, and their mother. It's only
when the people in power don't hold up their end of the deal—
like John and Fanny Dashwood—that it's clear how dangerous it
is to have so little control over your own fate.

During the night before my last full day in Paraguay, back in the
safety of Martín and Dorrie's house, something disturbed my
sleep. I heard a whining close to my ear. Then I felt the sting on
my neck.

As I'd toured the missions I'd coated up with bug spray. I'd
soaked and stayed vigilant when, before breakfast, I explored the
tangle of forest surrounding the alleged-Nazi-harboring hotel
near Encarnación. When I'd visited Martín's agricultural school,
the same. Ditto for every time I set foot outside of the house. So
of course, a mosquito had to bite me in the comfort of my own
bed after I'd showered.

I lay awake for hours. Now I was going to get Super Dengue. I
was going to die thousands of miles from home after all, in some
country no one from my immense family had ever set foot in.
I'd never see my mom again. I wouldn't get to apologize to her
for making light of her fears as I was traveling or for lying about
using a sun hat in Guatemala or for having that beer party in
junior high and throwing all the cans over the neighbor's fence.
I'd never see my sister or my brothers or their kids or any of my
friends, ever again. It would cost *a lot* to have my corpse shipped
back. Why hadn't I bought travel insurance?

I fretted myself into a state of exhaustion and finally dropped back to sleep. When I awoke, the hideous panic of the wee hours had subsided. Okay, so a mosquito bit me. What were the chances, really, that lightening would strike me twice?

"Don't worry about it," Martín and Dorrie reassured me. "There are dengue mosquitoes here, but they're much more common in the countryside. You'll be fine. And you're going to *love* Buenos Aires!"

Still, when I called my mother that afternoon to remind her I was heading to Argentina for my final Austen group, I made sure we had a nice long talk. And I thanked her for being so patient with me, so supportive of all the wacky ventures I'd embarked on over the years.

I didn't expect lightning to strike twice, but Emma never expected to wind up married to her own brother-in-law, either.

ARGENTINA:

Last Tango in Highbury

In which the author hunts down Jane Austen readers on the streets of Buenos Aires, meets a proud Argentinean, visits boodles of bookstores, has an encounter with a tango dancer, learns a bit of embroidery, gets a snow surprise, and, finally, reads Emma *with a bunch of lively, argumentative, cross-talking Argentineans.*

Chapter Sixteen

Guatemala: "When Argentineans see lightning, what do they think is happening? They think it's God, taking their picture."

Mexico: "How do Argentineans commit suicide? By jumping off their own big egos."

Ecuador: "Why don't Argentineans use hot water in the shower? Because it makes the mirror fog over."

Chile: "You're going to love Argentina! It's only got one drawback—it's full of Argentineans."

Paraguay: "How do you get rich overnight? Buy some Argentineans for what they're really worth, then sell them for what they *think* they're worth."

I arrived in country number six thoroughly prepped on what I should think about Argentineans. I'd heard it all in countries one through five from friends, acquaintances, and, in one case, a total stranger in an Internet café. Short version: they're arrogant.

Goodness knows I should have learned my lesson by now about making assumptions. But these weren't my assumptions— they came from folks I'd met on the road, beginning with Luis back in Guatemala, the first (but not the last) to pass on an "arrogant Argentinean" joke unsolicited. Leti from the Ecuador reading group, while warm and engaging, seemed pretty content with herself, but that was one person only. Secondhand stories should be treated with caution. Were the good people of Argentina getting Wickhamed by their fellow Latin Americans?

Still, I had to hope that another stereotype about Argentineans *would* be true—that they're voracious readers. I'd stepped off a plane in Buenos Aires without an Austen group arranged in advance and with no connections to set one up. I had a month; surely I could find people willing to join a book group in what's widely considered the literary capital of South America. And if yet another stereotype proved true—that Argentineans *adore* arguing with each other—then offering up a literary evening, verbal sparring welcome, should be just the thing for making new friends.

Back in Paraguay, Martín and Dorrie had recommended a building in Buenos Aires that rents apartments by the week. Anything they could afford would be pricey for me, but I couldn't resist spending at least part of my visit there in Emma style, so I went for it. Located in a posh neighborhood a short walk from the Avenida 9 de Julio, one of the city's main arteries, the building on Juncal was surrounded by chichi cafés and clothing stores with two or three tastefully arranged items per window—a sure sign that if you have to ask how much it costs, you can't afford it.

When I arrived, the doorman ran a practiced eye over my rumpled, never-stylish-in-the-first-place clothing and exchanged a look with the building manager, a stiffly elegant woman with a distinctive accent, which turned out to be French. Great. A displaced Parisian, in a country famed for snobbery. She looked thrilled to see the likes of me, battered suitcases and all.

"I know you'll love the apartment." She smiled tightly as she handed over the keys with the smug air of someone offering a much bigger Christmas present than the one they expect to get.

Too bad she didn't stick around to see what happened next. I rounded up all of the tasteful "accents" in the apartment and stashed them in a closet. From my overstuffed bags I pulled my purple Mexican fish blanket and various indigenous-patterned fabrics from Ecuador and Paraguay. Every beige surface in the place disappeared under riotous color. Then came my faithful entourage of traveling critters. Foremost was Señor Guapo the stuffed Chihuahua, the treasured gift from Diego. Next, the big-eyed owl statue, three wooden llamas, and the small copper Chilean alpaca. From Paraguay I'd brought a pudgy little family of clay birds that looked best roosting on the windowsill.

Home away from home—for the last time.

It was the homestretch for my mother as well, because I was finally in a country she wasn't too nervous about. *Dancing with the Stars* had taken care of that. As I settled onto the bed and called to report that I was still alive, she skipped her usual questions about airport delays, my seat on the plane, and if I had gotten any sleep during the flight. "Will you go out to see any shows with people dancing 'the Argentine tango?'"

A nap and a shower later, I descended into the lobby and spoke again with the doorman and manager. When I explained that I was a university professor carrying out a literary project, they both warmed up, apparently shifting me mentally from the "slob" category to "eccentric academic."

"Oh, you've come to the right city for literature," Vivienne the manager assured me, while the doorman proceeded to mark up a map to show neighborhoods with the highest concentration of bookstores.

"This city is full of bookstores," he assured me. "But along Corrientes, about eight blocks from here, you'll find one after another."

Because of the unexpected turn of events back in Paraguay, I'd given away the copies of *Emma* I'd planned to use in Buenos Aires. So, even before hunting down Austen readers, I needed to make sure I had enough books for them. In no time I located a store with three copies of *Emma*. They could, the clerk promised, have three more the following day.

Ecstasy over the sheer number of bookstores I found whisked off the rest of my travel weariness. Santiago had been impressive, but now I could see why even my Chilean friends traveled here just to buy books. In a single stretch of about eight blocks on Corrientes, heading west from the Avenida 9 de Julio, there were more than twenty bookstores. Some had only new books; others, used; and some, both. There were stores with every kind of classic you could want, translated from any language; stores focused on Latin American politics, history, and literature; stores specializing in overstock with new books for less than two dollars apiece; stores with used books stacked precariously from floor to ceiling; stores with antiquarian books guarded jealously behind glass. And this was just the beginning, just a single neighborhood!

In all fairness, it's probably worth mentioning that there's plenty aside from bookstores in Buenos Aires. *Fin-de-siècle* architecture from Argentina's golden era, 1880 to 1920, is the kind of thing that might attract some tourists, plus there's no shortage of tempting shops, cafés, and restaurants. And packing these shops, cafés, and restaurants (and, of course, the bookstores), one finds perhaps the most appealing thing of all—those fabled beings who think God wants to take their picture, who can't bear to have their mirrors fogged up, etc.—Argentineans themselves.

Of all the traveling I've done in my life, the only other country that had me ogling the passing locals so much was Italy. Italians have the charming custom of dressing their best and strolling the city streets not only to see the sights but to be seen. In fact, they have a name for this—*passeggiati*. When both political and economic turmoil forced tens of thousands of Italians to emigrate at the turn of the nineteenth century, many went to the United States and leaped into the melting pot. Most who didn't went to Argentina. Three or four generations later, Italian blood runs strong in Argentina, and it shows. A noteworthy percentage of men and women alike in Buenos Aires dress handsomely, carry themselves with confidence, and know how to make the most of what they've got.

"It's not just the women who get plastic surgery here. Men do, too," a chic store clerk informed me one day when we'd gotten to talking about just how many well-preserved older gentlemen one sees in Buenos Aires. "Even the ones who aren't fags," she added. I tried not to wince at the not-so-polite term "*maricón*," given that she was trying to be helpful.

So there they were, in all their splendor—Argentineans. Or more to the point, *porteños*, as the inhabitants of Buenos Aires are called, given that it's a port city. And more to the point still, *porteños* in a prosperous neighborhood. The very long ride from the airport had shown me that Buenos Aires is massive, and I didn't have any illusions about what some of the neighborhoods must be like. But I was where I was. Leti from the Ecuador group would fit right in on Corrientes, browsing the shops, whiling away her time in the cafés with the cultured and the coifed.

Now I needed to determine which five or six of these folks would be up for reading *Emma*. Emma is Austen's own experiment with "handsome, clever, and rich," so I hoped she'd go over better here than she had in Paraguay. Bookstores seemed the right neighborhood to start. The handsome twentysomething who'd sold me my *Emma* copies had been pleasant, but when I tried to engage him on the subject of local literature, it became clear that he could just as easily have been selling shoes.

Used shops were probably a better bet. Keeping a used bookstore afloat is a labor of love, and I needed to find booklovers, not just booksellers. I bypassed several stores that somehow didn't look promising and entered one with a motherly woman at the counter penciling prices into a stack of books. After browsing until I'd found something appealing in a bargain bin, I approached and put in my bid for Austen.

"Oh, *cariño*, I'd love to be in a reading group! And I love women authors. But I just don't have time." As I paid for my book and thanked her, she added, "You know, there's a nice store two blocks down, on one of the side streets. *Librería Romano*, it's called. You should try them."

I set off down the street but hadn't gotten far when I heard a voice behind me calling, "*Señora! Señora!*" The kindly bookseller, having hurried out after me, pressed something into my hands and said, "*Bienvenida a Buenos Aires!*" She bustled off again before I could get out more than a surprised "*Gracias!*" I found myself holding a small pack of cards with the label "*Naipes Gauchescos Argentinos.*" *Gauchos* are, in a rough translation, Argentinean cowboys. Well, still no readers, but I now had a lead, a very sweet welcome, and something to entertain myself with in the apartment.

Turning down what I hoped was the right street, I found

the store. It was 10:58 a.m., and two sharply dressed men were gazing in the window like dogs outside a butcher shop, waiting for it to open. No 7:00 a.m. schedules in Buenos Aires. A sign centered in the glass, just below eye level, read:

EN ESTA LIBRERÍA

EL PRESIDENTE

DE LOS ARGENTINOS

SIGUE SIENDO

DOMINGO F. SARMIENTO

"In this bookstore the president of the Argentineans is still Domingo F. Sarmiento" (note to self: ask). After a short wait we were allowed in by a tall, dark, and silent type who immediately sat back down again behind the store's computer. As I debated whether to speak to him, a cheerful voice called up from the store's basement level, and, suddenly, Edmund Gwenn from the 1940 *Pride and Prejudice* emerged—short, portly, with a glint in his eye and a book in each hand. Could this be a magic tunnel to the library at Longbourn?

"I'm Ernesto Romano," he introduced himself. From that point on I only understood about half of what he said. With each new country in Latin America came a new accent, and my comprehension level dipped, sometimes precipitously, until I readjusted. Argentineans have the most distinctive accent in all of South America, a singsong, lilting Spanish that sounds for all the world like Italian—presumably an ethnic inheritance from their biggest European influence after Spain. Plus, their "y" and "ll" sounds are more of a "sh," so that "*yo*" sounds like "ssshoo" and a common word like "*ella*" (meaning "she") becomes "eeessshaaa," rather than the "eya" sound of Mexican Spanish. To further complicate matters, they don't use "*tu*" as a familiar form, they use "*vos*," which comes with a whole other set of conjugations for the second person familiar.

But goodwill is goodwill in any language, and clearly, I'd come to the right place.

"A book group—what a nice idea!" Ernesto said. "You can do it here, if you'd like. Come down and see my basement." I'm filling in a few words here and there, but that was the basic idea—and being led down the stairs required no translation. "This is my Sarmiento library. Look, there's a table here. You can use this space!"

When I asked if he'd like to take part, he declined but offered up his girlfriend, Carolina. "I imagine she'd like to join you. And you should ask my employee Hugo, upstairs. He loves British literature!"

After profuse thanks and a promise to let him know when the date was set, I tried for Reader Number Two. But waiting for Hugo to finish something at the computer, I was dubious; there was nothing inviting about his manner. With thick dark hair and the heaviest eyebrows I'd seen in some time, he looked, well, like what I'd been told to expect from an Argentinean—handsome and arrogant. If I had to play "which star does he look like," it would be Chris Noth, aka Mr. Big, with some extra pounds on him—dark, intense eyes, strong Roman nose, intriguing lips.

When he finished his task, he looked up at me expectantly. That seemed to be all the invite I would get, so I plunged in, my Spanish taking more bad turns than usual as I explained my project. He stared at me, practically unblinking, his solemn expression unaltered.

"And so, the novel that I want to read with everybody here is *Emma*," I concluded. He continued to study me silently. *Whew.* Well, there was always the next bookstore.

Finally, one of his eyebrows moved upward. "Why *Emma*? Why not *Northanger Abbey*?"

I gawked.

"You've *read it*, of course?" he asked, a second bushy eyebrow rising to join the first, misreading my silence.

"Of course! In fact, well, it's my favorite. Of course I've read it. I'm just surprised that...you have." Fabulous—Amy's Big Parade of Assumptions, coming to a city near you. I blundered on. "It's just that her other books are more popular. *All* of her other books."

"English Gothic literature is very interesting to me, and *Northanger Abbey* is an important parody from the classic period." As he leaned back against his seat and crossed his arms, my stomach gave a funny little lurch. In his handsome, challenging gaze I saw a flash of Luis, my long-lost sparring partner from Antigua.

I'd come to the right place, that was clear.

We talked books for a stretch, then I realized I'd better let him get back to work. He never cut loose with anything resembling a smile, but he seemed interested in the conversation and agreed to give *Emma* a try, despite its lack of Gothic horrors. I promised to drop off copies of the novel the next day. On impulse, as I was pulling the door shut behind me, I looked back to see if he was watching me leave.

He wasn't.

Day two of the hunt for Austen readers also went well. Enough time had gone by since I'd been attacked in my bed by a mosquito in Asunción that I believed I'd live after all. I spent the morning wandering around an open-air book fair in the Plaza Italia, and although I didn't sign on any new readers, I bought so many books I had to get a taxi to haul them back to the apartment.

The only dark cloud over the day passed when I returned to the *Librería Romano* to drop off three copies of *Emma* just as Hugo the clerk was trying to put a "Back in Five Minutes" sign on the door to run an errand. I'd secretly been looking forward to seeing him again, but he seemed distinctly cross at being interrupted, so I handed over the books and bolted before he could change his mind about the group.

Following up on an inspiration to try for more readers, I went to the National Library. Something of an eyesore in the Recoleta, an otherwise attractive, upscale neighborhood, the library was designed in the 1960s and built on land cleared by the demolition of Juan and Eva Perón's personal residence. "Evita" and her husband remain beloved to this day by millions of Argentineans (and by lovers of musical theater who don't really know who the heck they were), but others hate them like poison, and as soon as the 1950s post-Perón government got a chance to flatten Juan and Eva's house, they went for it. From the ruins sprouted the library, looking for all the world like a concrete mushroom with windows.

With a mother who's a librarian, I know where the nerve center of a library is: reference. The person who greeted me there was a petite blue-eyed blond who introduced herself as Teresa. She only let me get partway through my Austen spiel before she interrupted.

"Oh, I adore book groups! And I've already read some

Austen. That would be lovely!" She promised to bring along two friends who she was sure would want to join in. All three, she told me, were Jewish and interested in Hebrew language and literature. We arranged to meet later that week for lunch so that I could deliver the books and learn a bit more about these newest *Emma* recruits.

Slipping back into librarian mode, Teresa reached for a pen and began writing down Argentinean authors I should read, before I could even ask. "Borges, of course you know him. Borges I'm not even going to write down," she said with a wave of her hand. Aside from Shakespeare, there are few authors who dominate their country's literature the way Jorge Luis Borges does in Argentina. Despite having died in 1986 at age 86, he still rules the world of the essay and short story the way Colombia's Gabriel García Marquez dominates the novel. Borges is arguably Latin America's most important literary intellectual, and he and his circle of writers are a prime reason for the literary fame of Buenos Aires.

Teresa handed me the list. "All of these authors are good," she said, "but my favorite, I have to tell you, is Bullrich, Silvina Bullrich. If you like Austen, I know that you'll love her novels!"

The name sounded familiar, and when I returned to the apartment, sure enough, I already had *Teléfono Ocupado* ("Line's Busy") by Bullrich, which I'd bought at the Plaza Italia book fair because, quite frankly, I liked the cover. Judging books by their covers is seriously underrated, and any book nerd who claims never to have done it is probably *lying*.

"Austenesque" is a seriously abused term in the United States, one mostly employed to sell books just as one sells knockoff perfume: "If you like Chanel No. 5, you'll LOVE [insert 'item for sale' here]!!!" The latest variation on this old ploy is "If you like Austen, you'll LOVE Austen with [insert 'zombies/vampires/yeti' here]." Numerous writers touted as "a modern-day Austen" have nothing more in common with her than the fact that somebody ends up married by the novel's conclusion.

If *Teléfono Ocupado* were one of today's ubiquitous Austen updates, it would have Emma married to Mr. Knightley in a comfortable, passionless marriage, sitting around all day taking boring phone calls from Miss Bates or Harriet Martin or her sister Isabella, people for whom she has affection but from whom she feels alienated. Then things would heat up when John Knightley's secretary calls to blackmail Emma, threatening to reveal her torrid affair with Mr. Knightley's brother prior to her marriage, back when Emma had gone off to London to discover herself and wound up working as a dancer in a nightclub. So… not very Austenesque.

Still, it's an interesting novel, good for someone learning Spanish. If you took *Teléfono Ocupado*'s theme of "too much time on the phone not really connecting" and substitute "too much time on Facebook, etc.," then the translation into the twenty-first century is pretty much seamless.

After a pleasant lunch with Teresa I decided to celebrate the fact that I now had five readers, all with *Emma* in hand. The San Telmo district is a magnet for tourists from abroad and from Argentina's other cities, thanks to an open-air market with stalls for antiques, handmade jewelry, and other types of crafts. There are dozens of small shops in the blocks surrounding the plaza with similar wares. The area is not as upscale as Palermo, a shopping hot spot more dedicated to clothing. San Telmo is rougher around the edges, a little more old Buenos Aires, tango and all.

That nippy winter day the pedestrian areas were packed. Street performers, each with a strategically located tip jar, competed for attention. A man in his sixties glided across the cobblestoned streets, tangoing languidly with a life-sized stuffed doll strapped to his body, marking a large circle of territory with his dips and turns. When a young woman tried to dodge through rather than fight the crowds around him, he tangoed her into a doorway on one side of the narrow street, rubbing against her in a way that would have been extremely lewd if there hadn't been a third party (albeit made of cloth) between them. Yet he never once made eye contact, pretending archly as though he hadn't seen her at all and was simply occupied with his faithful fabric partner.

Other tango dancers worked style rather than humor. Within a five-block radius, at least four different handsome couples glided across the cobblestones, dancing first with each other and then, after whetting the public's appetite, drawing new partners from the crowd and posing for photographs, all the while keeping an eye on their tip jars. Despite enjoying the display I couldn't help but feel sorry for the women, gorgeous in their billowy black skirts and tight-fitting, cleavage-enhancing tops, but ill-dressed for the chilly weather.

Stopping into a café bathroom, I interrupted a street dancer adjusting her stockings with one sleek, muscled leg propped up on the sink. Dressed all in black with a red scarf at her waist and beaded red feathers holding her dark hair slicked down in a tight bun, she wore dramatic makeup that would have looked cartoon-ish on the average woman—but she was anything but average.

I'm not in the habit of complimenting strangers in bathrooms, yet I couldn't stop myself. "You look so beautiful," I blurted out.

"Yes, it's true," she smiled, straightening her leg and smoothing down her skirt. There was no arrogance in her statement, no coyness—just unflinching confidence. "But, you know, I'm freezing my *tail* off out there."

I rejoined the crowd in San Telmo's small central square and was examining some handcrafted necklaces when I casually exchanged a glance with the woman next to me. Then we exchanged noisy cries of "Oh my *gaaawd!*" and big hugs. It was Tabitha, one of the students from Chile. She hadn't taken classes with me, but she was a close friend of Emily, the Canadian student.

"Emily's here, too. Sneak up on her!" Tabitha urged, giggling. Many of the students had had post-Chile tours planned. It was inevitable that some would wind up in a touristy part of alluring Buenos Aires, but I was thrilled we'd managed to cross paths.

Emily was checking out earrings several stalls down, and when I tapped her on the shoulder, she exclaimed and gave me a big surprised hug as well. After browsing a bit more, we took a taxi to *El Ateneo*. Originally a theater, the enormous, ornate structure had been converted into a bookstore, apparently the largest in Latin America. We exchanged school gossip in the store's café, set up where the former stage had been, and they caught me up on their recent travels through Bolivia and Peru.

"What about Taylor?" I asked. I hadn't had any email from her since Chile, and I'd been wondering what she'd decided about her hitchhiking venture.

"I heard that she stayed in Valparaiso after classes ended then went home," Tabitha said. "I think the plan is to improve her Spanish then come back for another trip."

I felt both relieved and a little sad. Hitchhiking straight through to Denver would have been madness—yet she had been so energized, so inspired by her time in Chile, that going straight home must have been a letdown for her. But if the spark that had been lit by her time in Chile (and by *El Che*) was really still burning, she'd find a way back. A true traveler always does.

"Silvina Bullrich?" Hugo snorted with disgust. After playing tourist I'd returned to the *Librería Romano*, despite my less-than-warm reception when I'd dropped off the *Emma*'s for him and the owner's girlfriend. I was still writing faithfully to Diego back in Mexico, and in the cold of an Argentinean winter, I fondly remembered steamy hikes in the jungle and lazy days floating in the sea by Diego's side. But I couldn't put Hugo out of my mind, distant (and grumpy) though he was. I went back to the bookstore with the flimsy excuse of wanting more reading recommendations and to update him on developments with the group.

"Bullrich—well, it's your time." He dismissed Teresa's recommendation with a shrug. "But there are lots of women writers here better and more important than Bullrich. Victoria Ocampo, for one. And if you're interested in classic literature, you need to read nineteenth-century women authors. Juana Manso, Eduarda Mansilla, Juana Manuela Gorriti. We have so many."

At long last, I'd finally found a country where women writers were making names for themselves in the same century as Austen. None of them is famous today, but Argentineans serious about literature, Hugo assured me, know who they were. They laid a foundation the best women writers of the twentieth century could build on, just as Austen carried forward (and bested) the successes of predecessors like Fanny Burney and Ann Radcliffe.

Along with their own talents, an important factor supporting women's success in Argentina was the intellectual climate fostered by that nineteenth-century president who, according to the bookstore's sign, was still in charge more than a hundred years after his death—Domingo Sarmiento. A scholar as well as a politician, Sarmiento, born in 1811, published on travel and other topics and made education a priority during his presidency, opening numerous schools and public libraries. His core idea that true democracy depends on an educated public seems obvious today but horrified the powerful, wealthy class, who preferred to keep their workers poor and ignorant.

And, scandal of scandals, Sarmiento dramatically improved women's education. Learning about him went a long way toward explaining what's distinctive about Argentinean culture. Women writers and artists from all over Latin America headed to Buenos Aires if they wanted to get published and be taken seriously, well into the twentieth century.

Then Hugo hauled out the heavy artillery for a nerdy American—Nancy Drew. I'd been hunting for translations of Nancy Drew since Guatemala, with no trace of the girl sleuth.

"Spaniards love to pretend they're the first to translate foreign literature into Spanish," Hugo said, pulling a face. "But along with lots of other works, Nancy Drew mysteries were translated here in the early sixties, well before they were in Spain."

When I finally got my hands on some copies later on, I was amused to see how Nancy's cup size magically plumped up south of the equator. The cover art for the translation of *The Bungalow Mystery* even has her in a nightie.

"Spain spent decades under a dictatorship after their civil war in the late 1930s, and that affected what works could be translated," Hugo explained. "But it's no excuse for them to ignore Argentinean literary accomplishments and pretend we have no culture except for Borges."

Pride, I thought, studying his handsome face as he waited for my reaction—pride in the best sense of the word, in the sense that Austen celebrates. He was proud of his country, proud of their strong tradition of education and literature and opportunities for women (and yes, even of Nancy Drew). And why not? Pride and arrogance are not the same thing, after all.

"I've been very impressed by everything I've learned here about literature," I assured him. "And I've never seen so many wonderful bookstores in any city, North or South America."

As he nodded and lifted his chin a notch higher still, I thought—well, a *bit* of arrogance isn't such a bad thing, either.

CHAPTER SEVENTEEN

As it turns out, there were Janeites in Buenos Aires well before I showed up. Poking around on the Internet, I came across a web page for JASBA—the Jane Austen Society of Buenos Aires. I emailed the contact address and that same day got an enthusiastic invitation for coffee from the president, Nadine.

It's human nature to fill in the visual blanks when you've exchanged mail but haven't met someone in person. I imagined Nadine was somewhere between forty and fifty, since anyone older was unlikely to use email regularly and anyone younger, unlikely to belong to a nerdy Jane Austen group, let alone serve as president. She'd have lovely dark hair and dark eyes and clothing that would make me jealous, and her scarf would be draped just so.

I got the stylish part right. Nadine spotted me quickly despite my best efforts to blend in and look chic in a scarf from Chile and some new clothes purchased the day before in Buenos Aires. Her carefully coiffed hair was an attractive shade of red, discreetly applied from a bottle—because she was clearly over eighty. So much for my assumptions about age and email. Nadine had the bright spirit, however, of a much younger woman.

"How lovely of you to contact us!" she cried, giving me a quick kiss on the cheek and drawing me to a table. She then switched into English, and I was surprised by her lack of accent until she explained that her father was American and her mother, French. "But I married a handsome Argentinean, and here I am, still! So, tell me all about your travels."

It felt good to speak English but when the waiter took our orders, we found our way back into Spanish. "We're a small group but very sociable," she explained. "How can you love Jane Austen and not be sociable? You must meet our founder, Mr. Dudgeon. He's not as young as he used to be, so we'll have to go to his house."

Coming from Nadine, I had to wonder just how old Mr. Dudgeon was.

I got the answer a week later when he invited me to a JASBA meeting at his apartment: ninety-three. But he, like Nadine, had the energy of a younger person as he led his Austen guests into his spacious ground floor apartment in an immense nineteenth-century building. There was something Dickensian about the high-ceilinged rooms, a bit musty from age and ringed with overflowing bookshelves. Modern Buenos Aires bustled by out-side, but Mr. Dudgeon's apartment felt suspended in time. A grave-looking print of a young Winston Churchill was promi-nently displayed in his dining room, and in the living room was a handsome portrait of Mr. Dudgeon himself done in the 1940s.

"That artist was quite famous in her day, my dear," Mr. Dudgeon explained in English when I complimented him on it. "She exhibited it in Paris after the war, between a portrait of the Pope and someone else famous." He gave a chuckle and added, "'A Man of No Importance,' my label read."

Mr. Dudgeon, who had emigrated from England in the mid-1930s, may have been "of no importance" compared to a pope, but he lay claim to a valuable literary credential in Argentina;

he'd been a friend of Borges for years and had published in *SUR*, Latin America's premier literary magazine from the 1930s through the 1980s. His survey of British literature, written in Spanish and tailored toward Argentineans, still circulated in used bookstores.

That afternoon in Mr. Dudgeon's quaint apartment, I asked him about Borges, but he wanted to stick with Jane Austen.

"We have a very nice newsletter, you know," he said proudly. "You must write something for us. Anything you like, my dear, as long as it's good. Promise me you will."

As I gave him my assurances, Nadine added, "We try to get together once a month, but we don't always manage." The two other members of the group sharing the couch with her nodded ruefully. "We do have a very nice Austen essay contest. You may have read about it on our web page."

Mr. Dudgeon harrumphed. "Computers. I don't like them. I'm just as happy writing someone a card, you know."

"If it hadn't been for JASBA's website, I would never have found you," I couldn't resist saying.

"Yes, my dear, that's true enough," he agreed. "These young ladies can handle things like web pages, but they're not for me." The "young ladies" in question exchanged a smile. Susana, the only member present who was Argentinean by birth, was in her mid-fifties. Nadine was in her eighties and Doris, the group's treasurer, past seventy. "And now, let's eat," he urged.

Mr. Dudgeon led us into his dining room for sandwiches, cakes, and tea. As we settled around the table, I asked, "Are you interested in the other types of literature about Austen, like the sequels and updates, or do you focus in your group on the novels themselves?"

"The novels are the most important thing, of course. But the films are crucial now, too, my dear." Mr. Dudgeon observed, helping himself to a sandwich. "Unparalleled in number, even by Dickens, and so many of them first rate. Of course, nothing replaces reading. I've been enjoying Agatha Christie lately. Did you know there's no mention of her in the *Cambridge History of English Literature*? Simply disgraceful."

Slowly clearing the table of satisfying food, we discussed Austen and Argentina and, after we made our way back into Mr. Dudgeon's living room, the beauties of Scotch, neat—although no one partook but our host. Perhaps the secret to his longevity?

"You can be very useful to us, my dear," he said as he settled into a high-backed chair directly in front of his portrait, a striking contrast between youthful good looks and, as Austen might put it, respectable old age. "A link to the States, you see. Let's have you as our U.S. liaison, shall we? An Austen liaison."

"What about 'correspondent?'" Nadine suggested. "I think 'U.S. correspondent' sounds better."

The group debated which title would be more fitting, and when "correspondent" was finally deemed the best, I was happy to agree. As so often happened during my travels, I was touched by the openness of people in Latin America—whether or not they were born there. I hadn't known a soul in this room a week earlier, and here we were, enjoying each others' company and making plans to stay in touch.

When Nadine signaled that she thought Mr. Dudgeon might be tiring, we ladies rose to leave. "Don't forget that article you promised us, my dear!" Mr. Dudgeon urged as he gave me a parting peck on the cheek.

"Patrick Dudgeon is *still alive?*"

Shortly after tea with the Janeites, Hugo—to my surprise and delight—invited me to lunch with two of his closest friends. Gabriela, a pretty woman in her thirties with short, curly brown hair and a sweet demeanor, owned her own bookstore. Roberto, an earnest, slender man a bit older than Hugo, helped her manage the place. Roberto read English well and was a huge fan of British and American lit. "I read Patrick Dudgeon's survey years ago, as well as articles he's published over the years," Roberto explained. "I had no idea he was still around! How on earth did you meet him after just showing up here?"

I was marveling myself at how smoothly things had gone since I'd arrived, a bit of new place panic aside. Not only had I socialized with the friendly Janeites and their founder, but I had already been to a play and a movie with Teresa from the National Library. And here I was talking books with book dealers. I had to admit, however, that my interest in Hugo was becoming more personal than professional. I took it as a good sign that he'd invited me to meet some of his friends, but since they were fellow book nerds, maybe he was just trying to help with my project. When I'd met Diego, he made clear from the first that he was interested in me—but Hugo was another matter. I didn't know how to say "Friend Zone" in Spanish, but I suspected I was there.

And that was good, right? I was already making email plans with Diego for his visit to California. Even in a city where I'd had amazing luck meeting warm, welcoming people, I still missed Diego's cheerful energy. I could just imagine how thrilled Diego would be to walk the crowded streets of Buenos Aires and share in my excitement about the city. Hugo was a different story altogether. However much he knew about books (and vampire films and the U.S. library system), he was, in fact, a pretty grumpy guy.

Swapping bookstore war stories made that amusingly clear. When Gabriela and Roberto learned that I'd worked for years for a book dealer, first in West Virginia and later in Florida, they were curious about the book business in the United States. We exchanged stories about, among other things, difficult customers—and no one had as many doozies as Hugo.

"I could have been fired from the store immediately," he said, tackling his second plate of entrees at the *tenedor libre* style restaurant. This means "free fork," or, as we'd say in English, all you can eat. "Argentineans are famous for arguing about everything, and it's no different in bookstores. Maybe it's worse in bookstores. Anyway, I threw someone out my very first week."

The customer's offense? Losing his cool over C. S. Lewis's *Chronicles of Narnia*. Somehow they got on the subject and Hugo referred to the Christian allegory of the books ("The noble, merciful lion is killed by his foes and comes back in spirit, even stronger? Of course it's an allegory!"). The customer took offense and demanded that Hugo retract his offensive statement. Then it went something like this:

Hugo: In my opinion those books *are* a Christian allegory, and you need to stop shouting.

Angry Zealot: You can't say that! That's blasphemy! And I'll shout if I like!

Hugo: Not in this store, you won't. You need to leave.

Angry Zealot: Who are *you* to throw me out?!

Hugo: The police can do it, if you'd rather—or I can do it with a few swift kicks.

Angry Zealot: I'm calling the owner! You're going to be fired!

Enter Ernesto, aka jolly Edmund Gwenn as Mr. Bennet. Since Hugo had worked there less than a week, he couldn't be sure how things would turn out, but Ernesto saved the day.

"My goodness, I'm so sorry!" exclaimed Ernesto when the customer returned the next day, demanding Hugo's head on a platter. Tsk-tsking like a disappointed grandpa, Ernesto set to work. "Poor Hugo is such an antifascist that he gets carried away with himself sometimes. It's really quite shocking! Come now, let's take a look at this over here…" Lulled by Ernesto's soothing manner and guileless, placid expression, the man didn't register that he'd just been called a fascist (kind of the same way he hadn't registered that Lewis's works are a Christian allegory). And so began a beautiful relationship between Hugo, dubbed on the Internet by one irate customer as "*el tirano*"—the tyrant—and Ernesto, who could always put customers in their place without losing his perpetual smile.

"It's a vice of ours," Roberto smiled, "this need to argue about everything. Remember, Hugo, the author who got mad because you were charging only five pesos for a used copy of his book? And Ernesto calmly walked the guy over to a five peso edition of Shakespeare? 'Don't confuse price with value, my friend!' Ernesto bests people all of the time without ruffling their feathers. But when Hugo's riled, everybody knows it."

As for me, I was thrilled to be in a place where people cared enough about books to duke it out verbally over allegory and literary value!

Wrangling wasn't limited to book clerks and their clients, I soon came to learn. There were rivalries between booksellers, as well. Shortly after my lunch with Hugo and his friends, I found my way into yet another bookshop.

"You've come all the way from California and here you are in my humble store? How lovely!" The owner was a handsomely dressed man in his late fifties with thick salt-and-pepper hair, a neatly trimmed beard, and a slightly rakish air. "Come and have a cup of coffee!" He led me to the back of the store where another woman, already enjoying a coffee, sat paging slowly through a book. Doing a double take, I saw that it was a Spanish translation of Claire Tomalin's biography of Jane Austen.

Seriously.

I had fallen into a literary rabbit hole, with Austen readers popping out of every hedge. As the owner set about making me a coffee, the woman introduced herself as Cristina. Somewhere in her sixties with jet-black hair and a strikingly pale complexion, she had a refined way about her that reminded me of Leti in Ecuador.

"You're here doing a book group? I adore book groups!" She set Tomalin aside and invited me to sit beside her. "Of course it all depends on the people. Sometimes the conversations just turn into group therapy, and that's a bore. And so many people can't move past narrative when they talk about a novel. What fascinates me is language itself. My mother was French, and I do French-to-Spanish translations."

Perhaps I should introduce her to Nadine. Intrigued, I did the only reasonable thing—I invited her to join the group.

"*Mi amor*, that would be wonderful! But I don't have a copy of *Emma*."

She was *not* getting away. I promptly wrote down the address of the *Librería Romano*. "There's a spare copy at this bookstore. You could go today and pick it up from Hugo, the clerk. Just tell him I sent you."

The owner swooped in, a look of distress on his face as he handed me my coffee. "You're doing a book group at Romano's? Well, I'm jealous! You could do it here, you know. This is a fine bookstore. Why not do it here, right, Cristina?" Cristina took a noncommittal sip of her coffee. He frowned, then turned his smile back on and continued, "Well, it's just that Ernesto and I, we've got a bit of a…friendly competition going on." Somehow, when he said the word "friendly," he looked anything but. "There's room here!"

Employing tact can be difficult in one's own language, let alone a second. As best as my Spanish allowed, I told him I appreciated his offer but didn't want to offend anyone by making a change. While he'd been generous to invite me in for coffee, there was something about him I found a little shady. Whether to change my mind or to show me what I was missing by slighting his store, he then slipped into a private office and returned with some of his best treasures to show off, including a Virginia Woolf first edition.

"These are a bit pricey, as you can imagine," he said archly; pricier than you could afford, his look implied. Perhaps it was my imagination, but I'm pretty sure I saw Cristina roll her eyes ever so gently in his direction before smiling at me and turning her attention back to Austen.

Too much backstory. Time to be going. I browsed the shelves and bought something (in my modest price range…) that looked interesting. Then I took my leave after exchanging contact information with Cristina and urging her to stop by Romano's for the copy of *Emma*.

"Of course I will, *mi amor*!"

I'd repeatedly been warned that since it's considered rude to decline invitations in Latin America, knowing when "yes" means "no" is tricky business. Nearly a year into my travels, I was still clueless at detecting the difference. But Cristina seemed like a very interesting woman, so I would just have to keep my fingers crossed.

Back in Mexico when I had achieved Book Overload, Diego had taken me out for an evening of boxing to change things up. Probably the appropriate choice in Buenos Aires would be to watch a soccer match or take tango lessons. But I wanted to do something more Austenesque and, in particular, something inspired by lodging in a ritzy *Emma* neighborhood. Promenading around one afternoon, I spotted a small shop where a group of women were gathered around a table, chatting and doing embroidery.

The attractive, middle-aged owner greeted me at the door. "You're welcome to join us," she smiled. "But if you're a beginner, it's best if you wait until my daughter is here. She's the one who teaches the group."

Liking the ambiance of the shop, stocked full of attractive fabric and patterns, I paid for a lesson in advance, pocketed the receipt, and returned two days later. The women stitching at the table welcomed me graciously, introducing themselves and asking questions about California. "You're welcome to see our work," a grandmotherly woman seated to my left offered, "but I'd recommend you start with a simpler pattern." She was embroidering a scene of the Virgin Mary and Jesus, while the woman on my right was stitching the name "María" into the center of a wreath of ivy. The others obligingly held up their projects—a farm scene with chickens and ducks, an overflowing fruit basket, and most attractive of all, an artistic spray of delicate flowers on silk done in tones of dark gold, chartreuse, and burnt orange.

Needlework of all sorts figures into Austen's novels since any woman of her day, regardless of class standing, would be expected to sew. A poor woman's skills would run the gamut from making her family's garments to creating whatever curtains, table linens, or bedclothes the family income could sustain. An "accomplished" woman of means would be expected to produce decorative work and keep her pretty hands from idleness— perhaps, like Lady Bertram from *Mansfield Park*, with "some long piece of needlework, of little use and no beauty."

Throughout her surviving letters Austen refers to this bonnet she's retrimming or that gown she's refurbishing. If you visit Chawton Cottage you can enjoy, among other things, seeing a delicate embroidered handkerchief worked by Austen's own hand and an elaborate patchwork quilt she made with her mother and Cassandra. As striking a thought as it may be for fans today, it's likely Austen spent at least as many hours a day sewing as she ever did writing—or more.

I'd never hit that sort of balance, but I could at least dabble in the classically feminine world of the sewing circle. I bought a needle and fabric and, with the owner's help, selected a simple pattern of violets in a basket while the others carried on without the teacher, who finally rushed in fifteen minutes late.

"Darling, we're going to have a new student today," the owner said as her daughter swept past. "She's a visitor from the United States."

"Some *Yanki* tourist?" the slender twentysomething said with undisguised annoyance, dropping her coat and scarf onto a chair without having turned to look at the group. "That's just great, Mother. You're kidding, right?

"No, darling, I'm not kidding. She's already here." Her smile stretched uncomfortably at her daughter's behavior. "*And* she speaks Spanish."

Bingo! One of the best things about learning another language is the opportunity to surprise people who don't expect you to speak it. For as much as you hear about anti-Americanism in Latin America, I'd expected moments like this long before— but either people were very discreet or just not as interested in *gringa*-bashing as international gossip might lead you to believe. It's probably the former, but I'm enough of a cockeyed optimist (i.e., American) to go for the latter.

I decided to run with the situation, giving the cranky young teacher my biggest Dorky American Tourist smile while calling out, "*Hola!*" She still couldn't manage to wipe the irritation off her face, despite the obvious prompting from her embarrassed mother, so I rubbed it in further, thrusting my hand cheerfully in the air and waving at her. *Yes, that's right. I sure am crass!*

The woman stitching Mary and Jesus gave me a reassuring pat on the arm, murmuring something about "young people," and the rest of the ladies redoubled their efforts to be kind. When it became clear that the teacher intended to reward my aggressive *Yanki* friendliness by ignoring me, the ladies offered advice, and slowly my little basket of violets took shape.

Despite a promising start, I began to make one mistake after another, and my violets wilted on the fabric. Stitchery and I, it seemed, were not cut out for each other. My sister Laurie has mastered pretty much every needle art despite flunking junior high home economics (more for mouthing off to the teacher than for lack of skill; hassling teachers runs in our family, even for those of us who turned out to *be* teachers). When Laurie settled down to married life at age eighteen, she not only learned to knit—she bought Angora rabbits, fed them from her own garden, taught herself how to spin, turned their fur into thread, and *then* knitted.

Alas, talent with stitchery was clearly not genetic. I returned for another lesson, and Señorita Sourpuss was just as neglectful as ever. I smeared the violets around a bit more with my needle, then, after enjoying the progress of the other ladies' fruit, religious figures, and chickens, I decided to finish the "lesson" and move on. I'd never rival Austen or any of her characters for needlework, even Lady Middleton, but I'd passed two pleasant hours gossiping and learning new *porteño* slang. Especially interesting was how the women used the phrase "*qué bárbaro, qué baaarbaro!*" every second or third sentence both to indicate "how wonderful!" and "how terrible!" A very flexible word.

As it turned out, I needed to abandon more than the leisure of the embroidery circle. When I sat down and worked on my finances for the month, I realized I would have to renounce my ritzy apartment and downgrade.

Well, if Austen's Miss Bates could survive her slide from wealth into genteel poverty with good cheer, so could I.

I paged through a city guide and settled on a hotel along the Avenida de Mayo, the broad artery that leads to the city's central square, the Plaza de Mayo. Fortunately they had space for the rest of my visit, and when I finished out the week I'd prepaid in my current accommodations, I packed my retinue of fanciful animals and fabrics and bid *au revoir* to the staff.

The new hotel wasn't exactly "genteel poverty," but it also wasn't the style I'd become accustomed to. On Juncal I'd had a spacious bathroom, a dining area, a full kitchen, and a very attractive living room. Now I had a single room so narrow I could hardly drag my suitcases through the space between the bed and wall. Since I'd been thrilled to find anything in the city center in July, I'd failed to notice how the wallpaper was peeling and the exposed floorboards in front of the bathroom swayed underfoot like the deck of ship. The shower curtain was too short, which led to a soaked floor with each shower. An odor of sewage, which I'd also failed to notice when I'd agreed on the room, permeated everything.

As self-pity swept over me, I felt an accompanying wave of belated travel panic. What had I been thinking, blowing my money on that expensive apartment? Why hadn't I searched out some middle ground? There wasn't even room in this new place to display my llamas! What was I even doing there? And what if nobody showed up for the group, after my hanging around for weeks, spending money? Hugo *el tirano* might just throw me out of the bookstore anyway the next time I showed up, if he decided he didn't like *Emma*.

Arrrrghh!

Maudlin, I fled the room and boomeranged back to my old neighborhood for a Marianne-style wallow. Ah, the streets where I'd lived! Eventually I wandered into a church, one of the most gorgeous I'd seen in all of my travels, a spot I had already visited several times. I sat quietly, absorbing the tranquility of the surroundings. Finally, having calmed down somewhat, I headed for the door, pausing to gaze at an ornate statue of the Virgin Mary with offerings of rosaries draped over her, a painted label at her feet: "*Yo soy la protectora de los desamparados*"—I am the protector of the helpless.

Descending the staircase, I walked past a teenage girl sitting with a baby. She raised a hand toward me. Still wrapped up in my own problems, I continued for half a block then jerked myself to a halt in the center of the sidewalk.

I'd done plenty of work with nonprofits in the United States, and employees at shelters advise not to give money to people on the street; you're most likely fueling an addiction. But this wasn't California with its numerous soup kitchens. Who knows what kind of safety nets there were in Argentina? I headed back and handed the girl enough money to eat for the day while well-dressed locals leaving the church passed her by without a glance. Maybe they had compassion burnout. Maybe they'd given her money on the way in. Maybe they wrote a big check to a shelter every month. Or maybe not. *¿Quién sabe?* Who knew?

My mother was raised Catholic; my father converted when he was in the Air Force. Visiting the Vatican was a powerful moment for him, a moving renewal of his adopted faith. As for my mother—she unexpectedly found herself shocked at the sight of such outrageous wealth. "Don't tell your father I said this," she confessed later, "but I kept thinking about how many people they could feed if they'd just sell off a few treasures."

Indeed. I'd had that same schizophrenia since the moment I'd set foot in Latin America, given the contrast between the striking loveliness of historic churches and the often desperate poverty of the general population. On the one hand, most churches were open long hours, and people could visit and feel ownership in the beautiful communal space, rich with memories of baptisms, weddings, and funerals. On the other hand, each elaborate statue or ornate cross could be translated into a scholarship fund for parishioners' kids, couldn't it? And shouldn't God be there, crosses or no crosses, statues or no statues, if there *was* a god?

I had no answers, especially not that day.

One of the most subtle, insightful moments in *Emma* happens after she and Harriet have delivered aid to some needy villagers. "These are the sights, Harriet, to do one good," Emma says as they leave the miserable abode. "How trifling they make everything else appear!—I feel now as if I could think of nothing but these poor creatures all the rest of the day; and yet, who can say how soon it may all vanish from my mind?"

A wise woman, Emma, however foolishly she behaved at times. She knew that even her acts of charity were self-serving—how helping others allowed her to help herself, how the sight of their misery intensified the glow of her own good fortune. In her heart she knew that the pain she felt for the suffering of others would fade the closer she moved back toward her own circle, her own people.

And what about my circle, my people? I'd been so far from them for so long. I traversed several blocks before I found a cybercafé with both computers and phone cabins. First, I wrote to Diego, telling him how much I missed him, despite feeling conflicted with guilt over my growing interest in Hugo *el tirano*. I told Diego how cold it was, just so he wouldn't feel too badly about not being there. More than half a year back, in what now seemed like another world, he'd told me, "I'm glad you don't live in Pennsylvania anymore. I'm not cut out for cold weather. Not even for a visit. I need the sun!"

Then I called my mother. I was feeling dangerously needy but was saved from having her detect that in my voice (and cycle into concern for me) by the fact that she'd been watching golf, which always sent her into a happy monologue. "Angel Cabrera is Argentinean, you know. Have you talked with people about Angel Cabrera? He won the U.S. open. I think he's the first Argentinean to win it. I don't like it when anybody beats Tiger, of course, but this Angel seems like a gentleman. Very handsome, too. But not as handsome as Tiger."

My reserved, extremely modest mother had, after my father's death, developed a sort of schoolgirl crush on Tiger Woods (before The Fall). A woman who never cared about sporting events aside from sacred Steelers games, she'd begun spending hours in front of the TV learning shot types and club preferences.

If that made her happy, so be it. Hearing her voice, birdies and bogeys and all, made me happy.

I returned to the new room determined to count my blessings and focus on the positives: the great central location and, best of all, the balcony. Stepping outside, I surveyed the crowded Avenida de Mayo below, then gazed up at the sky. I'd made it home in good time since it clearly was about to rain.

As the sky opened up I realized, suddenly, that it wasn't rain falling at all. It was *snow*. Snow in Buenos Aires. I was under the impression that it didn't snow here, although the day certainly felt cold enough for it. As the thick, wet flakes fell faster, people on the sidewalk two stories below began to exclaim in surprise.

I went to the phone and called reception. The woman was laughing as she picked up the receiver.

"Does it usually snow here?" I asked.

"It *never* snows here!" Reception had a view of the glass double-doors facing the street, so I knew she realized my question wasn't hypothetical.

When I stepped back out, the couple with the adjoining balcony were outside embracing, gazing up at the whitening sky. They turned as they heard me appear and greeted me with delight in their voices.

"It's just so beautiful!" the woman said, stretching out both hands to catch flakes. "I've never seen snow!"

On the streets below, happy chaos was erupting. The usual hectic pace of traffic slowed as people grappled with the strange new weather condition. The shops and cafés emptied, the sidewalks suddenly full of adults-turned-children, running, laughing, and trying to scrape together snowballs. For a native Pennsylvanian, it wasn't much of a snow—too wet for effective snow warfare, too thin for a serious accumulation. But this wasn't Pennsylvania.

In 1918, Rudyard Kipling was reading Jane Austen novels aloud to his family to ease the pain of the Great War. In 1918, the first scholarly edition of Austen's novels by Oxford's press was still five years in the future. Virginia Woolf was eleven years shy of publishing her famous description of Austen in *A Room of One's Own*. Austen herself had been dead for 101 years; Mr. Patrick Dudgeon was four. And it snowed in Buenos Aires.

That, according to the evening news, was the last time it had.

Yes, I had a wet shower floor. My room smelled sewage-y. The slits and gouges in the wallpaper formed themselves into creepy patterns if you looked at them long enough. And yes, people would go hungry or homeless (or both) that night, and I couldn't do a damned thing about it. All this was undeniable.

So was the snow outside my balcony and the noisy joy of the people on the street below, people who no doubt had their problems, too.

CHAPTER EIGHTEEN

Shortly before my final Austen group I stopped by Edmund Gwenn's bookstore, ostensibly to see if Cristina, my latest invite for the group, had come by for *Emma*. Good news—she had! When I mentioned wanting to visit La Boca, Hugo offered to take me on his day off. "You shouldn't go alone. Some areas there aren't safe." I'll admit it; that was just what I'd been hoping he'd say.

A colorful dockyard neighborhood, La Boca was once infamous for seedy tango bars, brothels, and crime. Now with a noticeable police presence to protect the tourist dollars, it's a hugely popular spot, with distinctive nineteenth-century architecture. Some buildings are renovated to period style, others decked with riotous pastel colors and enormous murals. As in San Telmo, tango dancers work the streets along with other entertainers, from roving Brazilian drummers to the inevitable artists dressed as statues who swing into motion for a coin.

Before Hugo arrived I spent the morning primping in the tiny bathroom, trying to avoid the huge puddle dumped out by my shower. He came by at ten, and, after a lengthy bus ride, we had coffee in La Boca then visited a museum with a fascinating collection of ships' figureheads. Later we found ourselves walking the full length of the docks, mostly out of service. A scattering of artists were there with easels set up to capture the picturesquely decaying warehouses and rusting hulks of abandoned ships.

By evening we'd covered a lot of ground, verbally and on foot. We talked Gothic literature, Argentinean politics, and the 1960s vampire soap opera *Dark Shadows*, among other topics, first over coffee, then lunch, then dinner, then late-night ice cream. Somehow it was eleven o'clock by the time Hugo walked me back to my hotel.

"Do you realize we just spent thirteen hours together?" I said, stopping outside the main doors.

His expression softened. "Well," he said with a smile, one of the few I'd seen from him. "That's a record for me. I'm just not sociable. I'm very close to my friends, but I don't have many. But with you, the day went by so fast."

And that was the moment he would lean in for a kiss. Everything about the day—the intense conversations, the meals, everything—had felt like a date. We locked eyes as the pedestrian traffic swirled past us. 11:00 p.m. is early for Buenos Aires; plenty of people would have barely finished dinner.

"I'm looking forward to the group," he said. His deep, richly accented Spanish made even the most mundane statement sound sexy. I caught myself leaning forward, ever so slightly.

Then he said good night and turned abruptly to find a taxi.

All right, then…no kiss. How *could* I have read him so wrong?

My parting with Hugo a few days earlier hadn't ended quite like I'd hoped, but I still had Austen.

"This is Susie. She's very excited to talk about *Emma*!" Teresa introduced her friend before taking a seat in the spacious basement of the *Librería Romano*. "But I'm afraid our other friend couldn't make it."

My final Austen group, at long last, was underway.

"I'm sorry I wasn't able to join you and Teresa for that film on Edith Piaf," Susie said as she gave me a greeting kiss on the cheek. "I heard you had a nice time." A pleasant-looking woman in her mid-fifties, she had dark eyes and extremely short, curly brown hair that made a striking contrast with Teresa's blue eyes and long blond locks. In demeanor as well they were a study in opposites. Where Teresa was animated to the point of appearing a bit jumpy, at times, Susie was cool and collected. Both women were nicely dressed but more like the average American than some of the other women I'd met in Buenos Aires.

"The movie was fabulous," I admitted as I showed her to a seat in the circle. "The audience actually sang along with '*La vie en rose*' and '*Je ne regrette rien*.' They even clapped at the end."

Susie and Teresa had met when Susie's husband and Teresa found themselves in the same Yiddish class, which Teresa had pursued to complement her advanced study of Hebrew. Buenos Aires has Latin America's largest Jewish population, a community of approximately 250,000. Unfortunately, the city also has a history of anti-Semitism. Our gathering that evening fell on the anniversary of the bombing in 1994 of AMIA, an important Jewish cultural center. Eighty-five people were killed. Because the investigation was badly botched—on purpose, many suspected—no one was ever convicted for the massacre. Teresa's Polish ancestors had immigrated to Argentina to escape anti-Semitism, but ugly ideologies cross borders.

"Who else will be joining us?" she asked, pulling her copy of *Emma* from an attractive handbag.

"The owner's girlfriend Carolina should be here any minute," I responded. "Also, a woman named Cristina who I met at another bookstore. Hugo, who works here, will be down shortly, too. He has to watch the shop until Ernesto and Carolina get here."

As if on cue, Hugo descended the stairs with a frown. "Carolina forgot which date we were meeting," he said, unable to keep irritation from creeping into his tone. "She scheduled something else, instead. My boss is here now, but I'll go back upstairs to wait for Cristina."

Next cue, Cristina: "Here I am! I'm here!" she cried from the top of the stairs. "You didn't start without me, did you?"

She descended, scooted past Hugo, and took a chair. Before I had a chance to make introductions, *bang*—we were off to the races. The readers jumped in to discuss *Emma* before I could even get the digital recorder on.

"What really got my attention," began Cristina, while twisting in her seat to take off her scarf and jacket, "is how the characters treated each other." Now that I had more time to observe her, I could see that Cristina, attractively dressed and elegantly made up, was older than I'd first assumed, closer to seventy than to sixty. Her voice had a thin, reedy quality, but there was nothing feeble about her opinions and her capacity to express them.

"I had a hard time keeping track of all those characters," Teresa cut in. "I had to write them down to sort them out."

With that, the cross-talking began. I thought the Ecuador group had been rough in that respect. Now I was more thankful than ever I had the recorder. It was just as well I hadn't invited more people and that two hadn't shown up, after all—no one would have been able to hear anybody else for all of the eagerness to discuss the work. Everyone was speaking at once about the basic relations among the characters when Hugo cut across through sheer volume.

"My favorite among the female characters was Jane Fairfax," he said.

The women stopped talking and observed him, curious. "Why?" Teresa asked.

"She has all of the sensibility Emma lacks."

"Such as?" Teresa pursued.

"Artistic sensibility, for instance," he offered.

"That's right," Cristina agreed. "Emma—"

"She's a kind of Celestina," Hugo continued. This, I later discovered, was a matchmaking busybody from classic Spanish literature. "But she's not as bad as Mrs. Elton, whose only motivation is social climbing. Emma is actually the opposite of her, because when she realizes she's hurt someone, like when she messes things up by pushing Mr. Elton on Harriet, Emma tries to make it right. Mrs. Elton doesn't feel anything for anyone."

"But Mr. Knightley, he's a sort of protector," Cristina began, leaning forward eagerly in her chair.

"Almost like something from the Middle Ages," Hugo agreed, picking up the idea. "What he feels for Emma is a kind of love that isn't spoken about and isn't really sexual. It's almost metaphysical."

"Absolutely," Cristina concurred.

Hugo continued: "And it can last a lifetime, this kind of love. That's what he has to offer Emma, since she's obviously not going to fall in love with him sexually. In fact, when she fantasizes about men, it's that younger one."

A lot of academic ink has been spilled on the subject of sexuality in *Emma*, since there's something just a bit too parental in the Emma/Mr. Knightley pairing, in comparison to the obvious chemistry between Lizzy and Mr. Darcy. Hugo's idea of respect-ful, courtly love was intriguing.

"That's right. Emma thinks about the good-looking one," Cristina agreed, while Susie and Teresa nodded.

"Exactly," Hugo continued. "But in the end, like a good Englishwoman—" I turned to him, curious to hear where this was going, and Hugo cleared his throat and clarified. "Like *any* woman might, Emma chose intelligence over good looks. Something that lasts."

Raising the idea of what a woman wants in a man led to a discussion of Austen herself. Cristina asked if she had ever been married. I clarified some details about her life, especially in response to Teresa asking if Austen was a feminist, an issue that had come up in several of the other groups as well.

With a look at her friend Susie, who was listening attentively but had yet to make any comments, Teresa stated, "I think Austen had an incredible intuition for the psychology of women. She was way ahead of her time. Almost all women have something of Emma in them."

"There's universality, it's true," Hugo overlapped.

"Our strengths and our weaknesses, they're all there," Teresa continued. "Women, all of us, we've got a bit of each of those different women Austen created."

Now it was official. Without any prompting from me—just like in Guatemala, Mexico, Ecuador, Chile, and Paraguay, to one degree or another—the readers in Argentina felt the connection between Austen's world and their own.

"That's why we can still read her today," Cristina agreed. "It's definitely not traditionally feminine, the kind of rebelliousness in Emma's character."

"When she's talking about other women, for instance," Teresa said, "I really get the feeling that she's just saying out loud what lots of women would like to say but don't. Maybe because of being raised to be 'polite' or our nervousness about being honest."

"The kind of things Emma says about Jane Fairfax, for instance?" I asked. And about Miss Bates, I was about to add, when Teresa responded, "Exactly."

"Emma does finally come to understand Jane Fairfax, though." Hugo commented. "Everyone responds to her arrival in their closed-off little social circle. Some see her as an interloper, but for others, she's a kind of mirror. She lets people see their own weaknesses or vices, which, until she showed up, they didn't even realize they had. She forces people to understand themselves better."

I was struck by Hugo's insight into the role Jane Fairfax performs in the novel. Sometimes being forced to look in the mirror is a daunting prospect, and she definitely sets off shockwaves around her. Teresa seemed to concur.

"Emma responds by creating that fantasy, the idea that Jane must be the lover of her best friend's husband," she observed.

"Jane was whose lover?" Cristina asked, surprised.

"Nobody's lover. It was just what Emma imagined," Teresa clarified.

Susie, nodding wryly, finally joined the conversation. "Well, that's what happens at times among women."

"We speculate out loud with friends about things," Teresa added.

Hugo raised an eyebrow, apparently surprised to hear women repeating a less-than-flattering stereotype about their own gender. "Well, I'm at a disadvantage on this subject since I'm the only man here."

Before we could head further down that road, the sound of

chipper electronic music made us all jump. Susie, looking embarrassed, made an apologetic gesture and reached into her bag to turn off her cell phone. Our conversation immediately fractured into two, with Cristina turning to ask me about other British literature while Hugo and Teresa began to debate the difference between what Emma says versus what the narrative voice reveals about her.

After a few moments, Hugo seemed to realize that I was unsure how to refocus our conversation.

"Ladies, please," he interrupted, and after a beat of silence, we found ourselves making all of the introductions we'd bypassed earlier.

"What's your name?" Cristina asked Hugo. Teresa stepped in and introduced him, then herself, then Susie. "And you," Cristina asked me, laughing at her own forgetfulness. "You know, I don't even remember *your* name!"

"Amy," I said.

"Emmy? Really?" Cristina exclaimed. There is no hard "a" sound in Spanish equivalent to what we use in English for the name Amy. In every Latin American country I'd visited people called me Emmy, and I had long since given up correcting anybody. On an Austen-inspired trip, I'd come to see it as kind of appropriate. "Emma, Emmy; Emma, Emmy!" Cristina repeated, giving me a wink.

Hugo drew us back into the book with a new line of thought. "About this translation," he began, reaching under his chair to set his copy on his lap.

"I think this is a very good translation," Susie spoke up.

At the same time that Hugo agreed, Teresa shook her head. "Good? I don't think it's so good."

"It's horrid!" Cristina concurred. Suddenly everyone was talking at once, with Cristina repeating "Horrid!" while Hugo tried to defend the translation.

"I'm a translator—I know what I'm talking about!" As Cristina cut through the discussion with that declaration, it occurred to me that language and translation were hallmarks of this particular group, just as poets had predominated in Chile. Unlike Cristina, Hugo hadn't published his work, but translation was a long-standing hobby. While his spoken English was weak his reading skills were excellent, and he'd been translating science fiction and Gothic stories from English into Spanish for decades. He'd passed several stories on to me, curious to have my opinion. Teresa didn't publish translations, but she taught Hebrew lessons, which gave her a special sensitivity to language, as well. Susie and I were the amateurs that night.

Hugo and Cristina continued debating the translator's tendency to use a style that apparently comes out as stilted in Spanish. "He says in the introduction," Hugo said, "that he's trying to maintain the style of the period."

"You can't reproduce an English style in Spanish," Cristina declared flatly. "It's impossible." She offered up several examples of wording she thought was especially bad, including the sentence "*La indudable convicción de lo sano que era comer gachas.*"

Susie made a humorous face. "What does '*gachas*' mean?"

Cristina threw her hands up in exaggerated confusion, as if to say, "That's my point!"

I'd certainly never heard the word "*gachas*" before, but considering the rest of the sentence, "the firm conviction of the healthfulness of eating *gachas*," I realized that we must have entered Mr. Woodhouse territory.

"I think it's like porridge," Hugo speculated, "but that's a Scottish dish."

Having no idea how to translate "thin gruel" into Spanish, I explained instead that it was a bland dish nobody except a serious hypochondriac would eat voluntarily.

Hugo nodded then cut me off to point out that one shouldn't judge the translation by a few awkward words. Cristina cut him off in turn. "I can find you twenty or thirty like that!" Teresa, Susie, and I fell silent as the two argued on. Hugo asserted that Valverde, the translator, was one of the best currently working in Spain. Cristina conceded that he was better with dialogue than description. In no time they had sidetracked into a new issue, with Cristina claiming that Borges had translated Virginia Woolf's *The Waves* and Hugo arguing that his mother had done the actual work while Borges took the credit. They talked on simultaneously for several minutes, neither listening to the other, while the rest of us tried to follow along.

"Well, one thing's for sure—it would have been easier to translate from French or Italian," Cristina said, circling back to Austen. "But if this translation had been a bit freer, if he hadn't tried to reproduce the structure of English sentences, it would be better. It's just too stilted."

Teresa tried to jump in, but Hugo's voice carried over hers. "That formality is part of the novel," he insisted. "We're used to much lighter, quicker writing today, but a translation like that of *Emma* would change everything. In Austen's day you'd savor a novel like this, page by page, for a month. But we had to read this quickly to have it done for this evening, and that makes the weightiness of the style more noticeable."

"Well, that's true," Cristina agreed, "but—"

"What I was trying to explain," Teresa interrupted, "is that Austen's formal style is more than a product of her time period. It's a conscious choice. It's her way of creating a specific environment, the slow pace, of that country village. It's deliberate. But her way of balancing that, it seems to me, is her use of short chapters. That really keeps things moving, because—"

Hugo and Cristina both talked over Teresa, Hugo to second her point about the effectiveness of the chapter divisions, Cristina to continue lambasting the translation. Susie and I exchanged glances as Teresa, impatient, weighed back in.

"Look, if we all keep talking at the same time, Amy's never going to understand a word of it!"

Susie took advantage of the brief silence that ensued. "Yes, it's a slow novel, but it's about basic things, about little events, one after another. None are major, but they build on each other, as the days pass for Emma. One day some question arises, some little happening, a new personality surfaces who changes things, and that's how we're hooked."

Teresa nodded enthusiastically. "And if you're reading carefully, you'll realize that in those little details Austen offers, there are hints of things that will happen down the road."

On that point, Cristina agreed. "The plot does draw you in."

"But when it comes down to it, the surprises aren't really surprises in the end," Susie added. "Mr. Knightley, he's really kind of a Pygmalion type, and when he's always correcting Emma's faults, it's clear how things will turn out between them."

"But it's interesting how this novel destroys the myth of the fairy tale," Teresa said. "Nobody marries Prince Charming. Everybody ends up with somebody at their same social level, somebody—"

"Everything in its place," Hugo agreed. This set off a debate, however, about the Mr. and Mrs. Elton pairing, since she's distinctly more vulgar even though she's the one with more money.

"It's important to clarify what you mean by levels—economics and culture are two different things," Teresa pointed out. "We still have stratification to this day on both levels."

No one begged to differ on that point.

"But on the cultural level, things get worse all the time here," Cristina lamented. "I've got three daughters-in-law, and they never lift a book. They can't understand how I can read all day. There's no culture, no culture anymore…"

I immediately wondered about her sons—how often did they lift a book? As if reading my mind, Hugo said, "Well, the fact is, there are a lot more women than men attending universities here. Just imagine, knowing that before, women couldn't even get in."

Since we'd shifted so completely from Highbury to Argentina, I asked, "Is it true, historically, that women had better opportunities in Buenos Aires than in other cities in Latin America?"

Susie, typically quiet, didn't hesitate to state, "Buenos Aires has always had a much higher level of culture than other Latin American capitals."

I could imagine readers from my other groups—especially the Chileans—wincing to hear such a bald statement. And Luis, that sharp-tongued lover of literature from Antigua, what would he have said? I suspect he would have been forced to agree—then he would have capped off the point with a nice "arrogant Argentinean" joke (he'd been, in fact, my best source for them). But there were no arguments on that point in the room. Cristina added, "But from here, we've always, *always* been looking to Paris."

"Always," Teresa and Susi echoed, while Hugo raised an eyebrow and shrugged. He wasn't disagreeing, but I knew that his cultural preferences lay more with Great Britain than France.

"I recently learned about the British invasion of Buenos Aires," I said. "It was fascinating to think that the British tried to take over this country."

"Some people here say the mistake was driving the British out." Hugo smiled wryly. "Others disagree and are glad we stuck with the Spanish." That topic got us back in the ballpark of Austen, but since everyone was still talking at the same time, Teresa once again blew the whistle on us. Susie stepped into the momentary quiet to ask about the social status of a governess.

After we spent some time talking about work for women and Jane Fairfax, Hugo asked, "There's been kind of a revival of interest in Austen in the last twenty years, hasn't there?"

"Definitely. It has to do with feminism, as one factor," I explained. "And it's been fascinating, because she's really the only writer to have a serious literary reputation *and* a huge popular following."

"That is unusual," Hugo agreed, and the point sent him off into an anecdote about an episode of an American TV show he'd seen where a boy gives his girlfriend a copy of *Pride and Prejudice* as a birthday present.

"I want to get back to the characters again," Teresa said, giving me a smile. "Emma and her sister. The one is so well delineated and the other is kept in the background."

"The father definitely likes Emma more, you can see," Susie added.

"That father is almost sinister, he's so manipulative," Hugo jumped in. Cristina rolled her eyes and gestured as he spoke, agreeing heartily as he continued: "With his invented sicknesses, he's got Emma trapped, and he even manages to get Mr. Knightley under his own roof when Emma marries him. Anything that hurts the father will hurt Emma, and he knows it."

As Susie added, "He's an absolute manipulator," Hugo capped off his own point by saying, "He's so utterly passive that he's *active*."

"Austen's secondary characters are really a marvel," Teresa said. Cristina agreed, and the two began simultaneously offering examples that interested them.

"All of her characters, really, are just so well drawn," Susie finally cut across their talk. "With each one, there's a fine stroke to every line about them."

Susie's painting metaphor was dead on. Nodding enthusiastically, I explained, "Austen's own vision of what she was doing, according to something she wrote in a letter, was painting on ivory, which was used for miniatures, with a very fine, with a fine—" I waved my hand in the air as if painting.

"Brush?" Teresa offered the word in Spanish.

"That's it. Sir Walter Scott published a very positive review of her work and later wrote that it was a pity a writer with a true gift for fine detail had died so young." I thought back to the moment I'd experienced in front of the church on the day it had snowed, with the young woman and her child. "Her portrait of Emma is extraordinary. Did you notice that part where Emma has gone to visit the poor, and she's thinking about how moved she is by their plight, but yet, she knows—"

"That in a short while, they'll fade from her mind," Cristina finished the sentence for me, nodding in admiration for Austen's skill. What a memory Cristina had—but the strength of Austen's characterizations helps them stay with you.

"The portraits of those interactions are so strong in that small town," Susie agreed.

"There's something I've heard," I said, "speaking of small towns. '*Pueblo chico*—'"

"*Infierno grande!*" cried all four in flawless chorus then burst out laughing. Small town, big hell was clearly not just a Paraguayan saying.

"But it's not hell in Austen's vision," I quickly pointed out, and Susie added, "There's more boredom than anything."

"What's so striking is how this small town," Hugo offered, "isn't just one place—it's any small town in rural England. In fact, it could be any small town anywhere. The generosity, the problems, the love, the jealousies, all of these things are what we'll deal with as long as human beings exist."

"That's one of the reasons the physical descriptions of the houses, of the countryside, are so vague," I agreed, "because—"

"They're practically nonexistent," Hugo interrupted. "They don't matter. Austen wasn't interested in sketching the country-side. She was drawing psychological landscapes. It's the opposite of a writer like Emily Brontë. The countryside is so central to what's she's writing about, it's almost—"

"It's a character, really," I cut in.

"Exactly!" Hugo said. I began to notice, as he and I enthused over Austen's skill on this point, that Teresa and Susie were giving the two of us speculative looks, while Cristina smiled knowingly. I'd certainly hoped that some chemistry was developing between Hugo and me—especially right before the-kiss-that-never-happened. Were the ladies clueing in to something here, or was *that* my imagination, too?

"Just look at the titles," Hugo continued. "*Wuthering Heights.*

The place is a character, it controls the characters. In *Emma*, it's the woman who's in charge."

"Speaking of that name and her role, here's something I noticed," Teresa offered. "Emma actually means 'mother' in Arabic. And she's really like a mother to people in that village."

Hugo's eyebrows shot up, and he nodded. "Interesting. But it must be a coincidence. It doesn't seem likely Austen would have known that." The two debated that issue for several minutes, until Cristina drew us off onto another line of thought.

"Which of the two main women is Jane Austen? Is it Emma or is it Jane Fairfax?" The group wrangled over this subject. I thought back to the women in Guatemala, who'd been so interested in this topic, as well—especially Mercedes, who'd turned out to be the star of that discussion. After listening to their points, I cut in, as I had in Antigua and in Ecuador, as well, to suggest that writers in Austen's time period didn't necessarily have the same relationship modern writers often do with their work.

"That could be, *mi amor*," Cristina nodded. "But you know what Virginia Woolf said—who am I going to write about, if not myself? But now, I have to tell you. I didn't used to like Jane Austen." She reached over and patted my knee affectionately as she made her point. "I was forced to read her too early. Austen really isn't for fourteen-year-olds, you know."

The others agreed, and Teresa took that moment to thank me. "We wouldn't have all met each other if you hadn't organized this talk! And I really enjoyed reading this Austen novel."

Hugo suddenly looked at his watch and winced. "We've been down here for almost three hours! My boss is going to kill me!"

Since everyone had met Ernesto on the way in and could see that he wouldn't hurt a fly, that set us all laughing.

"I want to take you all out to dinner," I said. "No arguments on that! But please, let me get a picture first."

Easier said than done. Cristina made a point about Russian novels that Hugo contested, and they were off. Getting everyone to look at the camera took numerous attempts because each time one of them would stop talking to smile and pose, the other would lean over and slip in a point about Dostoevsky or Pasternak or Solzhenitsyn, and I'd catch someone in profile, mouth open.

This struggle had everyone laughing again but finally, I got my shot. As Teresa, Susie, and Cristina gathered up their coats and scarves and books, Hugo put the chairs back where they belonged. Watching them so engaged in conversation, I experienced a sudden, intense swell of sadness.

Why sadness, when the group had gone so well? Because—after a year's worth of meeting enthusiastic booklovers, of hearing what readers thought about Austen's characters and plots and her distinctive talents, of watching readers draw endlessly fresh connections between their own lives and Austen's world—after a year's worth of finding new ways myself to look at Austen as I saw her through a kaleidoscope of distinctive perspectives—it dawned on me that this, finally, was it.

The last group was done.

I suggested a nice restaurant two blocks away. Hugo had to close the bookstore before he could join us, so I didn't want him to have to travel too far. But it was not to be. Teresa named a well-known *parrilla* or "grill" restaurant in a distant neighborhood, and since tearing into each other verbally had apparently put them in the mood for tearing into meat, the ladies outvoted me. Teresa wrote down the name and location for Hugo. I'd spent enough time around him to realize he was masking impatience when he saw the address.

"I'll be there as soon as I can," he said.

We piled into a taxi. Teresa and Cristina began talking about reading in French as I leaned back against the seat. I watched the lights of the city slip past outside the window and thought back to Paraguay. I'd loved meeting with the teachers in Asunción, but they so disliked Emma that it completely colored the discussion. Given that I'd learned one of my best "arrogant Argentinean" jokes from those young women, they'd probably have a good laugh to learn that, even though Hugo preferred Jane Fairfax, all of the readers in Buenos Aires felt quite at home with Austen's highbrow Emma.

One part of that evening's discussion, in particular, continued to resonate with me—Hugo's points about how the people of the village were the focus and the physical location, secondary. There's a word in Spanish that can't be fully translated: *pueblo*. No one word in English embraces every meaning that a Spanish speaker hears. *Pueblo* means "village," but it also means "people." When the Argentineans who adored Evita Perón referred to her as the "*protectora del pueblo Argentino*," they didn't mean she was out guarding people's houses with a twelve-gauge; they meant she had the people of the country in her heart. The place can't be separated from the people. People are what make a village (or a nation), not the houses and the fences, the hills and the fields.

Austen didn't know Spanish, but it's clear from her works that she knew, that she lived, a concept near and dear to the hearts of *latinos* and *latinas*. The landscapes of your life are the people around you. It's true, you need to know the physical geography of your village—which paths lead where, which bridge to avoid, which houses have dogs that bite. But if you *really* want to get around well, study the people. If you're Emma, you need to learn which matches will produce a stable marriage, according to the lay of the land. Harriet Smith with Mr. Martin works; Harriet Smith with Mr. Elton would produce a shaky matrimonial edifice. You need to learn who to trust. Any character in any Austen novel needs to learn to deal with obstacles that aren't going away, like the Mrs. Eltons of the world or the Wickhams or the Willoughbys or the Lady Catherine de Bourghs.

I'd mastered the bus routes in Puerto Vallarta and the metro system in Chile. I'd learned the grid of cobblestoned streets in Antigua and the riverside walks in Guayaquil. But navigating the social waters in every country I visited was always more complex. We don't know a place until we know the people, and that takes time, patience, and serious reading skills. If you're not willing to see people on their own terms, you'll wind up like Sir John Middleton, nattering on about hunting dogs, unable to imagine that people have interests and needs and desires—ways of seeing the world—that differ from your own.

If I'd heard someone at an academic conference give a talk on how place and people are intertwined in Austen's world, I would have nodded and thought, "Sure, I know that." But sitting in that taxi, watching the driver weave adeptly through traffic in a city I had come to love for its beauty and energy and arrogance, listening to the singing *porteño* Spanish of the three women around me all talking at once, I thought: *pueblo*. Place. People.

After a twenty-minute ride we reached the restaurant. Hardwood surfaces dominated visually—varnished walls, heavily framed windows, thick wooden tables. Upscale-hunting-cabin seemed to be the theme. Several railed dining areas throughout the room were set above floor level and reached via short sets of stairs, which created a sense of intimacy for diners and divided up the enormous space. We got one of the raised areas, thanks to how few people were there. "Don't take that as a bad sign," Teresa said as we were seated. "It's not even eight yet. That's very early for us." Despite how heated the Austen discussion had gotten at times, there was clearly no ill will among the women, and we spent the hour before Hugo arrived gossiping about various things, including him.

"He's quite insightful," Cristina smiled. "And clearly a lover of literature. That's worth a lot in a man. I get the feeling you like him. Am I right?"

"He's very interesting," I admitted, "but I'm sort of already in a long-distance relationship with a man from Mexico. Diego was in my reading group there. He's a wonderful person, very sweet, very warm."

The ladies eagerly interrupted each other with questions until Cristina raised her thin voice to cut through the talk. "Well, I don't see a ring on your finger, *mi amor*. Until somebody puts one there, you're free to do as you like." My inner feminist balked at the implied possession, but I knew she meant well so I kept my thoughts to myself. Susie smiled, and Teresa raised her wine glass in salute.

When Hugo arrived, we ordered meat and more meat, which we washed down with wine and more wine. The beauty of city living is that nobody had to drive. Hours later as we made our way out onto the street to hunt down taxis, I thanked everyone profusely for being in the group while they thanked me for meat and wine—and quality time with Austen.

Wine goes to my head very quickly, one of several reasons I typically stick with beer. Before I knew it, I was speeding away from the group with the vague sense that I'd made more promises for visits than I could possibly keep in the few days that remained of my trip.

Waking up the next day with a blazing headache sealed the deal. I was down for two days with some kind of superduper-hangover-bug. Since there was no accompanying fever, I kept from panicking about dengue. Still, I was left with only enough time in Buenos Aires to keep a lunch date I'd set with Nadine of JASBA and to spend one final evening out. Susie had invited Teresa and me to a dinner at her house. Cristina had invited me to a poetry reading. Hugo had invited me to go bookshopping.

I broke the Girls' Honor Code: I spent the evening with Hugo. But not before a lovely farewell lunch with Nadine, who reminded me yet again about my promise to write a piece on Austen for JASBA's newsletter.

"I have a little something for you, something I didn't want Mr. Dudgeon to see." From her purse she pulled a broad, laminated bookmark with a digitally altered sketch of Jane Austen drinking *mate*, a South American drink similar to tea but stronger. *Mate* is an herb that you steep inside a distinctive container that's half thermos, half coffee mug, then sip through a metal straw. You can see Che Guevara enjoying it in the film adaptation of *The Motorcycle Diaries*. "A friend designed this for us, but we haven't shown Mr. Dudgeon yet," Nadine said with a naughty little smile. "I'm afraid he doesn't find this kind of thing amusing, but I thought you would."

Austen sipping *mate*—what a perfect souvenir of Argentina! I gave her a hug and promised not to tell on her.

After I made my apologies to Teresa, Susie, and Cristina by phone, I met Hugo in a café on Corrientes for one last book jaunt. Who knew how long it would be before I visited such a booklover's paradise again? I had already sent five boxes of books back to the States. I felt sure, though, there was room in my bags for a few more treasures.

And a good thing, too, because Hugo handed me a pretty little present as soon as I sat down: an attractive 1945 hardcopy edition of *La Abadía de Northanger*.

"I want you to have this," he said with a smile. "I should read it in English anyway next time."

While some book dealers close by 7:00 p.m., many along Corrientes stay open as late as 10:00 p.m. or even 1:00 a.m. It was a pleasure to browse the stores with Hugo, block after block. There's no city in the United States that I know of where stores stay open so late to accommodate the crowds of lingering, well-dressed people like one finds in Buenos Aires at night. Numerous theaters lined the street as well, contributing to the flow of noisy, animated pedestrians.

Goodness knows I had enough editions of Austen already, but how could I turn down *Orgullo y Prejuicio* with a stylized painting of Lizzy and Darcy flying through the air in modern wedding clothes on the cover?

"That publishing house does school editions, rewritten and abridged," Hugo pointed out. "That won't be useful for you."

"I like the cover," I smiled as I paid for it.

Next store. I also couldn't turn down *Persuasion* with a photo of a sultry blond who could have passed for a 1970s Bond girl, set against a bright red background.

"Oh please, no," Hugo again attempted to intervene. "That publisher puts out appalling trash. That *can't* be a good translation." When I met his eye and smiled again, he sighed and shrugged. "I get it. You like the cover."

The only sour note in the evening hit when we got on to the subject of *Dark Shadows* yet again, and Hugo lamented that Jonathan Frid, who'd played Barnabas Collins, wasn't alive to see the current revival of interest in the show. Panicked, I insisted that Frid had *not* died. Only a visit to the website *Dead or Alive* could settle this, and when we saw Internet proof that as of that moment, Barnabas lived, we heaved a simultaneous sigh of relief. What a pair of nerds! Then Hugo laughed—really laughed—for the first time since I'd met him, outside of the moments of merriment in the Austen group.

But linger as we might, we eventually found ourselves at the door of my hotel once more.

"Would you like to come up for a bit?" I asked before giving myself time to think about what I was doing. I wasn't necessarily inviting him into my bed, but we'd never had a bit of real privacy since we'd met.

He hesitated, then said, "Sure."

I showed him some of the special books I was packing in my carry-on, among them a first edition of Manuel Puig's *The Buenos Aires Affair* and an early edition of Eva Perón's strange autobiography, *La Razón de mi Vida*. We talked books then fell silent. Hugo, seated on my bed, studied me for a long moment, his dark gaze intense and his handsome features, strained. He leaned forward—would he finally try to kiss me? He looked so desperately like he wanted to share something. Maybe I should jump in and kiss *him?* Then I thought of Diego and again wondered what I was up to. According to the ladies over dinner—no ring, no problem. But that wasn't my style. I assumed Diego was dating other people while waiting for me, but we did still have a plan see each other this fall, something I'd very much been looking forward to.

While these thoughts were racing through my head, god only knows what Hugo was thinking—but finally, he made the first move.

He told me how happy he'd been to meet me, how much he'd enjoyed being with me, and that he had my email address. Then he stood up and left.

Yee—oooouch.

Maybe…I just didn't know the signals here? Perhaps Hugo was gay, and I'd misread his friendly overtures? As I heard the elevator doors open and close outside my room, whisking him street-ward, my addled brain careened into a *Scrubs*-style fantasy: my best buds from my fortieth birthday bash in Las Vegas suddenly appeared on the bed—in brightly colored PJs with their hair in slumber party pigtails—crowding the space where Hugo had just been sitting.

Cheryl, who had visited in Chile, can be something of a pessimist. She was nodding, "Yep, he's gay. Forget it. No dice." Jaque, ever cautious, was giving an inscrutable "Who's to say?" shrug, while Susan, the most adventurous, was winking, "Could still be interesting if he's bi!"

Then poof, they were gone, and I was alone again.

Had I been Frank Churchilled, *Clueless* style, or had I simply Emma'd myself? Gay or straight, Hugo wasn't interested. So much for my belief that as an Austen devotee, I had especially keen powers of observation. I'd felt *so* sure that Hugo had feelings for me. But hadn't I proven repeatedly throughout the year of travels that if there was a way to make a misstep, I'd be there? I guess I'd believed, too easily, that because my feelings had tipped over from friendship into romance that Hugo's had as well.

Okay, so I screwed up again. But a lot had gone right in Argentina. Most things, in fact. Without knowing a soul in the city, I located fascinating, insightful readers for my group. I took in fun cultural events with Teresa, who taught me that there is no way to say "I am" or "I have" in Hebrew. I was welcomed into the JASBA fold and broke bread with a man who'd known Borges and Victoria Ocampo; I even found a *SUR* from 1963 with one of Mr. Dudgeon's reviews. I saw tango dancers and lost track of happy hours wandering from one bookstore to another. I tormented an anti-Yankee embroidery teacher with my crassness and bad needle skills. I made friends with a proud, handsome, grumpy, nerdy *porteño* who never threw me out of his bookstore. I got to see how *Emma* held up across time and borders in a city that Austen's snootiest heroine would have simply adored. How could anybody "handsome, clever, and rich" not love a city where, according to the Latin American grapevine, most people believe "handsome" and "clever" are their birthright?

As for this last night—well, Emma's ego takes a bruising when she realizes that she and Frank Churchill are never going to happen as a couple, but she holds up just fine. Better things awaited.

I didn't know what my own better things *were* yet. But I felt pretty sure, they awaited.

The End and
the Beginning

D id you have good seats for the flights?"

Someone who didn't know my mother would think she was welcoming me home from a weekend's vacation. But I could hear the depths of relief and happiness in her voice at finally receiving a phone call from California, not from who-knows-where, plus-bats. It was all there in the undertones: *Oh thank God, you didn't die! Please don't do something like this again anytime too soon. My heart can only take so much!*

Emma's fretful father struggles to make gruel eaters out of everybody around him, never understanding their resistance. "One half of the world," Emma tries to explain, "cannot understand the pleasures of the other." I was lucky to have a mother who, while she didn't always share my idea of what constitutes a good time, didn't push porridge. I'd cut my return too close to the beginning of my teaching semester to make a Pennsylvania visit before classes started, but I would definitely get in that family Christmas I'd promised myself back in Ecuador during my dengue-fueled, most maudlin holiday ever.

As for the return to California—*damnation, it felt good*. Yes, I'd loved the year in Latin America, but coming home was a world of comfort and familiarity. It was fabulous to reconnect with friends, move back into my own place, and pull all of my worldly goods out of storage. My chickens were another story, unfortunately…but some coyote mother and father did right by their own family when they'd found a weak spot in my friend's security fence.

Home at last, the reminders of my travels were everywhere, starting with the stacks of boxes in my office at the university plastered with colorful stamps from Mexico, Guatemala, Ecuador, Chile, Paraguay, and Argentina. Every box I'd sent to myself made it safely, although a few were a little battered around the edges. I was in nerd heaven hauling the books home, sorting them by country, then organizing them by publisher on my shelves (ha!—just kidding; I alphabetized them). Joining the house decorations I'd pulled from storage were various blankets and woven fabrics from every country I'd visited, along with Señor Guapo and a host of llamas, owls, alpacas, and pudgy clay birds.

Travel now colored my relationship with language as well. Having struggled so long to make myself understood in Spanish, it was an intense pleasure not to feel like a dummy most of the time. Using English was like running again after gimping along on a bad ankle for a year. Subtlety returned to my verbal arsenal, and I could make jokes above the kindergarten level. I had a newfound patience with anybody struggling with English. Living in a new language is exhilarating but *exhausting*, and considering how often people had helped me during my travels, I could definitely keep the good karma moving.

A new language opens doorways, too. I could now accost my *latino* and *latina* colleagues in Spanish, and they were entertained by the odd accent I'd acquired, an overlay of *gringa* with musical undertones of Chile and Argentina. Conversations in

Spanish all around me—in the grocery store, at the bank, on campus—turned from pretty noise into speech. My ears were alert to finally hear the secret things people discuss in Spanish specifically because they don't want others to understand. Here it is: "They've got good prices on almonds this week." "Can you believe how long this line is?" "Jesus, my classes suck this semester." Not so secret, after all.

And what about Austen? Had I learned what I'd set out to learn—whether Latin American readers would connect with Austen the way people in the States do? The quick answer was most did, some didn't. While certain readers were dubious about how well Austen's characters might fare if transported into modern Guayaquil, Santiago, or Buenos Aires, discussions of her works had led seamlessly into conversations about the local culture, in one way or another, in every group. Austen's world hadn't felt like the fascinating but distant Planet of the Brontës to the readers. Mrs. Bennet was alive and well in Antigua, Emma could push people's buttons in Asunción, and Elinor could break hearts in Santiago (or at least one heart, anyway—but Elinor never asked for much).

For all of the emotion Austen's characters generated, on the manhandling issue I'd only had one score: Oscar and Ignacio José in Ecuador had wanted to see Mr. Darcy beaten with a stick. If I left out Erna from Paraguay, who'd been born in the States, no one else invoked bodily harm during the reading groups— although verbal thrashings abounded. *¿Quién sabe?*—maybe it was a commentary on violence in American culture that U.S. readers were more likely to want to knock around Miss Austen's ladies and gents. A man in Ecuador once asked me, "What's the challenge in American football if players can use their hands?"

My reply: "What's the challenge in soccer if players can't get slammed to the ground legally?" Carmen Gloria in Chile was dumbfounded when I rattled off a list of names for the ritualized torment American kids routinely inflict on each other: wedgies, Indian rope burns, purple nurples, tittie twisters, wet willies, noogies, swirlies, and the super atomic wedgie, to name a few. She couldn't think of a single equivalent term in Spanish, and neither could anybody else I'd asked (yes, I went around asking things like that). We are, it seems, a violent people.

As I settled back into my routine at home and the university, I emailed readers and friends in the countries I'd visited to let them know I'd made it back safely.

And then there was Diego, poised to visit me in the States. Ever since I'd met Hugo, I'd been conflicted about Diego. I knew I cared about him—he was handsome, smart, cheerful, patient, and loving. Despite the dengue, living in Puerto Vallarta had seemed like a wonderful dream. But even after Hugo's tense, kissless exit from my Buenos Aires hotel, I could *not* get him out of my head.

So I called Cindy, a friend and colleague. We carried cups of coffee out to a shady spot on campus, and I explained the dilemma. She put me straight with a single question: "Which one is Mr. Darcy?"

Wow—I hadn't seen that coming, but I guess I should have. I'd been so curious about whether people in Latin America would enter Austenland that I hadn't realized I'd crossed the border myself.

Which was Mr. Darcy? Well, neither was filthy rich. Neither was going to make me mistress of Pemberley or the equivalent thereof. But the more I thought about it, the more apt the question seemed. Who is Mr. Darcy, really? Is he Mr. Perfect? No.

At his worst he's proud, insensitive, demanding, and socially awkward—but he's right for Lizzy Bennet, who at her worst is proud, judgmental, hasty, and flippant. It's all about *fit*. It dawned on me what the unspoken half of Cindy's question was, within the framework of *Pride and Prejudice*: "and which is Mr. Bingley?"

Mr. Bingley is relentlessly cheerful. He looks for the best in everyone. He loves getting out and socializing with all sorts of people—and he loves to dance. Mr. Bingley is…Diego.

The right fit for Mr. Bingley was sweet, good-natured, passive Jane. Was I sweet, good-natured, and passive? Hell no. I'd done my best to look on the bright side of things when I was with Diego, but I had a growing suspicion I'd stayed in Puerto Vallarta *just* the right amount of time. Anything more than three months, and Diego would have seen how nerdy, neurotic, judgmental, and cranky I can be, even without a raging tropical fever as an excuse. There was a reason my visit to Puerto Vallarta had felt like a dream: it kind of had been. I'd made a temporary home there, but I was still just a tourist in the land of sunshine. Anything more than three months, and Diego's perpetually bright temperament would have burned me out, I'm sorry to say, as I would have struggled, against my nature, to be sunshine-y myself.

I never felt that I would shock Hugo if I described somebody as a jerk or showed how impatient I still got at times, despite my best attempts at cultural adaptation, with slow restaurant service. Fact is, I did those things, and he *wasn't* shocked. I always felt comfortable with him, even functioning in a second language, because I could be my neurotic, judgmental, cranky self without feeling that it would bring him down—because he was prideful, combative, and grumpy himself. As for the nerd thing—Barnabas Collins? Come on. Anybody who loves *Dark Shadows* is a hopeless nerd. Johnny Depp is poised to put Barnabas Collins on the media radar again with a new film adaptation, but swashbuckling aside, Johnny Depp is actually the world's best-looking nerd.

Okay, so that was settled—Hugo was Mr. Darcy, and Diego was Mr. Bingley.

I wrote to Diego and admitted that I'd met somebody else. After a slightly longer than usual silence, he responded just the way I would have expected him to: "This makes me very sad, Amy, but what I want most of all is for you to be happy. You know my life is here, and if you've found somebody who can be with you in California, then I'm happy for you." His generosity made me feel even worse about how I may have hurt him. But with his warm heart, good looks, and perpetual optimism, somehow I didn't think he'd stay single too long.

So I'd come clean with myself (and Diego) about Hugo. The real problem remained. I'd found somebody I wanted to have with me in California—but judging from Hugo's behavior when we said good-bye, he didn't want *me*. And he lived in Argentina. Yet even without knowing Hugo's feelings, once I knew mine, I couldn't carry on with Diego.

But hope dawns eternal. When I'd arrived back in the States, there'd been an email message from Hugo awaiting me. "This is my first message to you from Argentina. I hope when you read it you're set up in your new house. *Un beso*, Hugo."

Un beso—there was my kiss. Then again, everybody runs around kissing everybody else in Buenos Aires, including guy-on-guy. Madonna, delicate flower that she is, was rumored to have been offended at how often she got kissed on the check by strangers when she was filming *Evita*. Still, I decided to be optimistic. I just couldn't get the idea out of my head that Hugo felt the same about me as I did about him, despite evidence to the contrary. Did that make me a cross-cultural stalker? As long as I wasn't hanging around outside his window and threatening other women who talked to him, I supposed I was still on safe ground.

The months passed, and we wrote to each other regularly, notes that got longer and more personal. As spring arrived, I decided to go for it—I asked him how he'd feel if I visited again in July. I also asked, only half joking, if he had a girlfriend or a wife hidden away somewhere (I wasn't seriously concerned about his having a boyfriend; that had just been wounded vanity on my part).

After I sent the note, I paced my apartment. What had I *done*? What if I scared him off and ruined our budding friendship? What if he did have a girlfriend? I checked my email compulsively that evening, to no avail. Was a delayed answer a good sign or a bad one? Typically if I have trouble sleeping, I relax by watching Universal horror films from the thirties and forties. That was a two-*Mummy* night.

Finally, Hugo's answer arrived the next afternoon. I was so anxious to read it I could hardly remember to breathe.

"I would love to see you again this summer. But here's what's going to happen if you come down here," he wrote. I could picture him typing away at the computer in the bookstore, where he often stayed on after hours, heavy brows knitted as he dove into a note that took up two full pages when I printed it. "If we see each other again, we're going to fall in love. That's what's going to happen. So you need to think about whether you want to come back here, because everything for us is going to get complicated."

So there it was. Once I tipped my hand, we both had cards all over the table.

I don't know how I made it through the weeks before I could finally set foot again in Buenos Aires and eyes, again, on Hugo. Having saved up during the year, I made reservations for a month in the Emma apartment on Juncal rather than my old Miss Bates option on the Avenida de Mayo.

Thanks to a late departure from the United States, I missed a connection in Chile, was put on a different flight, and arrived in Buenos Aires seven hours late. I couldn't find Hugo anywhere in the airport, so I took a taxi to my apartment, utterly exhausted, and crashed on the king-sized bed. An hour or so later reception buzzed me that I had a visitor. During the time it took the elevator to ascend to my room, I scrambled around madly to put on clothes, untangle my hair, and get a bit of color on my lips.

There, when I opened the door, was Hugo, apologizing profusely for having missed me at the airport. I'm going to invoke the standard Austen veil of discretion over that reunion—I'm still more Elinor than Marianne. Suffice it to say, we were happy to see each other. Very happy. And yes, Dear Reader, I *finally* got my kiss.

When the right moment arrived a few days later, I asked the question that had been bugging me for the better part of a year: "Why did you walk out of my room last summer without even trying to kiss me?"

Hugo nodded solemnly; he'd been expecting this. "I was afraid I'd never hear from you again after I did that. It would have completely offended most Argentinean women. But I just didn't want to start something when you were leaving the next day, and who knew if I would ever see you again? I don't take relationships lightly. Ever. That's just the way I am."

One of my favorite episodes of *Sex and the City* is called "Are We Sluts?" In it, Carrie Bradshaw begins power-fretting when Aidan, her new love interest, doesn't immediately hop into bed with her. He wanted to take things slowly. I hadn't necessarily expected that night with Hugo the year before to end in bed, but the sentiment was the same. Aidan was a gentleman, and so was Hugo. Given that Hugo's father had been a nightclub musician, Lady Catherine de Bourgh might not think so, but I certainly did.

While I'd been traveling in Latin America for a year I'd made silly assumption after silly assumption. Clueless on two continents—that was me. When Hugo had walked away from me a year ago, I'd assumed he wasn't interested in me romantically. Maybe that seemed like a safe enough assumption. After all, don't other episodes of *Sex and the City* teach that "he's just not that into you" if he doesn't vault the stairs into your bed once you've dropped a hint?

But I didn't ride that assumption out, and my gut had been right after all. Chalk it up to the Elinor in me. Even when Lucy Steele showed up, flaunting her secret engagement, Elinor just *knew* that Edward couldn't have been playing her false. She trusted her feelings, despite appearances. I hadn't given up hope when Hugo walked away. I just knew, somehow, that he cared for me. And sure enough, he did.

"Did you know right away that you liked me?" I asked a few days later as we returned to browse the bookstores on Corrientes. Conflicting emotions crossed his face. "To be honest, no," he finally answered, setting down the book he'd been looking at. "I thought you were a little irritating." Then he took me by the shoulders, right there in the bookstore. "But it didn't take long, you know, when I began to suspect you were interested in me. Are you mad at me for saying this?"

"For being honest? Never. I don't ask questions unless I want to hear the answer." I smiled and kissed him. "But for the record, I knew the day I met you that you were special. Right away. I really did."

"Well, thank god you didn't give up on me even after how grumpy I was the second time you came by the store. I can't believe how close I came to ruining everything!" He squeezed my hand and shook his head in alarm at the disturbing thought.

If he asked me directly, then I'd tell him. Honesty needs to cut both ways. But since he didn't ask, I didn't explain that he'd never really been in danger of ruining anything. I was too darned stubborn to cut and run because of a little grumpiness. Catherine Morland, goof that she is, hangs in there with Henry Tilney through some rough circumstances. The narrator of *Northanger Abbey* wryly confesses that although Henry came to love Catherine, it didn't happen at first sight: "A persuasion of her partiality for him had been the only cause of giving her a serious thought." Something of an insult to a heroine, to be sure, but if Catherine could survive it, so could I.

The weeks flew by. Shortly before I had to return to the States, Hugo and I walked to the Plaza de Mayo. We settled in on a bench in front of the famous *Casa Rosada* or "Pink House"— Argentina's equivalent of the White House. This was the square where tens of thousands of Argentineans had gathered from around the country to demand the release of Juan Perón from military prison, an event that led to his becoming president and to his wife Eva Perón achieving worldwide fame.

On that day with Hugo, I couldn't think about all of the history that had been made in that important square, ringed with colonial architecture and attractive cafés; all I could think about was how I was getting on a plane again very, very soon.

Shall I invoke Austen once more? I adore the ending of *Northanger Abbey* when the narrator steps in to point out how there can't be much more suspense over the fate of her hero and heroine since the readers "will see in the tell-tale compression of the pages before them, that we are all hastening together to perfect felicity."

Austen is famously cagey about marriage proposals—she leaves her couples to their privacy in that most sacred of moments. But what the heck, I'll share. Ours went like this:

Hugo: I know you don't want to give up your job, so I want to tell you now—I'd be willing to come with you to the States.

Amy: That's wonderful! The easiest way for that to work would be for us to get married.

Hugo: Then let's get married.

Amy: Okay then.

And there you have it. Nobody happened to have a ring on them at the moment, but we worked that out later. The legal details turned out to be a *lot* more complicated than either of us could have imagined, but details are details. The most important thing—we'd found each other. Even if I had found him a bit faster than he'd found me. Even if we lived 6,000 miles (and a lot of immigration paperwork) apart.

Hugo's parents had both passed away years ago, so he would be able to move without too much complication, although leaving close friends behind would be hard. As for my mother, she was thrilled that I was getting married. She was even more thrilled when I made it clear Hugo would be coming to the United States, and not vice versa.

"I'm not sure how I would have managed if you'd moved to another country!" she said frankly. Once the big details were settled, it didn't take her long to ask, "So, does Hugo know how to dance the Argentine tango?"

The day I met Hugo, here's what I wrote in my travel notes: "And how is it, that of all the bookstores in the bookstore capital of Latin America, I happen to walk into one with a guy who says, 'Why *Emma?* Why not *Northanger Abbey?*'"

Despite the echo of that famous line from Casablanca, we didn't get a *Casablanca* ending, with a wrenching, permanent good-bye on a dark airport runway. We got an Austen ending. I'd had a beautiful visit with Diego, a solidly good man—a Bingley who deserved his very own Jane (and who, I felt sure, would find her).

But with Hugo, I was home.

Austen's happy endings aren't dopey. They're not fairy tales, as Teresa had pointed out during the Buenos Aires group. Anybody who's read *Sense and Sensibility* carefully knows that Elinor and Edward (and their cows) will struggle financially for the rest of their lives and that Lucy Ferrars, wealthy sister-in-law, will be twice as aggravating as conniving Miss Lucy Steele was. As for *Emma*, Emma and Mr. Knightley will keep getting into arguments— especially while they're stuck under Mr. Woodhouse's roof—as will Darcy and Lizzy from *Pride and Prejudice*, for sure. Lizzy will continue getting crap from Mr. Darcy's snooty aunt and continue slinging it back, as well (and sending Lydia off to a distant county isn't going to prevent that bad penny and her rotter husband from turning up to mooch money when things go sour, and they *will* go sour).

Believable happiness—that's what's in store for Austen's protagonists. They all find love, but it's love embedded in situations we can identify with: money woes, frustrating relatives, unavoidable personality clashes. That, I think, is why people keep coming back to Austen. That's why Austen resonated so richly for Nora, Élida, and the other ladies in Guatemala, who kept their faith in love despite gender discrimination that might make weaker women cynical. That's why Diego and his friends in Mexico, all struggling financially but doing it with strength and optimism, were so happy, above all, for patient, virtuous Elinor. That's why the members of the Ecuador group, with their literary director and their broad-ranging reading experiences, were still impressed with Austen's psychological realism. Wanting some believable happiness is what frustrated the Chilean writers when Austen ties things up so quickly between Marianne and Colonel Brandon; disliking Emma too much to want to see her happy kept the Paraguay readers from making it to the end of the book (and I'm afraid those young ladies, busy no doubt with family and with their own students, never did get back to me on *Emma*).

As for Argentina—ahhh, Argentina! The readers wrangled and tangled and argued so much we barely made it to a discussion of the novel's end. But did they find it believable? Absolutely.

I'd set off from California as a teacher and quickly realized what a student I still was. Austen's lessons about patience and careful reading had seemed *so* clear in my comfortable California classroom. I hadn't realized how my trip would really be a road test of values and beliefs I thought I had already absorbed from Austen: Don't judge too hastily; not everyone wants the same things out of life; people's circumstances color how they respond to *everything*; we're not all speaking the same language, even when we're speaking the same language.

Theoretically, I could have shown up in any six countries and had a great experience learning with Austen. But I was glad I'd chosen Latin America, and not just because that's where Hugo awaited. I was glad because now I could speak the most common second language in the United States. Now I knew one country from another south of the U.S. border, and I'd clued in to the many family squabbles among them, some lighthearted, like their soccer rivalries and the popularity of "arrogant Argentinean" jokes, others much more politically serious. I now knew better than to call myself an "American" in Spanish, since we're all Americans— South Americans, Central Americans, North Americans. In English, I'm an American; in Spanish, an *estado unidense* or "United States-er." Sounds better in Spanish, doesn't it?

I love teaching because I love learning, and none of us is a finished product. Ever. If I showed up in Germany or Thailand or Bora Bora with some Austen novels, I'd go through the same trial and error (emphasis on the "error") all over again, albeit not on the dating front. Learning is fun, as any book nerd knows. Maybe Germany or Thailand or Bora Bora wouldn't be such a bad idea after all; I never did get to find out what folks outside of the United States think of *Persuasion, Mansfield Park*, and my personal favorite, *Northanger Abbey*. It might also be fun to start a new hunt for Nancy Drew—and maybe learn a different language along the way.

And for those of you with a good memory, yes, Mr. Dudgeon got his Jane Austen article for the JASBA newsletter. When Hugo and I recently attended his ninety-seventh birthday party in Buenos Aires, we brought him a bottle of Johnny Walker Red. His response? "Isn't that just lovely! And about our next newsletter—you'll write another piece, won't you, my dear? We must keep busy, you know."

I agree. Introducing Hugo to his new home in the United States (and to his enormous new family!)—that happy beginning will keep us both very busy indeed.

READING GROUP GUIDE

1. While reading *All Roads Lead to Austen*, did you learn anything new or surprising about Jane Austen's life or about her novels?

2. The author chose to read three Austen novels two times each. What differences did you notice between the reactions of readers in Guatemala and those in Ecuador to *Pride and Prejudice*? How did the Mexico and Chile groups differ in their discussions of *Sense and Sensibility*? What were the most noticeable differences in how the Paraguay and the Argentina readers reacted to *Emma*?

3. The author mentions early on that she considers herself a feminist. Do you think this affects any of her interactions with people as she travels? Do you see any changes in her attitudes about gender issues in Latin America by the end of the book?

4. The author discusses how nervous her mother was about the author traveling alone in unfamiliar countries. How would your family members react if you decided to embark on an

extended trip? Would they be nervous? Supportive? Maybe a little jealous?

5. The author describes a run-in with some anti-Americanism in Argentina, when a young woman called her a "Yankee tourist." Do you think this is common problem for American travelers abroad? If so, what are some the causes? Is it worse in some parts of the world than others? Have you ever experienced it yourself while traveling?

6. The students the author taught in Chile were Americans and Canadians studying abroad. Do you believe that study abroad programs are important and valuable? Why or why not?

7. Translations of Austen's novels are available in every major language. Which other countries would be interesting places to read Austen's novels with local groups? Do you think there are countries or regions of the world where her stories and characters might not translate as well as they did in Latin America? If so, where? And why do you think so?

8. In the preface to the work, the author mentions that someone criticized her project for "superimposing" European literature on Latin American readers, a concern that her fiancé found patronizing. What is your opinion of this issue?

9. Which reading group discussion did you find the most interesting, memorable, or surprising—the one in Guatemala, Mexico, Ecuador, Chile, Paraguay, or Argentina? Why?

10. The author discusses how her serious, lengthy illness made her behave impatiently at times with people she met. Have you ever had a similar experience?

11. What are some of your favorite moments from the book? Who are some of the most memorable people the author meets during her travels and in her reading groups?

12. Does the author seem to be changed in some ways by her experiences in Latin America? Does she grow and mature? If so, how? Does her relationship with her mother change? If so, how?

13. If you could spend an entire year traveling and reading Jane Austen novels with people in new places, where would you go?

14. Overall, the readers in Latin America enjoyed Austen's novels and identified with her characters. Do you think this would have happened if the author had shared other authors with these same groups of readers? Would the readers in Mexico or Chile, for instance, have enjoyed Charles Dickens as much? Or Emily Brontë? If you are in a book group, are there authors you've read who might not translate well into Latin American cultures?

15. What similarities or differences do you see between Diego and Hugo? What did you like about each of the men? Why do you think Hugo won Amy's heart in the end?

16. The author mentions at the end of the section on Mexico that meeting the readers made her realize she'd had certain preconceptions about Mexicans that her experience led her to reconsider. Did the novel challenge you to reconsider any stereotypes or preconceptions you might have about Latin American countries or people who come from Latin American countries?

17. Does reading *All Roads Lead to Austen* inspire you to want to travel to Latin America? Why or why not? If it does, which countries seem most appealing, and why?

ACKNOWLEDGMENTS

I have so many people to thank for my Austen year—most of all, each and every reader from the groups in Guatemala, Mexico, Ecuador, Chile (Fernando, forgive me for revealing your Elinor secret!), Paraguay, and Argentina. Writers tend to say modest things like "I couldn't have done it without x, y, or z," and in this case, it's completely true. I'd like to thank Betsy and her husband and Martín and Dorrie for being such great hosts. Various colleagues helped along the way, including Katie Golsan, Luis Figueroa, Gene Bigler, and David Schmidt. As for the real Larry from Pittsburgh, I loved our Austen conversations, and thanks also to the adventurous students from Chile!

All of my wonderful Jane Austen students from the University of the Pacific have been an inspiration as well, especially those whose projects I mentioned here—Jamie Cunningham, Caleb Draper, Katelyn McGehee, Megan Olhasso, and Alyssa Soboleski.

Friends and family have been a huge help with elements of the project and with the manuscript, including Dolly Blair, Laurie Brady, Martín Camps, Cynthia Dobbs, David Dobbs, Anne Gossage, Susan Harman, James Lewis, Hannah Myers, Cindy Ostberg, Traci Roberts-Camps, Shawn Smith, Pat Thomas, and the fabulous travelin' Cheryl Wanko. Jaque Lyman went above and beyond to help—thanks *so* much. (I can't wait to return the favor with your next novel). Folks from the Writers Unlimited group in San Andreas, California, supported by the Calaveras County Arts Council, gave me good direction as I was finishing the work and designing the website, especially Rachel-Mikel ArceJaeger and Monika Rose.

I want to thank Caroline Cox not only for braving the earliest, shaggiest forms of the chapters, but also for introducing me to Lisa Adams, my wonderful, supportive, and very patient agent. Thanks, too, to Shana Drehs, my editor, as well as Deirdre Burgess, for helping an uptight Elinor try to get in touch with her inner Marianne.

As for Rob Hume—I owe you so much. I know this isn't the kind of book you trained me to write, but I hope you're not too horrified. And as for my mom—you were there, every step of the way. I hope your church friends don't give you too much grief for some of the stuff I admitted to doing here…

I'm very sorry to say that, along with Luis, two other friends I met on the road weren't there when I reached the end of it. Ani from the Guatemala group lost a battle with cancer and Nadine, who'd opened the doors of JASBA to me, also passed away. They are sorely missed.

Whatever weaknesses this book has, I'm sure some friend, colleague, or editor tried to talk me out of them; I take credit for any and all problems. As for my husband, who transcribed two of the reading groups for me *and* taught me to speak Spanish with a funny accent—*¡qué suerte, mi amor, que al fin nos encontramos!*

About the Author

Amy Elizabeth Smith is from western Pennsylvania. She has a degree in music from West Virginia University, a PhD in English from Penn State, and teaches writing and literature at the University of the Pacific in Stockton, California. A lifetime member of JASNA (Jane Austen Society of North America), she's been publishing scholarly articles for years, but this is her first venture into travel writing. She's always plotting more trips. Anyone who would like to see some Chilean cow graffiti from Smith's travels can visit www.allroadsleadtoausten.com.